# HUMAN,

## ALL TOO

## HUMAN

### Menschliches,
### Allzumenschliches

# HUMAN,
## ALL TOO
## HUMAN

A Book
for Free
Spirits

# Friedrich
# Nietzsche

Translated by
Marion Faber, with
Stephen Lehmann

Introduction
and notes by
Marion Faber

University of
Nebraska Press
Lincoln and London

Copyright 1984, Index copyright 1986 by
the University of Nebraska Press
All rights reserved
Manufactured in
the United States of America

Library of Congress Cataloging in Publication Data
Nietzsche, Friedrich Wilhelm, 1844–1900.
Human, all too human.
Translation of: Menschliches, Allzumenschliches.
Includes index.
1. Man. I. Title.
B3313.M52E5    1984    128    83-25955
ISBN 0-8032-3309-4
ISBN 0-8032-8353-9 (pbk.)

Most recent printing indicated by first digit below:
4    5    6    7    8    9    10

# CONTENTS

# Acknowledgments

The translators would like to acknowledge their indebtedness to Erich Lehmann, Stephen Hannaford, Rüdiger Bittner, Martin Ostwald, and David Gill for their thoughtful corrections and suggestions.

Thanks, too, to the National Endowment for the Humanities and Swarthmore College for their generous support.

# Introduction

"*Human, All Too Human* is the monument of
a crisis," observed Nietzsche in *Ecce Homo*. It is a crisis in several
senses. From a biographical standpoint, the work grows out of a
change in Nietzsche's friendship with Richard Wagner. Since
1868, the composer had been Nietzsche's friend, mentor, and artistic ideal. He hosted the young philosopher at his home in Trib-
schen, near Lucerne, Switzerland—so often, in fact, that a room
in the Wagner household was reserved for Nietzsche. One imagines the Great Man regaling the admiring scholar with his own
rather fuzzy philosophical views. Nietzsche found in him "both
the will to worldly power . . . and a suggestion of the possible
transformation of such a will to power into artistic creativity."[1]
The relationship, which included an attachment on Nietzsche's
part to Wagner's wife, Cosima, grew ever more important to
Nietzsche and finally bordered on abject devotion. It is hard to
overestimate this early reverent bond, or indeed the lifelong importance of Wagner to Nietzsche.

In 1876, however, Nietzsche broke with Wagner. The loyalty
Nietzsche had felt gave way to an even stronger need for indepen-
dence, and the two strong egos could not coexist as equals.
Nietzsche was no longer willing or able to add fuel to Wagner's
fire with his own writing, as he had done in his first major work,
*The Birth of Tragedy out of the Spirit of Music* (1872), or to rhap-
sodize about Wagner's role in German culture, as he had done in
"Richard Wagner in Bayreuth" (early 1876), the fourth of his
*Untimely Meditations*. He was now compelled to reject Wagner,

1. Walter Kaufmann, *Nietzsche: Philosopher, Psychologist, Antichrist* (New
York: Meridian Books, 1956), pp. 154–55.

both as a man (the theatrical cult hero) and as a thinker (the newly pious, nationalistic anti-Semite). Furthermore, he recognized that Wagner's art had not been a sign of health in German culture, but rather "a baroque art of overexcitement and glorified extravagance."[2] After his departure from the Bayreuth Festival in August, 1876, Nietzsche's relationship with Wagner was never reestablished.

Another aspect of this biographical crisis is that, in this same year, 1876, the prodigious young professor of philosophy at Basel, who had attained his chair at the unheard-of age of twenty-four, was forced to leave the academy. His increasingly bad health (the onset of the syphilis which was to lead to his insanity in 1889) made it necessary for him to request a leave from his academic duties. His departure from academic life became final in 1879, when he retired on a pension. It was not only his health, however, but also his conviction that academic life was stifling and a hindrance to a true philosopher which prompted his departure. As he had already written in "Richard Wagner in Bayreuth," a philosopher must strive not merely to be a thinker, but primarily to be a human being; this latter goal would be better realized outside the confines of a scholarly existence.

Having left behind these two anchors in his life, Nietzsche came under the influence of a new friend, the German-Jewish psychologist Paul Rée. In 1873 Nietzsche had met Rée, whose *Psychological Observations* had impressed him. In fall 1876, he joined Rée in Sorrento, at the home of a wealthy patron of the arts, Malwida von Meysenbug. Here the two writers enjoyed a life free of obligations and distractions; they could turn all their energies to their work. Conversations increased Nietzsche's receptivity to Rée's psychological, materialistic interpretations of religion and morality, which Nietzsche termed "Réealism." He began work on *Human, All Too Human.* (Later Lou Salomé joined Rée and Nietzsche to form the notorious, short-lived *ménage à trois* that so incited the anger of Nietzsche's sister.)

In a biographical sense, then, the Nietzsche of 1876 was liberated from his former mentor, Wagner, as well as from the bonds of

---

2. Letter to Mathilde Maier, July 15, 1878, quoted in *Selected Letters of Friedrich Nietzsche,* selected and translated by Christopher Middleton (Chicago: University of Chicago Press, 1969), p. 167.

his academic life. He was living as a free philosopher, far from family, far from Germany, and enjoying the intellectual stimulation of a scientist—a psychologist who was a peer rather than a mentor. From this viewpoint, *Human, All Too Human* represents a coming of age for Nietzsche the man.

It is a coming of age for Nietzsche the philosopher, as well. To be sure, there is a coherence to Nietzsche's *oeuvre* which can be traced from the early tragic pessimism of *The Birth of Tragedy* through to the fragments of his *Nachlass*. Nevertheless, *Human, All Too Human* marks the beginning of a second period in Nietzsche's philosophy, for in it he rejects decisively the romanticism that had characterized his first major work. In rejecting romanticism, Nietzsche rejects not only the artist Wagner, but, perhaps more important, their common intellectual influence, Schopenhauer, as well. This rejection led to both an acceptance and a transcendence of the conclusion reached by Kant in *The Critique of Pure Reason* (1781): an acceptance, in that Nietzsche shared the view that any "real world" or "noumenon"—as opposed to the phenomena we know through our senses and our reason—is inaccessible to us. Nietzsche also went a step further by asserting that this real world was not only inaccessible but also of no significance to man. Romantic philosophers such as Fichte and Schopenhauer had concentrated on the noumenon, attempting to know it, somewhat as a Hindu attempts to know Brahman. Fichte (1762–1814) had sought to develop the world itself from out of reflection, self-consciousness, believing that such an initial turning inward was the crucial key. Schopenhauer, in *The World as Will and Idea* (1819), had posited the noumenon as a "will," a will to life, the subjective knowledge of one's body, which he believed was represented most purely by the art of music. In the world of appearances or idea (*Vorstellung*), individual wills were doomed to run into conflict with other wills, and to suffer. Thus the pessimism of his stance, the admonition to deny the will and renounce striving.

In his first work, *The Birth of Tragedy,* Nietzsche was still operating within this dualistic mode of thought, opposing what he saw as the root and essence of human experience, or the universal Dionysian aspect of life and creativity, to the individuated Apollonian world of forms and dreams. Of course, these dual terms cannot simply be inserted into the same one equation to explain

Kant, Fichte, Schopenhauer, and Nietzsche; still, in his theory of the Dionysian, in his defense of tragic pessimism, in the glorification of the vanished culture of ancient Greece, and in his hailing of Richard Wagner's art as the rebirth of the ideal art, blended of Dionysian essence and Apollonian form, Nietzsche was thinking very much along the lines of romanticism.

In *Human, All Too Human* this is no longer so. Nietzsche's new work is determinedly in the spirit of the eighteenth-century Enlightenment. Nietzsche is cutting the ties to his romantic past, and in the process taking up a monistic world view, the materialism which had impressed him earlier in Friedrich Albert Lange's work *The History of Materialism* (1864) and which his friend Rée also espoused.[3] Characteristic in this regard is the quotation from Descartes that Nietzsche cites in lieu of a preface to the first edition of *Human, All Too Human* (1878). For Descartes, the search for knowledge is the way to meaning and joy; Nietzsche too will henceforth eschew what Schopenhauer called "metaphysical need" and, like Descartes, proceed rather "to develop his reason." It is a scientific attitude that predominates: his first aphorism is entitled "A chemistry of concepts and feelings," indicating Nietzsche's attempt to overcome the heat of a romantic approach and take on the coolness of science. As Thomas Mann understood, Nietzsche's denial of the death-bearing romanticism of Wagner and Schopenhauer, despite his love for it, was a self-overcoming.[4] As Nietzsche himself might have said, it was a transformation of the spirit.

*Human, All Too Human* is not only a break with Nietzsche's philosophical past: this pivotal work also reveals the beginnings of several of the concepts that are crucial to his later philosophy. His notion of the will to power is here in embryo, as is his transcendence of conventional Christian morality. Although Zarathustra and the Eternal Recurrence have not yet occurred to him (these were to come later, in 1881), the "Free Spirit" who appears here is Zarathustra's precursor. Functioning above the masses, independent of all accepted conventions, he embodies a friend as

3. For a full discussion of Nietzsche's early study of materialism, see Karl Schlechta and Anni Anders, *Friedrich Nietzsche: Von den verborgenen Anfängen seines Philosophierens* (Stuttgart: Fromann Verlag, 1962).

4. Thomas Mann, "Vorspruch zu einer musikalischen Nietzschefeier," *Gesammelte Werke* (Frankfurt: Fischer, 1974), vol. 10 p. 182.

Nietzsche would have wished one, or Nietzsche himself, as he saw himself during this period.

There is a third aspect to the critical nature of *Human, All Too Human*. It marks a turning point in terms of Nietzsche's style, as well. As there is a beginning here philosophically, so Nietzsche's style in this work is also beginning to assume its ultimate form. The main characteristic of this new style is Nietzsche's use of the aphorism. The 638 aphorisms of *Human, All Too Human* range from a few words to a few pages, but most are short paragraphs. One critic has observed that they are designed to consternate the reader and expose him to a shock of recognition.[5] The sometimes purple prose notable in *The Birth of Tragedy* has now given way to a new tone—a new sensibility, one might say, in which daring of thought outvalues Wagnerian weight. As one of the foremost Nietzsche scholars, R. J. Hollingdale, points out, reading *Human, All Too Human* makes us feel as if we had "come out of a closed drawing room into a cold breeze."[6]

"Most thinkers write badly because they tell us not only their thoughts, but also the thinking of the thoughts," writes Nietzsche in Aphorism 188. Nietzsche himself is determined to be different. Even when he does expand on a theme, the density and intensity of his thought are remarkable. After some initial unevenness, his style is clear and direct: he settles at a high altitude of abstraction and remains there, varying his text with examples, but rarely, if ever, with excessive information, observations, or digressions.

There are, however, different tones within the overall spare contours. Occasionally, and usually at the end of a section, Nietzsche can wax rhapsodical (i.e., Aphs. 107, 223, 292, 628). He uses metaphors from mythology (Hesiod's good Eris, the veiled Isis) and from daily experience. There is no visible evidence of scholarly toil, but rather wide-ranging erudition, well-argued points, and flashes of wit.

The two poems that close this volume anticipate the verse at the beginning and end of his later work from this period, *The Gay Science* (1882). Though flawed as art, they do help to indicate the other fundamental philosophical position revealed by Nietzsche's

5. Beda Allemann, "Nietzsche und die Dichtung" in *Nietzsche: Werk und Wirkung*, ed. H. Steffen (Göttingen: Vandenhoeck und Ruprecht, 1974), p. 51.

6. R. J. Hollingdale, *Nietzsche* (London: Routledge and Kegan Paul, 1973), p. 56.

new style. His blend of verse, pathos, and scientific exposition demonstrates his rejection of the idea that the work of a philosopher must be to construct a system to explain the world. Unlike his predecessors Kant and Schopenhauer, Nietzsche follows the fundamental tenet, evident already here, that "everything has evolved" (Aph. 16), that truth—or better, truths—are therefore relative, shifting, never absolute. Given this insight, the aphorism, which allows for a loosely organized, shifting whole containing specific ideas but no iron-clad explanation for everything, constitutes the style that best represents his philosophy.

It is this attitude which has allowed existentialism to claim Nietzsche as one of its spiritual forefathers. The subjectivity of truth, the rejection of the primacy of any philosophical system, as well as the fusion of the literary and the philosophical—all demonstrate the affinity between Nietzsche and writers such as Sartre, Camus, and that other forerunner of the existentialist movement, Kierkegaard.

These three points of view—the biographical, the philosophical, and the stylistic—are closely interrelated. Wagner, for example, was both personal friend and cultural phenomenon; Schopenhauer, both the cherished philosophical companion of Nietzsche's youthful isolation and the author of a philosophy with objective shortcomings. The materialistic bent was both the intellectual direction Nietzsche had known earlier and was now ready to take, and one enthusiastically endorsed by his new friend Rée; the aphorism, both a sign of his personal liberation and the best expression of his new philosophical search after small but sturdy "humble truths" (Aph. 3). And although *Human, All Too Human* may be too fluid a work to be called "a monument," it does indeed—from all these points of view—symbolize the crisis Nietzsche experienced, a critical turning point in his life and thought.

## The Literary Context

However fresh and daring a work within the context of Nietzsche's career, *Human, All Too Human* is not the first work of its kind in world literature, nor even within the German tradition. It belongs to the genre of the aphorism, which had already been well established.

In the German tradition, Nietzsche's most important predecessor, appropriately enough, is a figure of the Enlightenment: Georg Christoph Lichtenberg (1742–99). His aphorisms, published posthumously in 1800, are, as Goethe observed, jests that mark the spot where a problem lies buried. In his work, Lichtenberg attempts to balance his own tendency to negativism with humor and practical rules of conduct. Nietzsche greatly admired Lichtenberg's writing, ahead of its time in its subject matter and views, and helped it to gain wider recognition. He had already quoted him in the first of his *Untimely Meditations,* and acknowledges him in *Human, All Too Human* with a citation in Aphorism 133.

The aphorism was also used during the period of early romanticism by theoretical writers such as Friedrich Schlegel and Novalis (whom Nietzsche cites in Aph. 142). Despite his admiration for them, their aphorisms, centered as they are on the transcendental and the mystical, do not bear as directly on Nietzsche's use of the genre as do those of the late romantic Schopenhauer, whose collection *Aphorisms for Practical Wisdom (Aphorismen zur Lebensweisheit,* 1851) anticipates Nietzsche. The tenor of Nietzsche's observations is almost totally opposite that of the pessimist Schopenhauer, who denies the reality of any pleasure and argues the cynical view that the best way to live is to escape pain, which *is* real; but Nietzsche's own work is indebted to Schopenhauer's for the strong sense of the writer's independent personal voice and emotional involvement in his work, for its psychological orientation, for its reliance on quotations from classical literature, and for its acknowledgment of the French aphorists.

It is above all this shared debt to the French tradition of the aphorism which is most important to *Human, All Too Human,* for Nietzsche's work is a deliberate turn westward. Whereas in "Richard Wagner in Bayreuth" Nietzsche had compared the Germans to the Greeks and seen in German art the rebirth of a Greek spirit, in this work he contends rather that it is the French who have inherited the birthright of the Greeks: "The Frenchman's nature is much more closely related to the Greek's than is the German's" (Aph. 221). Nietzsche cites the French aphorists Jean de La Bruyère and Prosper Merimée, and in Aphorism 221 he celebrates Voltaire as an artist to be admired and emulated (as opposed to Wagner, or that romantic French figure also discussed in the work, Rousseau). The extreme act of apostasy, from the point of view of Wagner and his circle, was the dedication to Voltaire on the one hundredth anniversary of the French skeptic's death.[7] Besides his need to defy Wagner, Nietzsche's wish to counteract the widespread chauvinism of the years following the Franco-Prussian War may have helped decide him on this pro-French stance of 1876. The removal of the dedication in the 1886 edition suggests that it was ultimately too radical a turn westward, even for Nietzsche. He himself says in *Ecco Homo* that his honoring Voltaire in this way was in truth a step toward his own self-discovery.

At the beginning of the second section (which in an early rough draft was to be the beginning of the entire work), Nietzsche mentions La Rochefoucauld. It is clear that he is named here at the outset as a model, the epitome of the aphorist, a master of the type of writing unjustly held in low esteem by the Germans of Nietzsche's day. Nietzsche is trying to revive the Frenchman's art, an art like that of cameo making, underappreciated but requiring great skill and expertise.

We know that Nietzsche had a copy of La Rochefoucauld's *Sentences et maximes* (1665) in his library, and that he had been reading it shortly before beginning to write *Human, All Too Human,* on the train ride to Sorrento, in fact. (This may have been at the suggestion of Paul Rée, an admirer of La Rochefoucauld.)[8] More than that of the other French aphorists mentioned by Nietzsche, it is La Rochefoucauld's work that lies behind his own. Instead of making a general comparison, it might be illuminating to examine an aphorism from each writer, on the same topic—gratitude—to see in some detail what Nietzsche has done with the tradition he inherited. La Rochefoucauld's Aphorism 298 runs as follows:

7. The dedication on the title page reads as follows: "Dedicated to the memory of Voltaire on the celebration of the anniversary of his death, May 30, 1778." On the reverse of the page is the following motto: "This monologue of a book, which was written during a winter's sojourn (1876 to 1877), would not be made public now, if the proximity of May 30, 1878, had not aroused the all-too-keen desire to offer personal homage at the right moment to one of the greatest liberators of the spirit."

8. For more about Nietzsche's relationship to French literature, see W. D. Williams, *Nietzsche and the French* (Oxford: Basil Blackwell, 1952).

La reconnaissance, dans la plupart des hommes, n'est qu'une forte et sécrète envie de recevoir de plus grands bienfaits. (In the majority of men, gratitude is nothing but a strong and secret desire to receive even greater favors.)

Nietzsche's forty-fourth aphorism reads:

> *Gratitude and revenge.* The powerful man feels gratitude for the following reason: through his good deed, his benefactor has, as it were, violated the powerful man's sphere and penetrated it. Now through his act of gratitude the powerful man requites himself by violating the sphere of the benefactor. It is a milder form of revenge. Without the satisfaction of gratitude, the powerful man would have shown himself to be unpowerful and henceforth would be considered such. For that reason, every society of good men (that is, originally of powerful men) places gratitude among its first duties.
>
> Swift remarked that men are grateful in the same proportion as they cherish revenge.

Although La Rochefoucauld's work includes passages longer than this one, and Nietzsche's shorter, both these aphorisms are typical of their authors in terms of length: Nietzsche does not generally attain the same brevity and grace as La Rochefoucald. His aphorisms do not usually build towards a *pointe* in the French sense; rather Nietzsche goes more thoroughly into the matter at hand. Even the lines of this most elegant of German writers seem a bit heavy-handed when compared to the chiseled sharpness, the balan˄ed reversals and rhythm of his French model.

What is most interesting, however, is the difference in the explanations for gratitude offered by the two writers. As always, both authors are disabusing man of his illusion that gratitude is as pure or selfless or straightforward as it would seem. But La Rochefoucauld emphasizes in gratitude the human desire to be self-seeking, to advance oneself, as through flattery. Egoism (*l'amour-propre*) is at the root of La Rochefoucauld's psychology of man, and gratitude is yet another manifestation of it, a means to gain advantage from others by one's behavior. In other aphorisms about gratitude he likens it to a kind of money, paid in the hope of making better loans in the future (Aph. 223) and he stresses the role of pride in the transaction (Aph. 225). La Rochefoucauld's life as an aristocrat close to the court of Louis XIV may well be part of the reason for his particular psychological insight into gratitude.

Like La Rochefoucauld, Nietzsche is exposing a secret reason for gratitude; he does not accept it at face value, but seeks a psychological explanation truer than any obvious one. But his metaphor is derived neither from the search to find favor with a monarch nor from commercial trading. Nor is self-love or pride salient here. Rather, Nietzsche, in an anticipation of his theory of the will to power, uses territorial metaphors of attack, of power struggles, to interpret what we call gratitude. The powerful man has been weakened by a kindness. By his gratitude he avenges himself on his benefactor, showing his own power, and thus demonstrating that gratitude and revenge—normally conceived as opposites— are fundamentally similar (another example of Nietzsche's monistic tendency, this time within the moral sphere). Other aphorisms dealing with gratitude (Aphs. 92, 323, 366) again conceive it in terms of weak and strong, of nobility of nature, rather than of egoism per se.[9] Tabling the question of the influence of a Bismarckian *Zeitgeist,* we can at least speculate that such a psychology of gratitude may be partially attributed to Nietzsche's own conception of his life as struggle—with himself, his illness, and the outside world.

Furthermore, Nietzsche's historical orientation is evident here, for in writing of "every society of good men (that is, originally of powerful men)" he reveals his invariable genealogical approach to subjects under investigation, whether metaphysical, religious, or moral. This kind of historical method both goes beyond La Rochefoucauld's, which is limited to his own particular time, place, and society, and at the same time puts limits on La Rochefoucauld's apparent universality by insisting on the *evolution* of every kind of behavior or conviction.

Nietzsche's use of the aphorism in this work, then, grows out of a tradition, one with which he was very familiar and for which he had great respect. It is his first essay into the new genre, and he

9. In Aphorism 50, Nietzsche himself improves La Rochefoucauld's analysis of pity as "stupidity" along these same lines, seeing pity rather as a tool for inflicting pain on others. Nietzsche's style of kneading the stuff of his aphorisms much more than La Rochefoucauld does is well represented in this aphorism.

incorporates acknowledgment of his masters into his work. (In German literature, the tradition continues with Franz Kafka, Walter Benjamin, and, more recently, Elias Canetti.) Yet Nietzsche's contribution to the genre is unique: the breadth of his vision is remarkable, for he covers a range of issues far greater than the social and psychological area of interest to La Rochefoucauld. To the cynicism typical of the genre, Nietzsche brings a new dimension by his combination of nihilistic energy with historical consciousness. Finally, he expands the genre to include not merely insights, but argument as well: where La Rochefoucauld twists a knife, Nietzsche hammers at the nailhead until it is firmly lodged.

## The Structure of the Work

The intent of *Human, All Too Human* is immediately evident from its title.[10] Reflecting all that we have outlined above, the title declares that this work will be concerned with material, psychological, and social truths. Furthermore, it suggests that human fallibilities—not strengths—are to be the focus of attention. The phrase itself is used at the outset, in Aphorism 35 (originally conceived as the first aphorism), when Nietzsche observes that maxims about human nature can help in overcoming life's hard moments. Thus there is also an implicit drive to overcome what is "human, all too human" through understanding it, through philosophy.

The work is divided into nine books, which can be loosely grouped around certain key themes or ideas. Sections One to Four are concerned, respectively, with metaphysics, morality, religion, and art. Nietzsche sets out to expose the erroneous assumptions that underlie men's beliefs in all four areas. As shown earlier, he attacks the philosophical theory that there is some "real world" as opposed to the world of appearances which we know, and this he does primarily in the first section, "Of First and Last Things." Nietzsche traces the origin of metaphysical beliefs to physiological causes, such as dreams (Aph. 13), to psychological causes, such as dissatisfaction with oneself (Aph. 17), or to lan-

10. Strictly speaking, the title *Menschliches, Allzumenschliches* means "*Things Human, All Too Human.*"

guage itself (Aph. 11). He concludes that we can know nothing positive about a metaphysical world, even if it should exist. In fact, our knowledge of it "would be the most inconsequential of all knowledge, even more inconsequential than the knowledge of the chemical analysis of water must be to the boatman facing a storm" (Aph. 9). In his book about this first section, Peter Heller writes that its theme is the philosopher's "bliss in the unhappiness of knowledge."[11] For in giving up metaphysical convictions the philosopher also gains the chance for greater freedom.

In Section Two, which anticipates his later genealogy of morals, and is indebted to Rée, whom he cites, Nietzsche goes on to outline the origin of our moral assumptions, exposing the falsity both of the Christian and of the Schopenhauerian idea of good and evil. Originally, according to Nietzsche, powerful men formed a community that was called good (Aph. 45), and justice originated in terms of equal powers (Aph. 92). Custom (*Sitte*) is seen as antedating morality (*Sittlichkeit*): in fact, morality is equivalent to conforming to custom (Aph. 96). "Evil" actions are in actuality innocent (Aph. 99), for man seeks his own well-being above all else, even if this results in harm to others.[12] Between good and evil there is therefore no difference in type, but only in degree. Contrary to Schopenhauer's belief, everything is the consequence of necessity, and all men of knowledge must swallow "the bitterest drop" (Aph. 107), man's complete lack of responsibility, both for his behavior and for his nature.

The third section analyses religious worship from a psychological viewpoint, not as the serving of any divine truth (Aph. 110), but rather as the attempt of a weaker party to control a stronger one (Aph. 111). Ultimately, even the saintly or ascetic way of life has nothing innately virtuous or saintly about it, but is yet another way for man to wage war: this time, against a part of himself. While not discounting the greatness of religious figures,

---

11. Peter Heller, "*Von den ersten und letzten Dingen*" (Berlin: De Gruyter, 1972), p. xxviii. This is the only thorough study of *Human, All Too Human* to date; although it is structured around the first section of the work only, it covers a vast range of issues and ramifications growing out of the work. See also Heller's *Dialectics and Nihilism* (Amherst: University of Massachusetts Press, 1966).

12. In this sense, Nietzsche, like La Rochefoucauld, acknowledges the importance of egoism as a human motivation (cf. Aph. 101).

Nietzsche assails Christianity as a barbaric form of thought desiring to "destroy, shatter, stun, intoxicate" (Aph. 114) rather than to enable man to feel self-respect in his relationship to a godhead.

In the fourth section, the aesthetic experience is taken to task. Here Nietzsche is concerned with the demystification of art, artists, and—though he is never mentioned by name—Richard Wagner in particular, for the word *artist* in this section is largely a cipher for Wagner. Championing preromantic artists such as Voltaire and Goethe, Nietzsche stresses the effort involved in art, the years of hard work, examining at length and ultimately debunking the notion of divine inspiration. He deflates the idea of "genius," a term so valued by Wagner. Instead, he concludes that "every human activity is amazingly complicated, not only that of the genius: but none is a 'miracle'" (Aph. 162). In this section, the rejection of all that Wagner meant to Nietzsche, as hero and as artist, is accomplished for the first (though not for the last) time.

In these four books, Nietzsche's famous "philosophizing with a hammer" is anticipated, for his prime aim is not so much to construct new systems of values or beliefs as to shatter—with some regret for their loss—the old, erroneous ways of thinking. However, in Section Five, on high and low culture, Nietzsche is no longer simply destroying. Rather, he also presents his own answer to the demolition he has just accomplished, formulating at some length and depth the idea of the "free spirit" (*Freigeist*), which is to evolve in his later works into the sage Zarathustra, one who is paving the way for the Superman, the ultimate form of man. Indeed, the subtitle of *Human, All Too Human* is "A Book for Free Spirits." In this section, Nietzsche outlines the function of the free spirit within a culture: it is his role to challenge the old, the conventional, to wound the society at its vulnerable spot (Aph. 224), to take upon himself the fear and censure of the society in order to promote its growth and development. This exposition of the free spirit occurs in the fifth of the nine sections, and thus at the midpoint or peak of its structure, emphasizing the importance of the free spirit as the symbol of the new, positive direction to Nietzsche's thought. The free spirit is essentially the philosopher as Nietzsche sees him, hovering above the human fray, coolly testing the culture for its truths and errors; for while there is no Truth for Nietzsche—neither in metaphysical, moral, religious, nor aesthetic terms—there are truths, and it is these which the free spirit will seek out, since to him, as to Descartes, "no honey is sweeter than that of knowledge" (Aph. 292).

Sections Six and Seven deal with the traditional domain of the aphorism: here Nietzsche comments, respectively, on man in society and on women and children. These aphorisms tend to be shorter and perhaps more facile than those in the other books. In Section Six, Nietzsche attempts to emulate La Rochefoucauld's worldliness about the manners of society. He observes the dodges and darts of conversation, the hypocrisy and cunning in everyday intercourse, and fires off some witty remarks: "One is twice as happy to dive after a man who has fallen into the water if people are present who do not dare to" (Aph. 325). In general, however, he seems rather ill at ease with this more mundane subject matter.

The same is true in the seventh section. Nietzsche's notorious misogynistic views are in evidence: Women are "so much more personal than objective" (Aph. 419); they "intrigue secretly against their husband's higher soul" (Aph. 434). One should also note that there are less hostile, more considered observations. Nietzsche knows, for example, that "everyone carries within him an image of woman which he gets from his mother" (Aph. 380). He affirms that a good marriage is based on the ability to converse: "Everything else in marriage is transitory, but most of the time in interaction is spent in conversation" (Aph. 406). He expresses hope for the future of women (Aphs. 416, 424). Yet—again with likely biographical overtones—Nietzsche concludes that marriage and the life of the free spirit are incompatible (Aph. 426).

In Section Eight Nietzsche analyzes the structures of power in the state. He discounts the hopes of Marxian social theory, seeing the claim of the lower classes for their just share not as an outcry for social justice, but only as the beast's roar at food he cannot have (Aph. 451). But he also shows his cosmopolitan, antinationalistic colors when he decries the necessity of war; even while acknowledging that war may be necessary to put new energy into a culture (Aph. 477), he laments that it is at the cost of the lives of the finest, most able and promising of a nation's youth (Aph. 481). The state, like religion, depends on a "mysterium"; it is Nietzsche's intention to be the harbinger of the end of this mysterium, too, and thus to proclaim "the death of the state" (Aph. 472).

The final section of the book concerns man alone with himself. There is a poetic quality to many of these aphorisms, almost a kind of mellow resignation at times: "However far man may extend himself with knowledge," he writes, "however objective he may appear to himself—ultimately he carries away with him nothing but his own biography" (Aph. 513). In an anticipation of *The Wanderer and His Shadow* (1880), and ultimately of the figure Zarathustra, we see Nietzsche as the solitary wanderer enjoying his own counsel. Toward the end of the section, he evokes the goddess Justice, the even-minded goddess he has sought to serve in this work. Aware of the tendency of his own nature to swing from the extreme of heated passion or enthusiasm to the other extreme of cold, rational calculation, he adores the Enlightenment ideal of temperate judgment. The work closes with praise of the forenoon. Biographically, the thirty-four-year-old may well have been thinking of his own life, almost *"nel mezzo del camin."* Philosophically, he may have had in mind this stage of his own thought: not yet at its zenith, but on the way to it, well beyond the romantic mists of its dawn. And stylistically, it is the forenoon of a clear, sunny, fresh prose voice energetically analyzing or thoughtfully musing on the nature of life and the human, all too human nature of man.

## Bibliographical History

This translation is of the first volume of Nietzsche's work *Menschliches, Allzumenschliches,* begun in Sorrento in winter, 1876. (An earlier form of the work, *The Plowshare,* a kind of notebook comprising roughly one third of the finished book, was completed in September, 1876.) The work was finished in Basel in 1878 and published by Ernst Schmeitzner. In 1879, *Assorted Opinions and Maxims* was published as an appendix to the work. This volume and *The Wanderer and His Shadow,* published separately in 1880, were joined together in 1886 to form what is now known as the second volume of *Human, All Too Human.* At that time Nietzsche also added the two poems which serve as a postlude to the first volume, and a preface, analyzing his own work from the perspective of his subsequent life and thought. He removed from the original title page the dedication to Voltaire and also deleted the quotation from Descartes which had stood in lieu of a preface.

Contemporary reception of the work was mixed. Not surprisingly, Richard Wagner and his circle were hostile. Nietzsche wrote to his friend Peter Gast in May, 1878, that the book had been "practically banned by Bayreuth."[13] But others recognized its merit at once; again not surprisingly, Paul Rée was pleased. More important, the venerable historian Jacob Burckhardt, who had become Nietzsche's admirer and friend in Basel, was enthusiastic. Writing to Gast on May 31, he called Nietzsche's work a "masterful [*souveränes*] book," and asserted that it would "increase the amount of independence in the world."[14] Nietzsche was gratified by Burckhardt's enthusiasm and wrote of it to others.

Today, *Human, All Too Human* is still one of Nietzsche's less familiar works, perhaps because in it the visionary Nietzsche is so overshadowed by the skeptical Nietzsche. It represents the extreme of his cool and detached side, and its voice is less overtly personal than in later works. Some would regard it as less profound, while to others, wary of profundity, this very fact may be its great attraction.

## The Translation

"*Untranslatable*. It is neither the best nor the worst of a work which is untranslatable" (Aph. 134). Despite this mild encouragement on Nietzsche's part, the task of translation has still been a formidable one. As if the challenge of rendering Nietzsche in another language were not great enough, it is not always clear what the text is in German; variants abound from one version of the manuscript to another, from edition to edition, from publisher to publisher. We have consulted several texts based on the 1886 edition; significant discrepancies are indicated in the footnotes.

The previous English translation of the work was done in 1909 by Helen Zimmern, author of books on Schopenhauer and Lessing. She had once met Nietzsche briefly, and later became the translator of this and other volumes for the only complete English-language edition of Nietzsche's work, edited by Oscar Levy and published in 1909–11. Because of Zimmern's antiquated

---

13. Quoted in Middleton, *Selected Letters,* p. 167.
14. Ibid.

Victorian style, Nietzsche comes to sound in her translation like a fusty contemporary of Matthew Arnold. Though he may indeed have been Arnold's contemporary, he was anything but fusty in this work, neither in its ideas nor in its style, which makes it one of the best examples of his pithy, incisive writing. Our new translation seeks to capture in modern English Nietzsche's detached and yet passionate tone.

Zimmern often has resourceful solutions to the problems in translating this text; but despite its overall accuracy, her translation contains numerous errors. In Aphorism 61, for example, the word *Schaf* (sheep) is rendered as "fool," which could be another possible meaning; but in this case the reference is to Sophocles' play *Ajax,* in which the mad hero does indeed charge a herd of sheep, taking them for soldiers. In several places there are possible misreadings. These, too, when significant, are noted in the footnotes.

Understandably, Zimmern's Victorian translation is also sometimes marred by bowdlerizations. She avoids the word "dung" (Aph. 121), for example, and more important, distorts Jesus's *Einbildung* (fantasy) that he was the son of God into an "idea" (Aph. 144). J. M. Kennedy, the editor of the volume, adds an unwanted color, too. For example, to Aphorism 603, which asserts that one cannot feel both love and respect for the same person at the same time, he adds a footnote: "Women never understand this." Nietzsche serves himself badly enough with his own such generalizations; we do not need Kennedy's two cents' worth, too.

Faithfulness to the text, then, both in its tone and its semantic meaning, was our first concern. And, as in any translation, we encountered some specific problems which need to be explained:

The word *Freigeist* is central to the work, and its translation is problematic. It could be rendered either "free thinker" or "free spirit." (*Freigeisterei* has no real alternative in English: it is "free-thinking.") In his subtitle, Nietzsche writes that *Human, All Too Human* is a book for "*freie Geister.*" The terms *Freigeist* and *freier Geist* are inextricably interrelated, if not interchangeable. But the plural *Geister* could only be translated as "spirits" (or "minds"), never as "thinkers"; thus we have chosen to render *Freigeist* as "free spirit."

There is another, more important reason for the choice, as well.

"Free thinker" implies something British, a no-nonsense atheism and anticlerical stance. The term *Geist,* suggesting Nietzsche's original debt to Schopenhauer and Wagner, demands the slightly ethereal overtones of the word "spirit." For Nietzsche was not *merely* a free thinker, but even in this work never ceased to respect the very lies he had stopped believing in. (The fact that "free spirit" in English also suggests something devil-may-care or flighty is a risk we have to take, and, for all that, it may not be entirely out of keeping with Nietzsche's intentions, either.)

The words *Sitte* (custom) and *Sittlichkeit* (morality) were also a problem. In Section Two, Nietzsche is able to preserve a playfulness with these terms, central to his moral history, a playfulness that is lost in the translation. In the German, the words themselves make clear the origins of the one in the other. While "mores" and "morals" are successful in certain cases, they do not work in others.

Unlike Walter Kaufmann, then, whose translations of Nietzsche have deservedly become classics, we have not tried to translate *Geist* as "spirit" whenever it appears, nor *sittlich* invariably as "moral." We have chosen as the context demanded. Nor have we emulated Kaufmann in our annotations; rather than wishing to offer a running commentary to Nietzsche's text, we are concerned primarily to identify references, explain terms, note discrepancies, offer the German original in certain cases, and point out some of Nietzsche's verbal games. To present a more readable English text, we have followed Kaufmann's example in breaking up long paragraphs into shorter paragraphs at those places where Nietzsche has indicated a break in thought with a dash.

As mentioned above, Nietzsche's play with words is integral to his art. Whenever possible, we have tried to render it in the text itself. But often there is a need to explain his untranslatable puns and other word games. This tendency on Nietzsche's part is most marked in the 1886 preface to the work. Here the translator sometimes even has the feeling that the potential of the German language for making new words by adding or changing prefixes actually determined the direction of Nietzsche's thought—that the conceit dictated the conception, so to speak. In this beautiful and moving self-examination, the reader might also have an uneasy feeling about such a preoccupation with words, their sound per se, as divorced from their conventionally accepted (or newly defined) meaning.

Nietzsche's insight into language and its detachment from that which is signified is one of the main reasons for the interest in Nietzsche on the part of many contemporary French critics. Michel Foucault, for example, speaks of Nietzsche in terms of a self-referential hermeneutic, a "région mitoyenne de la folie et du pur langage."[15] In his later works, Nietzsche's conviction about the arbitrary nature of language, its ultimate meaninglessness (Zarathustra: "*only* a fool, *only* a poet") is clear. And it is evident in Aphorism 11 of this work, as well: only late, Nietzsche writes, did men realize that "in their belief in language they have propagated a monstrous error." But this is only one aspect of Nietzsche's self-understanding. For communication is intended by the act of writing, even when the writer is as solitary and self-enclosed a character as Nietzsche. Zarathustra himself comes down from the mountain to speak to men. Nietzsche's despair at the lies of philosophers and poets, their inevitable lies, is countered by his continued exercise with words, with the aim of presenting a well-articulated, forceful philosophy to the world. His lifelong theme was one of overcoming: health is the overcoming of sickness; the values of one society are overcome by the next; each stage of an individual's life is a self-overcoming. Surely such a thinker did not regard his language merely as a web of illusions, but also—paradoxically—as the tool for the heroic overcoming of that very premise.

Today Nietzsche is enjoying a reception that parallels the earlier breadth of his influence around 1900. If *Human, All Too Human* is one of his less settled works, bulkier and less confident than later efforts, it is no less seminal, no less fascinating and engaging. This pivotal work is crucial to his development; we hope with this new translation to provide an essential complement to the body of his thought already available in good translation.

Marion Faber

15. Michel Foucault, "Nietzsche, Freud, Marx," in *Nietzsche,* Cahiers de Royaumont Philosophie no. 6 (Paris: Les Éditions de Minuit, 1967), p. 192.

# HUMAN,
## ALL TOO
## HUMAN

# Preface[1]

## I

Often enough, and always with great consternation, people have
told me that there is something distinctive in all my writings, from

1. In the place of this preface to the 1886 edition, the 1878 edition of *Human,
All Too Human* included the following quotation from René Descartes's *Discourse
on Method:*

### In Lieu of a Preface

". . . for a time I reviewed the various occupations of men in this life, trying
to choose out the best; and without wishing to say anything of the em-
ployment of others, I thought that I could not do better than continue in
the one in which I found myself engaged, that is to say, in occupying my
whole life in cultivating my Reason, and in advancing as much as possible
the knowledge of the truth in accordance with the method which I had
prescribed myself. I had tasted so much satisfaction since beginning to use
this method, that I did not believe that anything sweeter or more innocent
could be found in this life; every day I discovered by its means something
new which seemed to me sufficiently important, and not at all familiar to
other men. The joy which I had so filled my soul that all else seemed of no
account."

( . . . je m'avisay de faire un reveuë sur les diverses occupations qu'ont les
hommes en cete vie, pour tascher a faire chois de la meilleure; et sans que je
vueille rien dire de celles des autres, je pensay que je ne pouvois mieux que
de continuër en celle la mesme ou je me trouvois, c'est a dire, que d'em-
ployer toute ma vie a cultiver ma raison, et m'avancer, autant que je pour-
rois, en la connoissance de la verité, suivant la Methode que je m'estois
prescrite. J'avois esprouvé de si extremes contentmens, depuis que j'avois
commencé de me servir de cete Methode, que je ne croyois pas qu'on pust
recevoir de plus doux, ny de plus innocens, en cete vie; et descouvrant tous
les jours par son moyen quelques veritez, qui me sembloient assez impor-
tantes, et communement ignorées des autres hommes, la satisfaction que
j'en avois remplissoit tellement mon esprit que tout le reste ne me touchoit
point.)

*The Birth of Tragedy* to the most recently published *Prologue to a Philosophy of the Future.*[2] All of them, I have been told, contain snares and nets for careless birds, and an almost constant, unperceived challenge to reverse one's habitual estimations and esteemed habits. "What's that? *Everything* is only—human, all too human?" With such a sigh one comes from my writings, they say, with a kind of wariness and distrust even toward morality, indeed tempted and encouraged in no small way to become the spokesman for the worst things: might they perhaps be only the best slandered? My writings have been called a School for Suspicion, even more for Contempt, fortunately also for Courage and, in fact, for Daring. Truly, I myself do not believe that anyone has ever looked into the world with such deep suspicion, and not only as an occasional devil's advocate, but every bit as much, to speak theologically, as an enemy and challenger of God. Whoever guesses something of the consequences of any deep suspicion, something of the chills and fears stemming from isolation, to which every man burdened with an unconditional *difference of viewpoint* is condemned, this person will understand how often I tried to take shelter somewhere, to recover from myself, as if to forget myself entirely for a time (in some sort of reverence, or enmity, or scholarliness, or frivolity, or stupidity); and he will also understand why, when I could not find what I *needed,* I had to gain it by force artificially, to counterfeit it, or create it poetically. (And what have poets ever done otherwise? And why else do we have all the art in the world?) What I always needed most to cure and restore myself, however, was the belief that I was *not* the only one to be thus, to *see* thus—I needed the enchanting intuition of kinship and equality in the eye and in desire, repose in a trusted friendship; I needed a shared blindness, with no suspicion or question marks, a pleasure in foregrounds, surfaces, what is near, what is nearest, in everything that has color, skin, appearance. Perhaps one could accuse me in this regard of some sort of "art," various sorts of finer counterfeiting: for example, that I had deliberately and willfully closed my eyes to Schopenhauer's blind will to morality,[3] at a time when I was al-

2. *The Birth of Tragedy* was published in 1872. *Prologue to a Philosophy of the Future* is the subtitle of *Beyond Good and Evil,* published in 1886.

3. In "Schopenhauer as Educator" (1874). For Nietzsche's later response to

ready clear-sighted enough about morality; similarly, that I had deceived myself about Richard Wagner's incurable romanticism,[4] as if it were a beginning and not an end; similarly, about the Greeks; similarly about the Germans and their future—and there might be a whole long list of such Similarly's. But even if this all were true and I were accused of it with good reason, what do *you* know, what *could* you know about the amount of self-preserving cunning, of reason and higher protection that is contained in such self-deception—and how much falseness I still *require* so that I may keep permitting myself the luxury of *my* truthfulness?

Enough, I am still alive; and life has not been devised by morality: it *wants* deception, it *lives* on deception—but wouldn't you know it? Here I am, beginning again, doing what I have always done, the old immoralist and birdcatcher, I am speaking immorally, extra-morally, "beyond good and evil."

2

Thus I invented, when I needed them, the "free spirits"[5] too, to whom this heavyhearted-stouthearted[6] book with the title "Human, All Too Human" is dedicated. There are no such "free spirits," were none—but, as I said, I needed their company at the time, to be of good cheer in the midst of bad things (illness, isolation, foreignness, sloth, inactivity); as brave fellows and specters to chat and laugh with, when one feels like chatting and laughing, and whom one sends to hell when they get boring—as reparation for lacking friends. That there *could* someday be such free spirits, that our Europe will have such lively, daring fellows among its sons of tomorrow and the day after tomorrow, real and palpable and not merely, as in my case, phantoms and a hermit's shadow play: I am the last person to want to doubt that. I already see them *coming,* slowly, slowly; and perhaps I am doing something to hasten their

---

Schopenhauer's blind will to morality, see especially Aphorism 39.

4. In "Richard Wagner in Bayreuth" (1876). For Nietzsche's later response to Wagner's art, see especially Aphorisms 164, 165, 215, 219.

5. *die "freien Geister."* See Introduction.

6. *schwermütig-mutig*

coming when I describe before the fact the fateful conditions that I
*see* giving rise to them, the paths on which I *see* them coming?

### 3

It may be conjectured that the decisive event for a spirit in
whom the type of the "free spirit" is one day to ripen to sweet
perfection has been a *great separation,*[7] and that before it, he was
probably all the more a bound spirit, and seemed to be chained
forever to his corner, to his post. What binds most firmly? Which
cords can almost not be torn? With men of a high and select type,
it will be their obligations: that awe which befits the young, their
diffidence and delicacy before all that is time-honored and digni-
fied, their gratitude for the ground out of which they grew, for the
hand that led them, for the shrine where they learned to worship—their own highest moments will bind them most firmly and
oblige them most lastingly. For such bound people the great separation comes suddenly, like the shock of an earthquake: all at once
the young soul is devastated, torn loose, torn out—it itself does
not know what is happening. An urge, a pressure governs it, mas-
tering the soul like a command: the will and wish awaken to go
away, anywhere, at any cost: a violent, dangerous curiosity for an
undiscovered world flames up and flickers in all the senses. "Better to die than live *here,*" so sounds the imperious and seductive
voice. And this "here," this "at home" is everything which it had
loved until then! A sudden horror and suspicion of that which it
loved; a lightning flash of contempt toward that which was its
"obligation"; a rebellious, despotic, volcanically jolting desire to
roam abroad, to become alienated, cool, sober, icy: a hatred of
love, perhaps a desecratory reaching and glancing *backward,* to
where it had until then worshiped and loved; perhaps a blush of
shame at its most recent act, and at the same time, jubilation *that*
it was done; a drunken, inner, jubilant shudder, which betrays a
victory—a victory? over what? over whom? a puzzling, questioning, questionable victory, but the *first* victory nevertheless: such
bad and painful things are part of the history of the great separation. It is also a disease that can destroy man, this first outburst of
strength and will to self-determination, self-valorization, this will
to *free* will: and how much disease is expressed by the wild at-

7. *Loslösung*

tempts and peculiarities with which the freed man, the separated man, now tries to prove his rule over things! He wanders about savagely with an unsatisfied lust; his booty must atone for the dangerous tension of his pride; he rips apart what attracts him.[8] With an evil laugh he overturns what he finds concealed, spared until then by some shame; he investigates how these things look if they are overturned. There is some arbitrariness and pleasure in arbitrariness to it, if he then perhaps directs his favor to that which previously stood in disrepute—if he creeps curiously and enticingly around what is most forbidden. Behind his ranging activity (for he is journeying restlessly and aimlessly, as in a desert) stands the question mark of an ever more dangerous curiosity. "Cannot *all* values be overturned? And is Good perhaps Evil? And God only an invention, a nicety of the devil? Is everything perhaps ultimately false? And if we are deceived, are we not for that very reason also deceivers? *Must* we not be deceivers, too?" Such thoughts lead and mislead[9] him, always further onward, always further away. Loneliness surrounds him, curls round him, ever more threatening, strangling, heart-constricting, that fearful goddess and *mater saeva cupidinum*[10]—but who today knows what *loneliness* is?

### 4.

It is still a long way from this morbid isolation, from the desert of these experimental years, to that enormous, overflowing certainty and health which cannot do without even illness itself, as an instrument and fishhook of knowledge; to that *mature* freedom of the spirit which is fully as much self-mastery and discipline of the heart, and which permits paths to many opposing ways of thought. It is a long way to the inner spaciousness and cosseting of a superabundance which precludes the danger that the spirit might lose itself on its own paths and fall in love and stay put, intoxicated, in some nook; a long way to that excess of vivid healing, reproducing, reviving powers, the very sign of *great* health, an excess that gives the free spirit the dangerous privilege of being permitted to live *experimentally* and to offer himself to ad-

8. *er zerreisst, was ihn reizt.*
9. *führen und verführen ihn*
10. wild mother of the passions

venture: the privilege of the master free spirit! In between may lie
long years of convalescence, years full of multicolored, painful-
magical transformations, governed and led by a tough *will to
health* which already often dares to dress and disguise[11] itself as
health. There is a middle point on the way, which a man having
such a fate cannot remember later without being moved: a pale,
fine light and sunny happiness are characteristic of it, a feeling of a
birdlike freedom, birdlike perspective, birdlike arrogance, some
third thing in which curiosity and a tender contempt are united.
A "free spirit"—this cool term is soothing in that state, almost
warming. No longer chained down by hatred and love, one lives
without Yes, without No, voluntarily near, voluntarily far, most
preferably slipping away, avoiding, fluttering on, gone again, fly-
ing upward again; one is spoiled, like anyone who has ever seen
an enormous multiplicity beneath him—and one becomes the antithesis of those who trouble themselves about things that do not
concern them. Indeed, now the free spirit concerns himself only
with things (and how many there are!) which no longer *trouble*
him.

## 5

Another step onward in convalescence. The free spirit again
approaches life, slowly, of course, almost recalcitrantly, almost
suspiciously. It grows warmer around him again, yellower, as it
were; feeling and fellow-feeling gain depth; mild breezes of all
kinds pass over him. He almost feels as if his eyes were only now
open to what is *near.* He is amazed and sits motionless: where *had
he been,* then? These near and nearest things, how they seem to
him transformed! What magical fluff they have acquired in the
meantime! He glances backward gratefully—grateful to his trav-
els, to his severity and self-alienation, to his far-off glances and
bird flights into cold heights. How good that he did not stay "at
home," "with himself" the whole time, like a dull, pampered loaf-
er! He was *beside* himself: there is no doubt about that. Only now
does he see himself—and what surprises he finds there! What un-
tried terrors! What happiness even in weariness, in the old illness,
in the convalescent's relapses! How he likes to sit still, suffering,
spinning patience, or to lie in the sun! Who understands as he

11. *zu kleiden und zu verkleiden*

does the happiness of winter, the sun spots on the wall! They are the most grateful animals in the world, the most modest, too, these convalescents and squirrels, turned halfway back to life again—there are those among them who let no day pass without hanging a little song of praise on its trailing hem. And to speak seriously, all pessimism (the inveterate evil of old idealists and liars, as we know) is thoroughly *cured* by falling ill in the way these free spirits do, staying ill for a good while, and then, for even longer, even longer, becoming healthy—I mean "healthier." There is wisdom, practical wisdom in it, when over a long period of time even health itself is administered only in small doses.

## 6

About that time it may finally happen, among the sudden illuminations of a still turbulent, still changeable state of health, that the free spirit, ever freer, begins to unveil the mystery of that great separation which until then had waited impenetrable, questionable, almost unapproachable in his memory. Perhaps for a long time he hardly dared ask himself, "Why so apart, so alone? Renouncing everything I admired, even admiration? Why this severity, this suspicion, this hatred of one's own virtues?" But now he dares to ask it loudly, and already hears something like an answer. "You had to become your own master, and also the master of your own virtues. Previously, your virtues were your masters; but they must be nothing more than your tools, along with your other tools. You had to gain power over your For and Against, and learn how to hang them out or take them in, according to your higher purpose. You had to learn that all estimations have a perspective, to learn the displacement, distortion, apparent teleology of horizons, and whatever else is part of perspective; also the bit of stupidity in regard to opposite values and all the intellectual damage that every For or Against exacts in payment. You had to learn to grasp the necessary injustice in every For and Against; to grasp that injustice is inseparable from life, that life itself is determined by perspective and its injustice. Above all you had to see clearly wherever injustice is greatest, where life is developed least, most narrowly, meagerly, rudimentarily, and yet cannot help taking *itself* as the purpose and measure of things, and for the sake of its preservation picking at and questioning secretly and pettily and incessantly what is higher, greater, and richer. You had to see clearly the problem of *hierarchy,* and how power and justice and breadth of perspective grow upward together. You had to—." Enough, now the free spirit *knows* which "thou shalt" he has obeyed, and also what he now *can* do, what he only now *is permitted* to do.

## 7

That is how the free spirit answers himself about that mystery of separation and he ends by generalizing his case, to decide thus about his experience. "As it happened to me," he tells himself, "so must it happen to everyone in whom a *task* wants to take form and 'come into the world.'" The secret power and necessity of this task will hold sway within and among his various destinies like an unsuspected pregnancy, long before he has looked the task itself in the eye or knows its name. Our destiny commands us, even when we do not yet know what it is; it is the future which gives the rule to our present. Granted that it is *the problem of hierarchy* which we may call *our* problem, we free spirits; only now, in the noonday of our lives, do we understand what preparations, detours, trials, temptations, disguises, were needed before the problem *was permitted* to rise up before us. We understand how we first had to experience the most numerous and contradictory conditions of misery and happiness in our bodies and souls, as adventurers and circumnavigators of that inner world which is called "human being," as surveyors of every "higher" and "one above the other" which is likewise called "human being," penetrating everywhere, almost without fear, scorning nothing, losing nothing, savoring everything, cleaning and virtually straining off everything of the coincidental—until we finally could say, we free spirits: "Here is a *new* problem! Here is a long ladder on whose rungs we ourselves have sat and climbed, and which we ourselves *were* at one time! Here is a Higher, a Deeper, a Below-us, an enormous long ordering, a hierarchy which we *see:* here—is *our* problem!"

## 8

No psychologist or soothsayer will have a moment's difficulty in discovering at which place in the development sketched out above the present book belongs (or is *placed*). But where are there psychologists today? In France, certainly; perhaps in Russia; surely not in Germany. There are sufficient reasons for which the present-day Germans could esteem it an honor to be such; bad enough for a person who is constituted and has become un-German in this respect! This *German* book, which has known how to find its readers in a wide circle of countries and peoples (it has been on the road for approximately ten years), which must understand some kind of music and flute playing to seduce even unreceptive foreign ears to listen—precisely in Germany has this book been read most negligently, *heard* most poorly. What is the cause? "It demands too much," has been the reply, "it addresses itself to men who do not know the hardship of crude obligations; it demands fine, cosseted senses; it needs superfluity, superfluity of time, of bright heavens and hearts, of *otium*[12] in the boldest sense—all good things which we Germans of today do not have and therefore cannot give." After such a polite answer, my philosophy counsels me to be silent and inquire no further, especially since in certain cases, as the saying suggests, one *remains* a philosopher only by—being silent.[13]

Nice, Spring, 1886.

12. leisure

13. A reference to the medieval Latin distich: "*o si tacuisses / Philosophus mansisses.*"

# SECTION ONE
## Of First and Last Things[1]

I

*Chemistry of concepts and feelings.* In almost all respects, philosophical problems today are again formulated as they were two thousand years ago: how can something arise from its opposite—for example, reason from unreason, sensation from the lifeless, logic from the illogical, disinterested contemplation from covetous desire, altruism from egoism, truth from error? Until now, metaphysical philosophy has overcome this difficulty by denying the origin of the one from the other, and by assuming for the more highly valued things some miraculous origin, directly from out of the heart and essence of the "thing in itself."[2] Historical philosophy, on the other hand, the very youngest of all philosophical methods, which can no longer be even conceived of as separate from the natural sciences, has determined in isolated cases (and will probably conclude in all of them) that they are not opposites, only exaggerated to be so by the popular or metaphysical view, and that this opposition is based on an error of reason. As historical philosophy explains it, there exists, strictly considered, neither a selfless act nor a completely disinterested observation: both are merely sublimations. In them the basic element appears to be virtually dispersed and proves to be present only to the most careful observer.

1. "Last Things" (*die letzten Dinge*) refers to eschatology.
2. *Ding an sich:* the thing in itself, in Kant's *Critique of Pure Reason* (1781), refers to the existent as it exists independently of our knowledge; a noumenon, a thing of the mind rather than of the senses; that which a thing is when there is no human perception of it, i.e., when it is in "essence" rather than in "appearance."

All we need, something which can be given us only now, with the various sciences at their present level of achievement, is a *chemistry* of moral, religious, aesthetic ideas and feelings, a chemistry of all those impulses that we ourselves experience in the great and small interactions of culture and society, indeed even in solitude. What if this chemistry might end with the conclusion that, even here, the most glorious colors are extracted from base, even despised substances? Are there many who will want to pursue such investigations? Mankind loves to put the questions of origin and beginnings out of mind: must one not be almost inhuman to feel in himself the opposite inclination?

2

*Congenital defect of philosophers.* All philosophers suffer from the same defect, in that they start with present-day man and think they can arrive at their goal by analyzing him. Instinctively they let "man" hover before them as an *aeterna veritas,*[3] something unchanging in all turmoil, a secure measure of things. But everything the philosopher asserts about man is basically no more than a statement about man within a *very limited* time span. A lack of historical sense is the congenital defect of all philosophers. Some unwittingly even take the most recent form of man, as it developed under the imprint of certain religions or even certain political events, as the fixed form from which one must proceed. They will not understand that man has evolved, that the faculty of knowledge has also evolved, while some of them even permit themselves to spin the whole world from out of this faculty of knowledge.

Now, everything *essential* in human development occurred in primeval times, long before those four thousand years with which we are more or less familiar. Man probably hasn't changed much more in these years. But the philosopher sees "instincts" in present-day man, and assumes that they belong to the unchangeable facts of human nature, that they can, to that extent, provide a key to the understanding of the world in general. This entire teleology is predicated on the ability to speak about man of the last four thousand years as if he were eternal, the natural direction of all things in the world from the beginning. But everything has

3. eternal truth

evolved; there are *no eternal facts,* nor are there any absolute truths. Thus *historical philosophizing* is necessary henceforth, and the virtue of modesty as well.

### 3

*Esteeming humble truths.* It is the sign of a higher culture to esteem more highly the little, humble truths, those discovered by a strict method, rather than the gladdening and dazzling errors that originate in metaphysical and artistic ages and men. At first, one has scorn on his lips for humble truths, as if they could offer no match for the others: they stand so modest, simple, sober, even apparently discouraging, while the other truths are so beautiful, splendid, enchanting, or even enrapturing. But truths that are hard won, certain, enduring, and therefore still of consequence for all further knowledge are the higher; to keep to them is manly, and shows bravery, simplicity, restraint. Eventually, not only the individual, but all mankind will be elevated to this manliness, when men finally grow accustomed to the greater esteem for durable, lasting knowledge and have lost all belief in inspiration and a seemingly miraculous communication of truths.

The admirers of *forms,*[4] with their standard of beauty and sublimity, will, to be sure, have good reason to mock at first, when esteem for humble truths and the scientific spirit first comes to rule, but only because either their eye has not yet been opened to the charm of the *simplest* form, or because men raised in that spirit have not yet been fully and inwardly permeated by it, so that they continue thoughtlessly to imitate old forms (and poorly, too, like someone who no longer really cares about the matter). Previously, the mind was not obliged to think rigorously; its importance lay in spinning out symbols and forms. That has changed; that importance of symbols has become the sign of lower culture. Just as our very arts are becoming ever more intellectual and our senses more spiritual, and as, for example, that which is sensually pleasant to the ear is judged quite differently now than a hundred years ago, so the forms of our life become ever more *spiritual*—to the eye of older times *uglier,* perhaps, but only because it is unable to see how the realm of internal, spiritual beauty is continually deepening and expanding, and to what extent a glance full of intel-

---

4. Artists and aesthetes, as opposed to scientists.

ligence can mean more to all of us now than the most beautiful human body and the most sublime edifice.

## 4

*Astrology and the like.* It is probable that the objects of religious, moral, and aesthetic sensibility likewise belong only to the surface of things, although man likes to believe that here at least he is touching the heart of the world. Because those things make him so deeply happy or unhappy, he deceives himself, and shows the same pride as astrology, which thinks the heavens revolve around the fate of man. The moral man, however, presumes that that which is essential to his heart must also be the heart and essence of all things.

## 5

*Misunderstanding dreams.* In ages of crude, primordial cultures, man thought he could come to know a *second real world* in dreams: this is the origin of all metaphysics. Without dreams man would have found no occasion to divide the world. The separation into body and soul is also connected to the oldest views about dreams, as is the assumption of a spiritual apparition,[5] that is, the origin of all belief in ghosts, and probably also in gods. "The dead man lives on, *because* he appears to the living man in dreams." So man concluded formerly, throughout many thousands of years.

## 6

*The scientific spirit is powerful in the part, not in the whole.* The distinct, *smallest* fields of science are treated purely objectively. On the other hand, the general, great sciences, taken as a whole, pose the question (a very unobjective question, to be sure): what for? to what benefit? Because of this concern about benefit, men treat the sciences less impersonally as a whole than in their parts. Now, in philosophy—the top of the whole scientific pyramid—the question of the benefit of knowledge itself is posed automatically and each philosophy has the unconscious intention of ascribing to knowledge the *greatest* benefit. For this reason, all philosophies have so much high-flying metaphysics and so much wariness of the seemingly insignificant explanations of physics. For the im-

5. *Seelenscheinleib,* Nietzsche's neologism.

portance of knowledge for life *ought* to appear as great as possible. Here we have the antagonism between individual scientific fields and philosophy. The latter, like art, wishes to render the greatest possible depth and meaning to life and activity. In the sciences, one seeks knowledge and nothing more—whatever the consequences may be. Until now, there has been no philosopher in whose hands philosophy has not become an apology for knowledge. In this way, at least, every one is an optimist, by thinking that knowledge must be accorded the highest usefulness. All philosophers are tyrannized by logic: and logic, by its nature, is optimism.

## 7

*The troublemaker in science.* Philosophy divorced itself from science when it inquired which knowledge of the world and life could help man to live most happily. This occurred in the Socratic schools: out of a concern for *happiness* man tied off the veins of scientific investigation—and does so still today.

## 8

*Pneumatic explanation of nature.* Metaphysics explains nature's scriptures as if *pneumatically,* the way the church and its scholars used to explain the Bible. It takes a lot of intelligence to apply to nature the same kind of strict interpretive art that philologists today have created for all books: with the intention simply to understand what the scripture wants to say, but not to sniff out, or even presume, a *double* meaning. Just as we have by no means overcome bad interpretive art in regard to books, and one still comes upon vestiges of allegorical and mystical interpretation in the best-educated society, so it stands too in regard to nature—in fact much worse.

## 9

*Metaphysical world.* It is true, there might be a metaphysical world; one can hardly dispute the absolute possibility of it. We see all things by means of our human head, and cannot chop it off, though it remains to wonder what would be left of the world if indeed it had been cut off. This is a purely scientific problem, and not very suited to cause men worry. But all that has produced metaphysical assumptions and made them *valuable, horrible, plea-*

*surable* to men thus far is passion, error, and self-deception. The very worst methods of knowledge, not the very best, have taught us to believe in them. When one has disclosed these methods to be the foundation of all existing religions and metaphysical systems, one has refuted them. That other possibility still remains, but we cannot begin to do anything with it, let alone allow our happiness, salvation, and life to depend on the spider webs of such a possibility. For there is nothing at all we could state about the metaphysical world except its differentness, a differentness inaccessible and incomprehensible to us. It would be a thing with negative qualities.

No matter how well proven the existence of such a world might be, it would still hold true that the knowledge of it would be the most inconsequential of all knowledge, even more inconsequential than the knowledge of the chemical analysis of water must be to the boatman facing a storm.

## 10

*The harmlessness of metaphysics in the future.* As soon as the origins of religion, art, and morality have been described, so that one can explain them fully without resorting to the use of *metaphysical intervention* at the beginning and along the way, then one no longer has as strong an interest in the purely theoretical problem of the "thing in itself" and "appearance."[6] For however the case may be, religion, art, and morality do not enable us to touch the "essence of the world in itself." We are in the realm of idea,[7] no "intuition"[8] can carry us further. With complete calm we will let physiology and the ontogeny of organisms and concepts determine how our image of the world can be so very different from the disclosed essence of the world.

## 11

*Language as an alleged science.* The importance of language for the development of culture lies in the fact that, in language, man juxtaposed to the one world another world of his own, a place which he thought so sturdy that from it he could move the rest of

6. *Erscheinung* (see n. 2 to this section).

7. *Vorstellung.* Often translated as "representation." Schopenhauer himself used "idea."

8. A reference to Schopenhauer.

the world from its foundations and make himself lord over it. To the extent that he believed over long periods of time in the concepts and names of things as if they were *aeternae veritates,*[9] man has acquired that pride by which he has raised himself above the animals: he really did believe that in language he had knowledge of the world.[10] The shaper of language was not so modest as to think that he was only giving things labels; rather, he imagined that he was expressing the highest knowledge of things with words; and in fact, language is the first stage of scientific effort. Here, too, it is *the belief in found truth* from which the mightiest sources of strength have flowed. Very belatedly (only now) is it dawning on men that in their belief in language they have propagated a monstrous error. Fortunately, it is too late to be able to revoke the development of reason, which rests on that belief.

*Logic,* too, rests on assumptions that do not correspond to anything in the real world, e.g., on the assumption of the equality of things, the identity of the same thing at different points of time; but this science arose from the opposite belief (that there were indeed such things in the real world). So it is with *mathematics,* which would certainly not have originated if it had been known from the beginning that there is no exactly straight line in nature, no real circle, no absolute measure.

## 12

*Dream and culture.* Memory is that function of the brain which is most greatly impaired by sleep—not that it relaxes entirely, but it is brought back to a state of imperfection, as it might have been in everyone, when awake and by day, during mankind's primeval age.[11] Arbitrary and confused as it is, it continually mistakes things on the basis of the most superficial similarities; but it was the same arbitrariness and confusion with which the tribes composed their mythologies, and even now travelers regularly observe how greatly the savage inclines to forgetfulness, how, after he strains his memory briefly, his mind begins to stagger about,

9. eternal truths

10. Cf. Nietzsche, "On Truth and Lie in the Extra-Moral Sense" (1873).

11. Cf. Freud, *The Interpretation of Dreams.* In an addendum to the fifth edition of this work (1919), Freud refers to Nietzsche's concept of the dream as a means to knowledge of man's archaic heritage, "of what is psychically innate in him." (Standard Edition, V, p 549).

and he produces lies and nonsense simply because he is weary. But all of us are like the savage when we dream. Faulty recognitions and mistaken equations are the basis of the poor conclusions which we are guilty of making in dreams, so that when we recollect a dream clearly, we are frightened of ourselves, because we harbor so much foolishness within.

The utter clarity of all dream-ideas, which presupposes an unconditional belief in their reality, reminds us once again of the state of earlier mankind in which hallucinations were extraordinarily frequent, and sometimes seized whole communities, whole nations simultaneously. Thus, in our sleep and dreams, we go through the work of earlier mankind once more.

## 13

*The logic of dreams.* When we sleep, our nervous system is continually stimulated by various inner causes: almost all the organs secrete and are active; the blood circulates turbulently; the sleeper's position presses certain limbs; his blankets influence sensation in various ways; the stomach digests and disturbs other organs with its movements; the intestines turn; the placement of the head occasions unusual positions of the muscles; the feet, without shoes, their soles not pressing on the floor, cause a feeling of unusualness, as does the different way the whole body is clothed—after its daily change and variation, all of this strangeness stimulates the entire system, including even the brain function. And so there are a hundred occasions for the mind to be amazed, and to seek *reasons* for this stimulation. It is the dream which *seeks and imagines the causes* for those stimulated feelings—that is, the alleged causes. The man who ties two straps around his feet, for example, may dream that two snakes are winding about his feet. This is at first a hypothesis, then a belief, accompanied by a pictorial idea and elaboration: "These snakes must be the *causa*[12] of that feeling which I, the sleeper, am having"—thus judges the mind of the sleeper. The stimulated imagination turns the recent past, disclosed in this way, into the present. Everyone knows from experience how fast the dreamer can incorporate into his dream a loud sound he hears, bell ringing, for example, or cannon fire, how he can explain it *after the fact* from his dream, so that he

12. cause

*believes* he is experiencing first the occasioning factors, and then that sound.[13]

But how is it that the mind of the dreamer always errs so greatly, while the same mind awake tends to be so sober, careful, and skeptical about hypotheses? Why does he think the first best hypothesis that explains a feeling is enough to believe in it at once? (For when dreaming, we believe in the dream as if it were reality; that is, we take our hypothesis for fully proven.)

I think that man still draws conclusions in his dreams as mankind once did *in a waking state,* through many thousands of years: the first *causa* which occurred to the mind to explain something that needed explaining sufficed and was taken for truth. (According to the tales of travelers, savages proceed this way even today.) This old aspect of humanity lives on in us in our dreams, for it is the basis upon which higher reason developed, and is still developing, in every human: the dream restores us to distant states of human culture and gives us a means by which to understand them better. Dream-thought[14] is so easy for us now because, during mankind's immense periods of development, we have been so well drilled in just this form of fantastic and cheap explanation from the first, best idea. In this way dreaming is recuperation for a brain which must satisfy by day the stricter demands made on thought by higher culture.

A related occurrence when we are awake can be viewed as a virtual gate and antechamber to the dream. If we close our eyes, the brain produces a multitude of impressions of light and colors, probably as a kind of postlude and echo to all those effects of light which penetrate it by day. Now, however, our reason (in league with imagination) immediately works these plays of color, formless in themselves, into definite figures, forms, landscapes, moving groups. Once again, the actual process is a kind of conclusion from the effect to the cause; as the mind inquires about the origin of these light impressions and colors, it assumes those figures and shapes to be the cause. They seem to be the occasion of those colors and lights, because the mind is used to finding an occasioning cause for every color and every light impression it receives by day, with eyes open. Here, then, the imagination keeps pushing

13. Cf. Freud, *Interpretation of Dreams* (Standard Edition) V, pp. 23–30.
14. *Das Traumdenken.*

images upon the mind, using in their production the visual impressions of the day—and this is precisely what dream imagination does. That is, the supposed cause is deduced from the effect and imagined *after* the effect. All this with an extraordinary speed, so that, as with a conjurer, judgment becomes confused, and a sequence can appear to be a synchronism, or even a reversed sequence.

We can infer from these processes, *how late* a more acute logical thinking, a rigorous application of cause and effect, developed; *even now,* our functions of reason and intelligence reach back instinctively to those primitive forms of deductions, and we live more or less half our lives in this state. The poet, too, the artist, *attributes* his moods and states to causes that are in no way the true ones; to this extent he reminds us of an older mankind, and can help us to understand it.

## 14

*Resonance.* All intense moods bring with them a resonance of related feelings and moods; they seem to stir up memory. Something in us remembers and becomes aware of similar states and their origin. Thus habitual, rapid associations of feelings and thoughts are formed, which, when they follow with lightning speed upon one another, are eventually no longer felt as complexes, but rather as *unities.* In this sense, one speaks of moral feelings, religious feelings, as if they were all unities; in truth they are rivers with a hundred sources and tributaries. As is so often the case, the unity of the word does not guarantee the unity of the thing.

## 15

*No inside and outside in the world.* Just as Democritus[15] applied the concepts of above and below to infinite space, where they have no meaning, so philosophers in general apply the concept "inside and outside" to the essence and appearance of the world. They think that with deep feelings man penetrates deep into the inside, approaches the heart of nature. But these feelings are deep only to the extent that they regularly stimulate, almost imperceptibly, certain complicated groups of thoughts, which we call deep. A

15. Greek philosopher, 460?–370? B.C.

feeling is deep because we hold the accompanying thought to be deep. But the deep thought can nevertheless be very far from the truth, as is, for example, every metaphysical thought. If one subtracts the added elements of thought from the deep feeling, what remains is intense feeling, which guarantees nothing at all about knowledge except itself, just as strong belief proves only its own strength, not the truth of what is believed.

## 16

*Appearance and the thing-in-itself.* Philosophers tend to confront life and experience (what they call the world of appearance) as they would a painting that has been revealed once and for all, depicting with unchanging constancy the same event. They think they must interpret this event correctly in order to conclude something about the essence which produced the painting, that is, about the thing-in-itself, which always tends to be regarded as the sufficient reason[16] for the world of appearance. Conversely, stricter logicians, after they had rigorously established the concept of the metaphysical as the concept of that which is unconditioned and consequently unconditioning, denied any connection between the unconditioned (the metaphysical world) and the world we are familiar with. So that the thing-in-itself does *not* appear in the world of appearances, and any conclusion about the former on the basis of the latter must be rejected.[17] But both sides overlook the possibility that that painting—that which to us men means life and experience—has gradually *evolved,* indeed is still *evolving,* and therefore should not be considered a fixed quantity, on which basis a conclusion about the creator (the sufficient reason) may be made, or even rejected. Because for thousands of years we have been looking at the world with moral, aesthetic, and religious claims, with blind inclination, passion, or fear, and have indulged ourselves fully in the bad habits of illogical thought, this world has gradually *become* so strangely colorful,

16. Ontological principle that every existent, every objective reality, has a ground of existence (*Critique of Pure Reason* A201, A783, B246, B811). Thus, that the metaphysical world is the explanation of the existence of the world of appearances. Schopenhauer's earliest essay (1813) is "The Fourfold Root of the Principle of Sufficient Reason." Cf. E. F. J. Payne's translation (La Salle, Ill.: Open Court Publishing Co., 1974).

17. A reference to Kant.

frightful, profound, soulful; it has acquired color, but we have been the painters: the human intellect allowed appearance to appear, and projected its mistaken conceptions onto the things. Only late, very late, does the intellect stop to think: and now the world of experience and the thing-in-itself seem so extraordinarily different and separate that it rejects any conclusion about the latter from the former, or else, in an awful, mysterious way, it demands the *abandonment* of our intellect, of our personal will in order to come to the essential by *becoming essential*.[18] On the other hand, other people have gathered together all characteristic traits of our world of appearances (that is, our inherited idea of the world, spun out of intellectual errors) and, *instead of accusing the intellect,* have attacked the essence of things for causing this real, very uncanny character of the world, and have preached salvation from being.[19]

The steady and arduous progress of science, which will ultimately celebrate its greatest triumph in an *ontogeny of thought,* will deal decisively with all these views. Its conclusion might perhaps end up with this tenet: That which we now call the world is the result of a number of errors and fantasies, which came about gradually in the overall development of organic beings, fusing with one another, and now handed down to us as a collected treasure of our entire past—a treasure: for the *value* of our humanity rests upon it. From this world of idea strict science can, in fact, release us only to a small extent (something we by no means desire), in that it is unable to break significantly the power of ancient habits of feeling. But it can illuminate, quite gradually, step by step, the history of the origin of that world as idea—and lift us, for moments at least, above the whole process. Perhaps we will recognize then that the thing-in-itself deserves a Homeric laugh,[20] in that it *seemed* to be so much, indeed everything, and is actually empty, that is, empty of meaning.

## 17

*Metaphysical explanations.* A young person appreciates metaphysical explanations because they show him something highly

---

18. *wesenhaft*
19. A reference to Schopenhauer.
20. A loud, inexhaustible laugh; cf. *Iliad* 1.599, or *Odyssey* 7.326, 20.346.

meaningful in matters he found unpleasant or despicable. If he is dissatisfied with himself, his feeling is relieved if he can recognize in that which he so disapproves of in himself the innermost riddle of the world or its misery. To feel less responsible, and at the same time to find things more interesting: that is the twofold benefit which he owes to metaphysics. Later, of course, he comes to distrust the whole method of metaphysical explanation; then perhaps he understands that those same effects are to be obtained just as well and more scientifically in another way; he understands that physical and historical explanations bring about at least as much that feeling of irresponsibility, and that his interest in life and its problems is kindled perhaps even more thereby.

## 18

*Basic questions of metaphysics.* Once the ontogeny of thought is written, the following sentence by an excellent logician will be seen in a new light: "The original general law of the knowing subject consists in the inner necessity of knowing each object in itself, in its own being, as an object identical with itself, that is, self-existing and fundamentally always the same and unchangeable, in short, as a substance."[21] This law, too, which is here called "original," also evolved. Some day the gradual origin of this tendency in lower organisms will be shown, how the dull mole's eyes of these organizations at first see everything as identical; how then, when the various stimuli of pleasure and unpleasure become more noticeable, different substances are gradually distinguished, but each one with One attribute, that is, with one single relationship to such an organism.

The first stage of logic is judgment, whose essence consists, as the best logicians have determined, in belief. All belief is based on the *feeling of pleasure or pain* in relation to the feeling subject. A new, third feeling as the result of two preceding feelings is judgment in its lowest form.

Initially, we organic beings have no interest in a thing, other than in its relationship to us with regard to pleasure and pain. Between those moments in which we become aware of this relationship (i.e., the states of sensation) lie those states of quiet, of

21. From Afrikan Spir, *Denken und Wirklichkeit* (Thought and Reality) (Leipzig, 1873), which Nietzsche read in Basel in the year of its publication.

non-sensation. Then we find the world and every thing in it without interest; we notice no change in it (just as even now, a person who is intensely interested in something will not notice that someone is passing by him). To a plant, all things are normally quiet, eternal, each thing identical to itself. From the period of low organisms, man has inherited the belief that there are *identical things* (only experience which has been educated by the highest science contradicts this tenet). From the beginning, the first belief of all organic beings may be that the whole rest of the world is One and unmoved.

In that first stage of logic, the thought of *causality* is furthest removed. Even now, we believe fundamentally that all feelings and actions are acts of free will; when the feeling individual considers himself, he takes each feeling, each change, to be something *isolated,* that is, something unconditioned, without a context. It rises up out of us, with no connection to anything earlier or later. We are hungry, but do not think initially that the organism wants to be kept alive. Rather, that feeling seems to assert itself *without reason or purpose;* it isolates itself and takes itself to be *arbitrary.* Thus the belief in freedom of the will is an initial error of all organic beings, as old as the existence in them of stirrings of logic. Belief in unconditioned substances and identical things is likewise an old, original error of all that is organic. To the extent that all metaphysics has dealt primarily with substance and freedom of the will, however, one may characterize it as that science which deals with the basic errors of man—but as if they were basic truths.

### 19

*The number.* The laws of numbers were invented on the basis of the initially prevailing error that there are various identical things (but actually there is nothing identical) or at least that there are things (but there is no "thing"). The assumption of multiplicity always presumes that there is *something,* which occurs repeatedly. But this is just where error rules; even here, we invent entities, unities, that do not exist.

Our feelings of space and time are false, for if they are tested rigorously, they lead to logical contradictions. Whenever we establish something scientifically, we are inevitably always reckoning with some incorrect quantities; but because these quantities are at least *constant* (as is, for example, our feeling of time and space), the results of science do acquire a perfect strictness and certainty in their relationship to each other. One can continue to build upon them—up to that final analysis, where the mistaken basic assumptions, those constant errors, come into contradiction with the results, for example, in atomic theory. There we still feel ourselves forced to assume a "thing" or a material "substratum" that is moved, while the entire scientific procedure has pursued the task of dissolving everything thing-like (material) into movements. Here, too, our feeling distinguishes that which is moving from that which is moved, and we do not come out of this circle, because the belief in things has been tied up with our essential nature from time immemorial.[22]

When Kant says "Reason does not create its laws from nature, but dictates them to her,"[23] this is perfectly true in respect to the *concept of nature* which we are obliged to apply to her (Nature = world as idea, that is, as error), but which is the summation of a number of errors of reason.

To a world that is *not* our idea, the laws of numbers are completely inapplicable: they are valid only in the human world.

### 20

*A few rungs down.* One level of education, itself a very high one, has been reached when man gets beyond superstitious and religious concepts and fears and, for example, no longer believes in the heavenly angels or original sin, and has stopped talking about the soul's salvation. Once he is at this level of liberation, he must still make a last intense effort to overcome metaphysics. *Then,* however, a *retrograde movement* is necessary: he must understand both the historical and the psychological justification in metaphysical ideas. He must recognize how mankind's greatest advancement came from them and how, if one did not take this retrograde step, one would rob himself of mankind's finest accomplishments to date.

With regard to philosophical metaphysics, I now see a number

---

22. Besides Democritus, Nietzsche also mentions the work of Empedocles (5th c. B.C.) and Anaxagoras (500–428 B.C.) in connection with these problems (cf. *Philosophy in the Tragic Age of the Greeks,* par. 14).

23. Kant, *Prolegomena,* par. 36.

of people who have arrived at the negative goal (that all positive metaphysics is an error), but only a few who climb back down a few rungs. For one should look out over the last rung of the ladder, but not want to stand on it. Those who are most enlightened can go only as far as to free themselves of metaphysics and look back on it with superiority, while here, as in the hippodrome, it is necessary to take a turn at the end of the track.

### 21

*Presumed triumph of skepticism.* Let us accept for the moment the skeptical starting point: assuming there were no other, metaphysical world and that we could not use any metaphysical explanations of the only world known to us, how would we then look upon men and things? One can imagine this; it is useful to do so, even if one were to reject the question of whether Kant and Schopenhauer proved anything metaphysical scientifically. For according to historical probability, it is quite likely that men at some time will become *skeptical* about this whole subject. So one must ask the question: how will human society take shape under the influence of such an attitude? Perhaps the *scientific proof* of any metaphysical world is itself so *difficult* that mankind can no longer keep from distrusting it. And if one is distrustful of metaphysics, then we have, generally speaking, the same consequences as if metaphysics had been directly refuted and one were no longer *permitted* to believe in it. The historical question about mankind's unmetaphysical views remains the same in either case.

### 22

*Disbelief in the "monumentum aere perennius."*[24] One crucial disadvantage about the end of metaphysical views is that the individual looks his own short life span too squarely in the eye and feels no strong incentives to build on enduring institutions, designed for the ages. He wants to pick the fruit from the tree he has planted himself, and therefore no longer likes to plant those trees which require regular care over centuries, trees that are destined to overshade long successions of generations. For metaphysical views lead one to believe that they offer the conclusive foundation upon which all future generations are henceforth obliged to settle

24. "a monument more enduring than brass" from Horace, *Odes* 3.30.1.

and build. The individual is furthering his salvation when he endows a church, for example, or a monastery; he thinks it will be credited to him and repaid in his soul's eternal afterlife; it is work on the eternal salvation of his soul.

Can science, too, awaken such a belief in its results? To be sure, its truest allies must be doubt and distrust. Nevertheless, the sum of indisputable truths, which outlast all storms of skepticism and all disintegration, can in time become so large (in the dietetics of health, for example), that one can decide on that basis to found "eternal" works. In the meanwhile, the *contrast* between our excited ephemeral existence and the long-winded quiet of metaphysical ages is still too strong, because the two ages are still too close to each other; the individual runs through too many inner and outer evolutions himself to dare to set himself up permanently, once and for all, for even the span of his own life. When a wholly modern man intends, for example, to build a house, he has a feeling as if he were walling himself up alive in a mausoleum.

## 23

*Age of comparisons.* The less men are bound by their tradition, the greater the internal stirring of motives; the greater, accordingly, the external unrest, the whirling flow of men, the polyphony of strivings. Who today still feels a serious obligation to bind himself and his descendents to one place? Who feels that anything is seriously binding? Just as all artistic styles of the arts are imitated one next to the other, so too are all stages and kinds of morality, customs, cultures.

Such an age gets its meaning because in it the various world views, customs, cultures are compared and experienced next to one another, which was not possible earlier, when there was always a localized rule for each culture, just as all artistic styles were bound to place and time. Now, man's increased aesthetic feeling will decide definitively from among the many forms which offer themselves for comparison. It will let most of them (namely all those that it rejects) die out. Similarly, a selection is now taking place among the forms and habits of higher morality, whose goal can be none other than the downfall of baser moralities. This is the age of comparisons! That is its pride—but also by rights its sorrow. Let us not be afraid of this sorrow! Instead, we will conceive the task that this age sets us to be as great as possible. Then

posterity will bless us for it—a posterity that knows it has tran-
scended both the completed original folk cultures, as well as the
culture of comparison, but that looks back on both kinds of
culture as on venerable antiquities, with gratitude.

### 24

*Possibility of progress.* When a scholar of the old culture vows
no longer to have anything to do with men who believe in progress, he is right. For the old culture has its greatness and goodness behind it, and an historical education forces one to admit that
it can never again be fresh. To deny this requires an intolerable
obtuseness or an equally insufferable enthusiasm. But men can
*consciously* decide to develop themselves forward to a new culture, whereas formerly they developed unconsciously and by
chance. Now they can create better conditions for the generation
of men, their nourishment, upbringing, instruction; they can ad-
minister the earth as a whole economically, can weigh the
strengths of men, one against the other, and employ them. The
new, conscious culture kills the old culture, which, seen as a
whole, led an unconscious animal-and-vegetable life; it also kills
the distrust of progress: progress is *possible.* I mean to say, it is
premature and almost nonsensical to believe that progress must of
*necessity* come about; but how could one deny that it is possible?
Conversely, progress in the sense of the old culture, and by means
of it, is not even conceivable. Even if romantic fantasizing still
uses the word "progress" about its goals (e.g., completed, original
folk cultures) it is in any event borrowing that image from the
past: its thinking and imagining in this area lack all originality.

### 25

*Private morality, world morality.* Since man no longer believes
that a God is guiding the destinies of the world as a whole, or
that, despite all apparent twists, the path of mankind is leading
somewhere glorious, men must set themselves ecumenical goals,
embracing the whole earth. The older morality, namely Kant's,[25]
demands from the individual those actions that one desires from

25. A reference to the categorical imperative in Kant's *Critique of Practical
Reason* (1788), par. 7: "Always act in such a way that the maxims of your will
could function as the basis of a universal law of action."

all men—a nice, naive idea, as if everyone without further ado
would know which manner of action would benefit the whole of
mankind, that is, which actions were desirable at all. It is a theory
like that of free trade, which assumes that a general harmony
would have to result of itself, according to innate laws of meliora-
tion. Perhaps a future survey of the needs of mankind will reveal it
to be thoroughly undesirable that all men act identically; rather,
in the interest of ecumenical goals, for whole stretches of human
time special tasks, perhaps in some circumstances even evil tasks,
would have to be set.

In any event, if mankind is to keep from destroying itself by
such a conscious overall government, we must discover first a
*knowledge of the conditions of culture,* a knowledge surpassing all
previous knowledge, as a scientific standard for ecumenical goals.
This is the enormous task of the great minds of the next century.

## 26

*Reaction as progress.* Sometimes there appear rough, violent,
and impetuous spirits, who are nevertheless backward; they conjure up once again a past phase of mankind. They serve as proof
that the new tendencies which they are opposing are still not
strong enough, that something is lacking there; otherwise, those
conjurors would be opposed more effectively. For example,
Luther's Reformation proves that in his century all the impulses of
freedom of the spirit were still uncertain, delicate, juvenescent.
Science could not yet raise her head. Indeed, the whole Renaissance appears like an early spring, which almost gets snowed
away. But in our century, too, Schopenhauer's metaphysics
proved that the scientific spirit is still not strong enough. Thus, in
Schopenhauer's teaching the whole medieval Christian world
view and feeling of man could again celebrate a resurrection, despite the defeat, long since achieved, of all Christian dogmas. His
teaching is infused with much science, but what rules it is not
science but rather the old, well-known "metaphysical need."[26]
Certainly one of the greatest and quite inestimable benefits we
gain from Schopenhauer is that he forces our feeling for a time
back to older, powerful forms of contemplating the world and

26. Schopenhauer, *The World as Will and Idea,* pt. 2, bk. 1, chap. 17: "On the
metaphysical need of man."

men, to which other paths could not so readily lead us. History and justice benefit greatly. I believe that without Schopenhauer's aid, no one today could so easily do justice to Christianity and its Asian cousins; to attempt to do so based on the Christianity still existing today is impossible. Only after this great *achievement of justice,* only after we have corrected in such an essential point the historical way of thinking that the Enlightenment brought with it, may we once again carry onward the banner of the Enlightenment, the banner with the three names: Petrarch, Erasmus, Voltaire.[27] Out of reaction, we have taken a step forward.[28]

### 27

*Substitute for religion.* One thinks he is speaking well of philosophy when he presents it as a substitute religion for the people. In spiritual economy, transitional spheres of thought are indeed necessary occasionally, for the transition from religion to scientific contemplation is a violent, dangerous leap, something inadvisable. To that extent, it is right to recommend philosophy. But in the end, one ought to understand that the needs which religion has satisfied, which philosophy is now to satisfy, are not unchangeable: these needs themselves can be *weakened* and *rooted out.* Think, for example, of Christian anguish, the sighing about inner depravity, concern about salvation—all of these ideas originate only from errors of reason and deserve not satisfaction, but annihilation. A philosophy can be useful either by *satisfying* those needs or by *eliminating* them; for they are acquired needs, temporally limited, based on assumptions that contradict those of science. It is preferable to use *art* for this transition, for easing a heart overburdened with feelings; those ideas are entertained much less by art than by a metaphysical philosophy. Beginning with art, one can more easily move on to a truly liberating philosophical science.

27. Petrarch (1304–74) represents the Renaissance in this triumvirate; Erasmus (1466–1536), humanism; and Voltaire (1694–1778), of course, the Enlightenment.

28. *Wir haben aus der Reaction einen Fortschritt gemacht. Fortschritt,* literally "a step forward," also means "progress." Thus one could translate: "Out of reaction we have made progress."

## 28

*Disreputable words.* Away with those tedious, worn-out words "optimism" and "pessimism."[29] Every day there is less and less cause to use them; only babblers still cannot do without them. For why in the world should anyone want to be an optimist if he does not have to defend a God who *must* have created the best of all possible worlds, given that he himself is goodness and perfection? What thinking person still needs the hypothesis of a god?

Nor is there cause for a pessimistic confession, if one does not have an interest in irritating the advocates of God, the theologians or the theologizing philosophers, and energetically asserting the opposite claim, namely that evil reigns, that unpleasure is greater than pleasure, that the world is a botched job, the manifestation of an evil will to life. But who worries about theologians these days (except the theologians)?

All theology and its opposition aside, it is self-evident that the world is not good and not evil, let alone the best or the worst, and that these concepts "good" and "evil" make sense only in reference to men. Perhaps even there, as they are generally used, they are not justified: we must in every case dispense with both the reviling and the glorifying view of the world.

## 29

*Intoxicated by the blossoms' fragrance.* The ship of mankind, it is thought, has an ever greater draft, the more it is laden; it is believed that the deeper man thinks, the more delicate his feelings; the higher he esteems himself, the farther his distance from the other animals (the more he appears as the genius among animals), the nearer he will come to the true essence of the world and knowledge of it. This he does indeed through science, but he thinks he does it more through his religions and arts. These are, to be sure, a flower of civilization, but by no means nearer to the *root of the world* than is its stem. One does not understand the essence of things through art and religion, although nearly everyone is of that opinion. *Error* has made man so deep, delicate, inventive as to bring forth such blossoms as religions and arts. Pure knowledge would have been incapable of it. Whoever revealed to

29. A reference to Schopenhauer.

us the essence of the world would disappoint us all most unpleas-
antly. It is not the world as a thing in itself, but the world as idea
(as error) that is so rich in meaning, deep, wonderful, pregnant
with happiness and unhappiness. This conclusion leads to a philosophy of the *logical denial of the world,* which, by the way, can
be combined just as well with a practical affirmation of the world
as with its opposite.

## 30

*Bad habits in making conclusions.* The most common false conclusions of men are these: a thing exists, therefore it is legitimate.
Here one is concluding functionality from viability, and legit-
imacy from functionality. Furthermore, if an opinion makes us
glad, it must be true; if its effect is good, it in itself must be good
and true. Here one is attributing to the effect the predicate "gladdening," "good," in the sense of the useful, and providing the
cause with the same predicate "good," but now in the sense of the
logically valid. The reversal of the proposition is: if a thing cannot
prevail and maintain itself, it must be wrong; if an opinion tor-
tures and agitates, it must be false. The free spirit, who comes to
know all too well the error of this sort of deduction and has to
suffer from its consequences, often succumbs to the temptation of
making contrary deductions, which are in general naturally just
as false: if a thing cannot prevail, it must be good; if an opinion
troubles and disturbs, it must be true.

## 31

*The illogical necessary.* Among the things that can drive a
thinker to despair is the knowledge that the illogical is necessary
for man and that much good comes from it. It is so firmly lodged
in the passions, in speech, in art, in religion, and generally in
everything which endows life with value, that one cannot extri-
cate it without doing irreparable harm to these beautiful things.
Only the very naive are capable of thinking that the nature of man
can be transformed into a purely logical one;[30] but, if there were
degrees of approximation to this goal, how much would not have
to vanish along this path! Even the most rational man needs na-

30. Cf. Nietzsche's essay on David Strauss (1873), the first of the *Untimely
Meditations.*

ture again from time to time, that is, his *illogical basic attitude to all things*.

## 32

*Unfairness necessary.*[31] All judgments about the value of life have developed illogically and therefore unfairly. The impurity of the judgment lies first in the way the material is present (that is very incompletely), second, in the way it is assessed, and third, in the fact that every separate part of the material again results, as is absolutely necessary, from impure knowledge. No experience of a man, for example, however close he is to us, can be so complete that we would have a logical right to evaluate him *in toto*. All evaluations are premature, and must be so. Finally, the gauge by which we measure, our own nature, is no unchangeable quantity; we have moods and vacillations; yet we would have to know ourselves to be a fixed gauge if we were to evaluate fairly the relationship of any one thing to ourselves. Perhaps it will follow from all this that one ought not to judge at all; if only one could *live* without evaluating, without having disinclinations and inclinations! For all disinclination depends upon an evaluation, just as does all inclination. Man cannot experience a drive to or away from something without the feeling that he is desiring what is beneficial and avoiding what is harmful, without evaluating knowingly the merit of the goal. We are from the start illogical and therefore unfair beings, *and this we can know:* it is one of the greatest and most insoluble disharmonies of existence.

## 33

*Error about life necessary for life.* Every belief in the value and worth of life is based on impure thinking and is only possible because the individual's sympathy for life in general, and for the suffering of mankind, is very weakly developed. Even uncommon men who think beyond themselves at all do not focus on life in general, but rather on limited parts of it. If one knows how to keep his attention primarily on exceptions, that is, on the great talents and pure souls, if one takes their coming into existence to

31. This aphorism grows out of Nietzsche's notes to Karl Eugen Dühring's *Der Wert des Lebens im Sinne einer heroischen Lebensauffassung* (1865) (The Value of Life in an Heroic Sense).

be the goal of all world evolution and rejoices in their activity, then one may believe in the value of life—for one is *overlooking* other men, which is to say, thinking impurely. And likewise, if one does focus on all men, but takes only one type of drive, the less egoistical type, as valid and excuses mankind in respect to its other drives, then too one can hope something about mankind as a whole, and believe to this extent in the value of life—in this case, too, through impurity of thought. But whichever is the case, such a stance makes one an *exception* among men. Most men tolerate life without grumbling too much and *believe* thus in the value of existence, but precisely because everyone wills himself alone and stands his ground alone, and does not step out of himself as do those exceptional men, everything extrapersonal escapes his notice entirely, or seems at the most a faint shadow. Thus the value of life for ordinary, everyday man is based only on his taking himself to be more important than the world. The great lack of fantasy from which he suffers keeps him from being able to empathize with other beings, and he therefore participates in their vicissitudes and suffering as little as possible. On the other hand, whoever would be truly able to participate in it would have to despair about the value of life; if he were able to grasp and feel mankind's overall consciousness in himself, he would collapse with a curse against existence—for mankind, as whole, has *no* goals and consequently, considering the whole affair, man cannot find his comfort and support in it, but rather his despair. If, in everything he does, he considers the ultimate aimlessness of men, his own activity acquires the character of *squandering* in his eyes. But to feel squandered as mankind (and not just as an individual), as we see the single blossom squandered by nature, is a feeling above all feelings.

But who is capable of it? Certainly only a poet—and poets always know how to comfort themselves.

## 34

*Some reassurance.* But does not our philosophy then turn into tragedy? Does not truth become an enemy of life, an enemy of what is better? A question seems to weigh down our tongues, and yet not want to be uttered: whether one *is capable* of consciously remaining in untruth, or, if one *had* to do so, whether death would not be preferable? For there is no "ought" anymore. Morality to the extent that it was an "ought" has been destroyed by our way of reflection, every bit as much as religion. Knowledge can allow only pleasure and unpleasure, benefit and harm, as motives. But how will these motives come to terms with the feeling for truth? These motives, too, have to do with errors (to the extent that inclination and disinclination, and their very unfair measurements, essentially determine, as we have said, our pleasure and unpleasure). All human life is sunk deep in untruth; the individual cannot pull it out of this well without growing profoundly annoyed with his entire past, without finding his present motives (like honor) senseless, and without opposing scorn and disdain to the passions that urge one on to the future and to the happiness in it. If this is true, is there only one way of thought left, with despair as a personal end and a philosophy of destruction as a theoretical end?

I believe that a man's *temperament* determines the aftereffect of knowledge; although the aftereffect described above is possible in some natures, I could just as well imagine a different one, which would give rise to a life much more simple, more free of affects than the present one. The old motives of intense desire would still be strong at first, due to old, inherited habit, but they would gradually grow weaker under the influence of cleansing knowledge. Finally one would live among men and with oneself as in *nature,* without praise, reproaches, overzealousness, delighting in many things as in a spectacle that one formerly had only to fear. One would be free of appearance[32] and would no longer feel the goading thought that one was not simply nature, or that one was more than nature. Of course, as I said, a good temperament would be necessary—a secure, mild, and basically cheerful soul; such a disposition would not need to be on guard for tricks and sudden explosions, and its expressions would have neither a growling tone nor sullenness—those familiar bothersome traits of old dogs and men who have lain a long time chained up. Rather, a man from whom the ordinary chains of life have fallen in such measure that he continues to live on only to better his knowledge must be able to renounce without envy and chagrin much, indeed almost everything, that other men value. He must be *content* with that free, fearless hovering over men, customs, laws and the traditional

32. *die Emphasis*

evaluations of things, which is for him the most desirable of states. He is glad to communicate his joy in this state, and perhaps he has nothing else *to* communicate, which is, to be sure, one renunciation, one self-denial the more. But if one nevertheless wants more from him, with a benevolent shake of the head he will indicate his brother, the free man of action, and perhaps not conceal a little scorn: for that man's "freedom" is another matter entirely.

# SECTION TWO
## On the History of Moral Feelings

### 35

*The advantages of psychological observation.* That meditating on things human, all too human (or, as the learned phrase goes, "psychological observation") is one of the means by which man can ease life's burden; that by exercising this art, one can secure presence of mind in difficult situations and entertainment amid boring surroundings; indeed, that from the thorniest and unhappiest phases of one's own life one can pluck maxims and feel a bit better thereby: this was believed, known—in earlier centuries. Why has it been forgotten in this century, when many signs point, in Germany at least, if not throughout Europe, to the dearth of psychological observation? Not particularly in novels, short stories, and philosophical meditations, for these are the work of exceptional men; but more in the judging of public events and personalities; most of all we lack the art of psychological dissection and calculation in all classes of society, where one hears a lot of talk about men, but none at all *about man.* Why do people let the richest and most harmless source of entertainment get away from them? Why do they not even read the great masters of the psychological maxim any more? For it is no exaggeration to say that it is hard to find the cultured European who has read La Rochefoucauld[1] and his spiritual and artistic cousins. Even more uncommon is the man who knows them and does not despise them. But even this unusual reader will probably find much less delight in those artists than their form ought to give him; for not even the finest mind is capable of adequate appreciation of the art of the polished maxim if he has not been educated to it, has not been challenged by it

---

1. Duc François de la Rochefoucauld (1613–80). See Introduction.

himself. Without such practical learning one takes this form of creating and forming to be easier than it is; one is not acute enough in discerning what is successful and attractive. For that reason present-day readers of maxims take a relatively insignificant delight in them, scarcely a mouthful of pleasure; they react like typical viewers of cameos, praising them because they cannot love them, and quick to admire but even quicker to run away.

## 36

*Objection.* Or might there be a counterargument to the thesis that psychological observation is one of life's best stimulants, remedies, and palliatives? Might one be so persuaded of the unpleasant consequences of this art as to intentionally divert the student's gaze from it? Indeed, a certain blind faith in the goodness of human nature, an inculcated aversion to dissecting human behavior, a kind of shame with respect to the naked soul, may really be more desirable for a man's overall happiness than the trait of psychological sharpsightedness, which is helpful in isolated instances. And perhaps the belief in goodness, in virtuous men and actions, in an abundance of impersonal goodwill in the world has made men better, in that it has made them less distrustful. If one imitates Plutarch's[2] heroes with enthusiasm and feels an aversion toward tracing skeptically the motives for their actions, then the welfare of human society has benefited (even if the truth of human society has not). Psychological error, and dullness in this area generally, help humanity forward; but knowledge of the truth might gain more from the stimulating power of an hypothesis like the one La Rochefoucauld places at the beginning of the first edition of his *Sentences et maximes morales:* "Ce que le monde nomme vertu n'est d'ordinaire qu'un fantôme formé par nos passions, à qui on donne un nom honnête pour faire impunément ce qu'on veut."[3] La Rochefoucauld and those other French masters of soul searching (whose company a German, the author of *Psychological*

---

2. Plutarch of Chaeronea (A.D. 50–120). The purpose of his *Lives* was to exemplify private virtue in the careers of great men.

3. "That which men call virtue is usually no more than a phantom formed by our passions, to which one gives an honest name in order to do with impunity whatever one wishes."

*Observations,* has recently joined)[4] are like accurately aimed arrows, which hit the mark again and again, the black mark of man's nature. Their skill inspires amazement, but the spectator who is guided not by the scientific spirit, but by the humane spirit, will eventually curse an art which seems to implant in the souls of men a predilection for belittling and doubt.

## 37

*Nevertheless.* However the argument and counterargument stand, the present condition of one certain, single science has made necessary the awakening of moral observation, and mankind cannot be spared the horrible sight of the psychological operating table, with its knives and forceps. For now that science rules which asks after the origin and history of moral feelings and which tries as it progresses to pose and solve the complicated sociological problems; the old philosophy doesn't even acknowledge such problems and has always used meager excuses to avoid investigating the origin and history of moral feelings. We can survey the consequences very clearly, many examples having proven how the errors of the greatest philosophers usually start from a false explanation of certain human actions and feelings, how an erroneous analysis of so-called selfless behavior, for example, can be the basis for false ethics, for whose sake religion and mythological confusion are then drawn in, and finally how the shadows of these sad spirits also fall upon physics and the entire contemplation of the world. But if it is a fact that the superficiality of psychological observation has laid the most dangerous traps for human judgment and conclusions, and continues to lay them anew, then what we need now is a persistence in work that does not tire of piling stone upon stone, pebble upon pebble; we need a sober courage to do such humble work without shame and to defy any who disdain it. It is true that countless individual remarks about things human and all too human were first detected and stated in those social circles which would make every sort of sacrifice not for scientific knowledge, but for a witty coquetry. And because the scent of that old homeland (a very seductive scent) has at-

4. The German referred to is Paul Rée (1845–1901), whose *Psychological Observations* appeared in 1875. See Introduction.

tached itself almost inextricably to the whole genre of the moral maxim, the scientific man instinctively shows some suspicion towards this genre and its seriousness. But it suffices to point to the outcome: already it is becoming clear that the most serious results grow up from the ground of psychological observation. Which principle did one of the keenest and coolest thinkers, the author of the book *On the Origin of Moral Feelings,* arrive at through his incisive and piercing analysis of human actions? "The moral man," he says, "stands no nearer to the intelligible (metaphysical) world than does the physical man."[5] Perhaps at some point in the future this principle, grown hard and sharp by the hammerblow of historical knowledge, can serve as the axe laid to the root of men's "metaphysical need"[6] (whether *more* as a blessing than as a curse for the general welfare, who can say?). In any event, it is a tenet with the most weighty consequences, fruitful and frightful at the same time, and seeing into the world with that double vision which all great insights have.

## 38

*How beneficial.* Let us table the question, then, of whether psychological observation brings more advantage or harm upon men. What is certain is that it is necessary, for science cannot do without it. Science, however, takes as little consideration of final purposes as does nature; just as nature sometimes brings about the most useful things without having wanted to, so too true science, *which is the imitation of nature in concepts,* will sometimes, nay often, further man's benefit and welfare and achieve what is useful—but likewise *without having wanted to.* Whoever feels too wintry in the breeze of this kind of observation has perhaps too little fire in him. Let him look around meanwhile, and he will perceive diseases which require cold poultices, and men who are so "moulded" out of glowing spirit that they have great trouble in finding an atmosphere cold and biting enough for them anywhere. Moreover, as all overly earnest individuals and peoples have a need for frivolity; as others, who are overly excitable and

5. Paraphrased from Rée's book *On the Origin of Moral Feelings,* which appeared in 1877.

6. See n. 26 to Section One.

unstable, occasionally need heavy, oppressive burdens for their health's sake; so should not *we*—the *more* intellectual men in an age that is visibly being set aflame more and more—reach for all quenching and cooling means available to remain at least as steady, harmless, and moderate as we now are and thus render service to this age at some future time as a mirror and self-reflection of itself?

## 39

*The fable of intelligible freedom.*[7] The history of those feelings, by virtue of which we consider a person responsible, the so-called moral feelings, is divided into the following main phases. At first we call particular acts good or evil without any consideration of their motives, but simply on the basis of their beneficial or harmful consequences. Soon, however, we forget the origin of these terms and imagine that the quality "good" or "evil" is inherent in the actions themselves, without consideration of their consequences; this is the same error language makes when calling the stone itself hard, the tree itself green—that is, we take the effect to be the cause. Then we assign the goodness or evil to the motives, and regard the acts themselves as morally ambiguous. We go even further and cease to give to the particular motive the predicate good or evil, but give it rather to the whole nature of a man; the motive grows out of him as a plant grows out of the earth. So we make man responsible in turn for the effects of his actions, then for his actions, then for his motives and finally for his nature. Ultimately we discover that his nature cannot be responsible either, in that it is itself an inevitable consequence, an outgrowth of the elements and influences of past and present things; that is, man cannot be made responsible for anything, neither for his nature, nor his motives, nor his actions, nor the effects of his actions. And thus we come to understand that the history of moral feelings is the history of an error, an error called "responsibility," which in turn rests on an error called "freedom of the will."

7. In ancient Greece, Plato's world of ideas—as a model for the sensual world—was referred to as the "intelligible world." "Intelligible freedom" is the pure form of freedom, the idea of freedom. See *The World as Will and Idea*, bk. 4, par. 55.

Schopenhauer, on the other hand, concluded as follows: because certain actions produce *displeasure* ("sense of guilt"), a responsibility must exist. For there would be *no reason* for this displeasure if not only all human actions occurred out of necessity (as they actually do, according to this philosopher's insight), but if man himself also acquired his entire *nature* out of the same necessity (which Schopenhauer denies). From the fact of man's displeasure, Schopenhauer thinks he can prove that man somehow must have had a freedom, a freedom which did not determine his actions but rather determined his nature: freedom, that is, *to be* this way or the other, not *to act* this way or the other. According to Schopenhauer, "operari" (doing), the sphere of strict causality, necessity, and lack of responsibility, follows from *esse* (being) the sphere of freedom and responsibility. The displeasure man feels seems to refer to "operari" (to this extent it is erroneous), but in truth it refers to *esse,* which is the act of a free will, the primary cause of an individual's existence. Man becomes that which he *wants* to be; his volition precedes his existence.[8]

In this case, we are concluding falsely that we can deduce the justification, the rational *admissibility* of this displeasure, from the fact that it exists; and from this false deduction Schopenhauer arrives at his fantastic conclusion of so-called intelligible freedom. But displeasure after the deed need not be rational at all: in fact, it certainly is not rational, for its rests on the erroneous assumption that the deed did *not* have to follow necessarily. Thus, because he thinks he is free (but not because he is free), man feels remorse and the pangs of conscience.

Furthermore, this displeasure is a habit that can be given up; many men do not feel it at all, even after the same actions that cause many other men to feel it. Tied to the development of custom and culture, it is a very changeable thing, and present perhaps only within a relatively short period of world history.

No one is responsible for his deeds, no one for his nature; to judge is to be unjust. This is also true when the individual judges himself. The tenet is as bright as sunlight, and yet everyone prefers to walk back into the shadow and untruth—for fear of the consequences.

8. Ibid., bk. 4, par. 65.

## 40

*The super-animal.*[9] The beast in us wants to be lied to; morality is a white lie, to keep it from tearing us apart. Without the errors inherent in the postulates of morality, man would have remained an animal. But as it is he has taken himself to be something higher and has imposed stricter laws upon himself. He therefore has a hatred of those stages of man that remain closer to the animal state, which explains why the slave used to be disdained as a non-human, a thing.

## 41

*The unchangeable character.* In the strict sense, it is not true that one's character is unchangeable; rather, this popular tenet[10] means only that during a man's short lifetime the motives affecting him cannot normally cut deeply enough to destroy the imprinted writing of many millennia. If a man eighty thousand years old were conceivable, his character would in fact be absolutely variable, so that out of him little by little an abundance of different individuals would develop. The brevity of human life misleads us to many an erroneous assertion about the qualities of man.

## 42

*Morality and the ordering of the good.* The accepted hierarchy of the good, based on how a low, higher, or a most high egoism desires that thing or the other, decides today about morality or immorality. To prefer a low good (sensual pleasure, for example) to one esteemed higher (health, for example) is taken for immoral, likewise to prefer comfort to freedom. The hierarchy of the good, however, is not fixed and identical at all times. If someone prefers revenge to justice, he is moral by the standard of an earlier culture, yet by the standard of the present culture he is immoral. "Immoral" then indicates that someone has not felt, or not felt strongly enough, the higher, finer, more spiritual motives which the new culture of the time has brought with it. It indicates a backward nature, but only in degree.

9. *Das Ueber-Thier.*

10. Cf. Aristotle, *Nichomachean Ethics,* 6.13.1: "The several kinds of character are bestowed by nature," or Heraclitus: "Character is destiny."

The hierarchy itself is not established or changed from the point of view of morality; nevertheless an action is judged moral or immoral according to the prevailing determination.

## 43

*Cruel men as backward.* We must think of men who are cruel today as stages of *earlier cultures,* which have been left over; in their case, the mountain range of humanity shows openly its deeper formations, which otherwise lie hidden. They are backward men whose brains, because of various possible accidents of heredity, have not yet developed much delicacy or versatility. They show us what we *all* were, and frighten us. But they themselves are as little responsible as a piece of granite for being granite. In our brain, too, there must be grooves and bends which correspond to that state of mind, just as there are said to be reminders of the fish state in the form of certain human organs.[11] But these grooves and bends are no longer the bed in which the river of our feeling courses.

## 44

*Gratitude and revenge.* The powerful man feels gratitude for the following reason: through his good deed, his benefactor has, as it were, violated the powerful man's sphere and penetrated it. Now through his act of gratitude the powerful man requites himself by violating the sphere of the benefactor. It is a milder form of revenge. Without the satisfaction of gratitude, the powerful man would have shown himself to be unpowerful and henceforth would be considered such. For that reason, every society of good men (that is, originally, of powerful men) places gratitude among its first duties.

Swift remarked that men are grateful in the same proportion as they cherish revenge.[12]

## 45

*Double prehistory of good and evil.* The concept of good and evil has a double prehistory: namely, first of all, in the soul of the

11. Cf. the work of the biologists Karl Ernst von Baer (1792–1876) and Ernst Haeckel (1834–1919).

12. Actually a remark by Alexander Pope (cf. *Das Swift-Büchlein,* Berlin, 1847).

ruling clans and castes. The man who has the power to requite goodness with goodness, evil with evil, and really does practice requital by being grateful and vengeful, is called "good." The man who is unpowerful and cannot requite is taken for bad. As a good man, one belongs to the "good," a community that has a communal feeling, because all the individuals are entwined together by their feeling for requital. As a bad man, one belongs to the "bad," to a mass of abject, powerless men who have no communal feeling. The good men are a caste; the bad men are a multitude, like particles of dust. Good and bad are for a time equivalent to noble and base, master and slave. Conversely, one does not regard the enemy as evil: he can requite. In Homer, both the Trojan and the Greek are good. Not the man who inflicts harm on us, but the man who is contemptible, is bad. In the community of the good, goodness is hereditary; it is impossible for a bad man to grow out of such good soil. Should one of the good men nevertheless do something unworthy of good men, one resorts to excuses; one blames God, for example, saying that he struck the good man with blindness and madness.

*Then,* in the souls of oppressed, powerless men, every *other* man is taken for hostile, inconsiderate, exploitative, cruel, sly, whether he be noble or base. Evil is their epithet for man, indeed for every possible living being, even, for example, for a god; "human," "divine" mean the same as "devilish," "evil." Signs of goodness, helpfulness, pity are taken anxiously for malice, the prelude to a terrible outcome, bewilderment, and deception, in short, for refined evil. With such a state of mind in the individual, a community can scarcely come about at all—or at most in the crudest form; so that wherever this concept of good and evil predominates, the downfall of individuals, their clans and races, is near at hand.

Our present morality has grown up on the ground of the *ruling clans and castes.*[13]

## 46

*Pity more intense than suffering.*[14] There are cases where pity is more intense than actual suffering. When one of our friends is guilty of something ignominious, for example, we feel it more

---

13. Cf. *On the Genealogy of Morals* (1887), first essay.
14. *Mitleiden stärker als Leiden.*

painfully than when we ourselves do it. For we believe in the purity of his character more than he does. Thus our love for him (probably because of this very belief) is more intense than his own love for himself. Even if his egoism suffers more than our egoism, in that he has to feel the bad consequences of his fault more intensely, our selflessness (this word must never be taken literally, but only as a euphemism) is touched more intensely by his guilt than is his selflessness.

### 47

*Hypochondria.* There are people who become hypochondriacs out of compassion and concern for another; the kind of pity which results is nothing less than a disease. Similarly, there is a Christian hypochrondria which befalls those lonely, religious-minded people who continually visualize to themselves the suffering and death of Christ.

### 48

*Economy of kindness.* Kindness and love, the most curative herbs and agents in human intercourse, are such precious finds that one would hope these balsamlike remedies would be used as economically as possible; but this is impossible. Only the boldest Utopians would dream of the economy of kindness.

### 49

*Goodwill.* Among the small but endlessly abundant and therefore very effective things that science ought to heed more than the great, rare things, is goodwill. I mean those expressions of a friendly disposition in interactions, that smile of the eye, those handclasps, that ease which usually envelops nearly all human actions. Every teacher, every official brings this ingredient to what he considers his duty. It is the continual manifestation of our humanity, its rays of light, so to speak, in which everything grows. Especially within the narrowest circle, in the family, life sprouts and blossoms only by this goodwill. Good nature, friendliness, and courtesy of the heart are ever-flowing tributaries of the selfless drive and have made much greater contributions to culture than those much more famous expressions of this drive, called pity, charity, and self-sacrifice. But we tend to underestimate them, and in fact there really is not much about them that is selfless. The *sum* of these small doses is nevertheless mighty; its cumulative force is among the strongest of forces.

Similarly, there is much more happiness to be found in the world than dim eyes can see, if one calculates correctly and does not forget all those moments of ease which are so plentiful in every day of every human life, even the most oppressed.

## 50

*Desire to arouse pity.*[15] In the most noteworthy passage of his self-portrait (first published in 1658), La Rochefoucauld certainly hits the mark when he warns all reasonable men against pity,[16] when he advises them to leave it to those common people who need passions (because they are not directed by reason) to bring them to the point of helping the sufferer and intervening energetically in a misfortune. For pity, in his (and Plato's)[17] judgment, weakens the soul. Of course one ought to *express* pity, but one ought to guard against *having* it; for unfortunate people are so *stupid* that they count the expression of pity as the greatest good on earth.

Perhaps one can warn even more strongly against having pity for the unfortunate if one does not think of their need for pity as stupidity and intellectual deficiency, a kind of mental disorder resulting from their misfortune (this is how La Rochefoucauld seems to regard it), but rather as something quite different and more dubious. Observe how children weep and cry, *so that* they will be pitied, how they wait for the moment when their condi-

---

15. This aphorism is directed against Schopenhauer's exaltation of pity as the highest moral feeling (cf. *The World as Will and Idea,* Bk. 4, par. 67).

16. Je suis peu sensible à la pitié et voudrais ne l'y être point du tout . . . Cependant, il n'est rien que je ne fisse pour le soulagement d'une personne affligée. . . Mais je tiens aussi qu'il faut se contenter d'en témoigner et se garder soigneusement d'en avoir. C'est une passion qui n'est bonne à rien au dedans d'une âme bien faite, qui ne sert qu'a affaiblir le coeur, et qu'on doit laisser au peuple, qui, n'exécutant jamais rien par raison, a besoin des passions pour le porter à faire les choses. (I am not much moved by pity and would like to be not at all. . . . However, there is nothing I would not do to relieve a suffering person. . . . But I also maintain that one should be content to show it [pity] and carefully keep from having it. It is a passion which is useless to a well-developed soul, which serves only to weaken the heart, and which ought to be left to the masses, who, never doing anything out of reason, need passions to bring them to act.)

17. Cf. *The Republic* Bk. 3, 387–88.

tion will be noticed. Or live among the ill and depressed, and question whether their eloquent laments and whimpering, the spectacle of their misfortune, is not basically aimed at *hurting* those present. The pity that the spectators then express consoles the weak and suffering, inasmuch as they see that, despite all their weakness, they still *have* at least one *power: the power to hurt.* When expressions of pity make the unfortunate man aware of this feeling of superiority, he gets a kind of pleasure from it; his self-image revives; he is still important enough to inflict pain on the world. Thus the thirst for pity is a thirst for self-enjoyment, and at the expense of one's fellow men. It reveals man in the complete inconsideration of his most intimate dear self, but not precisely in his "stupidity," as La Rochefoucauld thinks.

In social dialogue, three-quarters of all questions and answers are framed in order to hurt the participants a little bit; this is why many men thirst after society so much: it gives them a feeling of their strength. In these countless, but very small doses, malevolence takes effect as one of life's powerful stimulants, just as goodwill, dispensed in the same way throughout the human world, is the perennially ready cure.

But will there be many people honest enough to admit that it is a pleasure to inflict pain? That not infrequently one amuses himself (and well) by offending other men (at least in his thoughts) and by shooting pellets of petty malice at them? Most people are too dishonest, and a few men are too good, to know anything about this source of shame. So they may try to deny that Prosper Merimée is right when he says, "Sachez aussi qu'il n'y a rien de plus commun que de faire le mal pour le plaisir de le faire."[18]

### 51

*How seeming becomes being.*[19] Ultimately, not even the deepest pain can keep the actor from thinking of the impression of his part and the overall theatrical effect, not even, for example, at his child's funeral.[20] He will be his own audience, and cry about his own pain as he expresses it. The hypocrite who always plays one and the same role finally ceases to be a hypocrite. Priests, for ex-

18. Prosper Merimée (1803–70), *Lettres à une inconnue*, 1:8. "Know that nothing is more common than to do harm for the pleasure of doing it."

19. *Wie der Schein zum Sein wird.*

20. Cf. Diderot, *Paradoxe sur le comédien* (1769).

ample, who are usually conscious or unconscious hypocrites when
they are young men, finally end by becoming natural, and then
they really are priests, with no affectation. Or if the father does not
get that far, perhaps the son, using his father's headway, inherits
the habit. If someone wants to *seem* to be something, stubbornly
and for a long time, he eventually finds it hard to *be* anything else.
The profession of almost every man, even the artist, begins with
hypocrisy, as he imitates from the outside, copies what is effective.
The man who always wears the mask of a friendly countenance
eventually has to gain power over benevolent moods without
which the expression of friendliness cannot be forced—and
eventually then these moods gain power over him, and he *is*
benevolent.

## 52

*The point of honesty in deception.* In all great deceivers there
occurs a noteworthy process to which they owe their power. In
the actual act of deception, among all the preparations, the horror
in the voice, expression, gestures, amid the striking scenery, the
*belief in themselves* overcomes them. It is this that speaks so mirac-
ulously and convincingly to the onlookers. The founders of religions are distinguished from those other great deceivers by the
fact that they do not come out of this condition of self-deception:
or, very infrequently, they do have those clearer moments, when
doubt overwhelms them; but they usually comfort themselves by
foisting these clearer moments off on the evil adversary. Self-deception must be present, so that both kinds of deceivers can have
a grand *effect.* For men will believe something is true, if it is evident that others believe in it firmly.

## 53

*Alleged levels of truth.* One common false conclusion is that because someone is truthful and upright toward us he is speaking
the truth. Thus the child believes his parents' judgments, the
Christian believes the claims of the church's founders. Likewise,
people do not want to admit that all those things which men have
defended with the sacrifice of their lives and happiness in earlier
centuries were nothing but errors. Perhaps one calls them levels
of truth. Basically, however, one thinks that if someone honestly
believed in something and fought for his belief and died it would

be too *unfair* if he had actually been inspired by a mere error. Such an occurrence seems to contradict eternal justice. Therefore the hearts of sensitive men always decree in opposition to their heads that there must be a necessary connection between moral actions and intellectual insights. Unfortunately, it is otherwise, for there is no eternal justice.

## 54

*The lie.* Why do men usually tell the truth in daily life? Certainly not because a god has forbidden lying. Rather it is because, first, it is more convenient: for lies demand imagination, dissembling, and memory (which is why Swift says that the man who tells a lie seldom perceives the heavy burden he is assuming: namely, he must invent twenty other lies to make good the first). Then, it is because it is advantageous in ordinary circumstances to say directly: I want this, I did that, and so on; that is, because the path of obligation and authority is safer than that of cunning.

If a child has been raised in complicated domestic circumstances, however, he will employ the lie naturally, and will always say instinctively that which corresponds to his interests. A feeling for truth, a distaste for lying in and of itself, is alien to him and inaccessible; and so he lies in complete innocence.

## 55

*To suspect morality because of belief.* No power can maintain itself if only hypocrites represent it. However many "worldly" elements the Catholic Church may have, its strength rests on those priestly natures, still numerous, who make life deep and difficult for themselves, and whose eye and emaciated body speak of nightly vigils, fasting, fervent prayers, perhaps even flagellation. These men shock others and worry them: what if it were *necessary* to live like that?—this is the horrible question that the sight of them brings to the tongue. By spreading this doubt they keep reestablishing a pillar of their power. Not even the most free-minded dare to resist so selfless a man with the hard sense for truth, and say: "You who are deceived, do not deceive others."

Only a difference of insight separates them from this man, by no means a difference of goodness or badness; but if one does not like a thing, one generally tends to treat it unjustly, too. Thus one speaks of the Jesuits' cunning and their infamous art, but overlooks what self-conquest each single Jesuit imposes upon himself, and how that lighter regimen preached in Jesuit textbooks is certainly not for their own benefit, but rather for the layman's. Indeed, one might ask if we the enlightened, using their tactics and organization, would be such good instruments, so admirably self-mastering, untiring, and devoted.

## 56

*Triumph of knowledge over radical evil.* The man who wants to gain wisdom profits greatly from having thought for a time that man is basically evil and degenerate: this idea is wrong, like its opposite, but for whole periods of time it was predominant and its roots have sunk deep into us and into our world. To understand ourselves we must understand *it;* but to climb higher, we must then climb over and beyond it. We recognize that there are no sins in the metaphysical sense; but, in the same sense, neither are there any virtues; we recognize that this entire realm of moral ideas is in a continual state of fluctuation, that there are higher and deeper concepts of good and evil, moral and immoral. A man who desires no more from things than to understand them easily makes peace with his soul and will err (or "sin," as the world calls it) at the most out of ignorance, but hardly out of desire. He will no longer want to condemn and root out his desires; but his single goal, governing him completely, to *understand* as well as he can at all times, will cool him down and soften all the wildness in his disposition. In addition, he has rid himself of a number of tormenting ideas; he no longer feels anything at the words "pains of hell," "sinfulness," "incapacity for the good": for him they are only the evanescent silhouettes of erroneous thoughts about life and the world.

## 57

*Morality as man's dividing himself.* A good author, who really cares about his subject, wishes that someone would come and destroy him by representing the same subject more clearly and by answering every last question contained in it. The girl in love wishes that she might prove the devoted faithfulness of her love through her lover's faithlessness. The soldier wishes that he might fall on the battlefield for his victorious fatherland, for in the victory of his fatherland his greatest desire is also victorious. The mother gives the child what she takes from herself: sleep, the best food, in some instances even her health, her wealth.

Are all these really selfless states, however? Are these acts of morality *miracles* because they are, to use Schopenhauer's phrase, "impossible and yet real"? Isn't it clear that, in all these cases, man is loving *something of himself,* a thought, a longing, an off-spring, more than *something else of himself;* that he is thus *dividing up* his being and sacrificing one part for the other? Is it something *essentially* different when a pigheaded man says, "I would rather be shot at once than move an inch to get out of that man's way"?

The *inclination towards something* (a wish, a drive, a longing) is present in all the above-mentioned cases; to yield to it, with all its consequences, is in any case not "selfless." In morality, man treats himself not as an "individuum," but as a "dividuum."

## 58

*What one can promise.* One can promise actions, but not feelings, for the latter are involuntary. He who promises to love forever or hate forever or be forever faithful to someone is promising something that is not in his power. He can, however, promise those actions that are usually the consequence of love, hatred, or faithfulness, but that can also spring from other motives: for there are several paths and motives to an action. A promise to love someone forever, then, means, "As long as I love you I will render unto you the actions of love; if I no longer love you, you will continue to receive the same actions from me, if for other motives." Thus the illusion remains in the minds of one's fellow men that the love is unchanged and still the same.

One is promising that the semblance of love will endure, then, when without self-deception one vows everlasting love.

## 59

*Intellect and morality.* One must have a good memory to be able to keep the promises one has given. One must have strong powers of imagination to be able to have pity. So closely is morality bound to the quality of the intellect.

## 60

*Desire to avenge and vengeance.* To have thoughts of revenge and execute them means to be struck with a violent—but temporary—fever. But to have thoughts of revenge without the strength or courage to execute them means to endure a chronic suffering, a poisoning of body and soul. A morality that notes only the intentions assesses both cases equally; usually the first case is assessed as worse (because of the evil consequences that the act of revenge may produce). Both evaluations are short-sighted.

## 61

*The ability to wait.* Being able to wait is so hard that the greatest poets did not disdain to make the inability to wait the theme of their poetry. Thus Shakespeare in his Othello, Sophocles in his Ajax,[21] who, as the oracle suggests, might not have thought his suicide necessary, if only he had been able to let his feeling cool for one day more. He probably would have outfoxed the terrible promptings of his wounded vanity and said to himself: "Who, in my situation, has never once taken a sheep for a warrior? Is that so monstrous? On the contrary, it is something universally human." Ajax might have consoled himself thus.

Passion will not wait. The tragedy in the lives of great men often lies not in their conflict with the times and the baseness of their fellow men, but rather in their inability to postpone their work for a year or two. They cannot wait.

In every duel, the advising friends have to determine whether the parties involved might be able to wait a while longer. If they cannot, then a duel is reasonable, since each of the parties says to himself: "Either I continue to live, and the other must die at once, or vice versa." In that case, to wait would be to continue suffering the horrible torture of offended honor in the presence of the offender. And this can be more suffering than life is worth.

## 62

*Reveling in revenge.* Crude men who feel themselves insulted tend to assess the degree of insult as high as possible, and talk about the offense in greatly exaggerated language, only so they can revel to their heart's content in the aroused feelings of hatred and revenge.

21. After Agamemnon awards Achilles' armor to Odysseus, Ajax, the hero of Sophocles' play, goes mad and charges a herd of sheep, thinking them soldiers. When he regains his sanity, he slays himself on his sword.

## 63

*The value of belittling.* Not a few, perhaps the great majority of men, find it necessary, in order to maintain their self-respect and a certain effectiveness in their actions, to lower and belittle the image they form of everyone they know. Since, however, the number of inferior natures is greater, and since it matters a great deal whether they have that effectiveness or lose it. . . .

## 64

*Those who flare up.* We must beware of the man who flares up at us as of someone who has once made an attempt upon our life. For *that* we are still alive is due to his lacking the power to kill. If looks could kill, we would long ago have been done for. It is an act of primitive culture to bring someone to silence by making physical savageness visible, by inciting fear.

In the same way, the cold glance which elegant people use with their servants is a vestige from those castelike distinctions between man and man, an act of primitive antiquity. Women, the guardians of that which is old, have also been more faithful in preserving this cultural remnant.

## 65

*Where honesty may lead.* Someone had the unfortunate habit of speaking out from time to time quite honestly about the motives for his actions, motives which were as good and as bad as those of all other men. At first, he gave offense, then he awoke suspicion, and at length he was virtually ostracized and banished. Finally, justice remembered this depraved creature on occasions when it otherwise averted or winked its eye. His want of silence about the universal secret, and his irresponsible inclination to see what no one wants to see—his own self—brought him to prison and an untimely death.

## 66

*Punishable, never punished.* Our crime against criminals is that we treat them like scoundrels.

## 67

Sancta simplicitas[22] *of virtue.* Every virtue has its privileges, one being to deliver its own little bundle of wood to the funeral pyre of a condemned man.

## 68

*Morality and success.* It is not only the witnesses of a deed who often measure its moral or immoral nature by its success. No, the author of a deed does so, too. For motives and intentions are seldom sufficiently clear and simple, and sometimes even memory seems to be dimmed by the success of a deed, so that one attributes false motives to his deed, or treats inessential motives as essential. Often it is success that gives to a deed the full, honest lustre of a good conscience; failure lays the shadow of an uneasy conscience upon the most estimable action. This leads to the politican's well-known practice of thinking: "Just grant me success; with it I will bring all honest souls to my side—and make myself honest in my own sight."

In a similar way, success can take the place of more substantial arguments. Even now, many educated people think that the victory of Christianity over Greek philosophy is a proof of the greater truth of the former—although in this case it is only that something more crude and violent has triumphed over something more spiritual and delicate. We can determine which of them has the greater truth by noting that the awakening sciences have carried on point for point with the philosophy of Epicurus,[23] but have rejected Christianity point for point.

## 69

*Love and justice.* Why do we overestimate love to the disadvantage of justice, saying the nicest things about it, as if it were a far higher essence than justice? Isn't love obviously more foolish? Of course, but for just that reason so much more pleasant for everyone. Love is foolish, and possesses a rich horn of plenty; from it

22. Holy simplicity.

23. Epicurus (341–270 B.C.): For documentation of Nietzsche's relation to Epicurus, see Walter Kaufmann's note in his translation of *The Gay Science* (New York: Vintage, 1974), p. 110.

she dispenses her gifts to everyone, even if he does not deserve them, indeed, even if he does not thank her for them. She is as nonpartisan as rain, which (according to the Bible[24] and to experience) rains not only upon the unjust, but sometimes soaks the just man to the skin, too.

## 70

*Executions.* How is it that every execution offends us more than a murder? It is the coldness of the judges, the painful preparations, the understanding that a man is here being used as a means to deter others. For guilt is not being punished, even if there were guilt; guilt lies in the educators, the parents, the environment, in us, not in the murderer—I am talking about the motivating circumstances.

## 71

*Hope.* Pandora brought the jar[25] with the evils and opened it. It was the gods' gift to man, on the outside a beautiful, enticing gift, called the "lucky jar." Then all the evils, those lively, winged beings, flew out of it. Since that time, they roam around and do harm to men by day and night. One single evil had not yet slipped out of the jar. As Zeus had wished, Pandora slammed the top down and it remained inside. So now man has the lucky jar in his house forever and thinks the world of the treasure. It is at his service; he reaches for it when he fancies it. For he does not know that that jar which Pandora brought was the jar of evils, and he takes the remaining evil for the greatest worldly good—it is hope, for Zeus did not want man to throw his life away, no matter how much the other evils might torment him, but rather to go on letting himself be tormented anew. To that end, he gives man hope. In truth, it is the most evil of evils because it prolongs man's torment.

24. Matthew 4:45. "His sun rises on the bad and the good, he rains on the just and the unjust."

25. According to Hesiod, Pandora brings a πιθος (*dolium* in Latin), a huge earthenware storage jar (not a box), as her dowry when she marries Epimetheus. Nietzsche uses the word *Fass,* suggesting a large, barrel-like container. For complete discussion of the versions of the legend, see Dora and Erwin Panofsky, *Pandora's Box* (New York: Harper and Row, 1962).

## 72

*Degree of moral inflammability unknown.* Whether or not our passions reach the point of red heat and guide our whole life depends on whether or not we have been exposed to certain shocking sights or impressions—for example a father falsely executed, killed or tortured; an unfaithful wife; a cruel ambush by an enemy. No one knows how far circumstances, pity, or indignation may drive him; he does not know the degree of his inflammability. Miserable, mean conditions make one miserable; it is usually not the quality of the experiences but rather the quantity that determines the lower and the higher man, in good and in evil.

## 73

*The martyr against his will.* In one party, there was a man who was too anxious and cowardly ever to contradict his comrades. They used him for every service; they demanded everything of him, because he was more afraid of the bad opinions of his companions than of death itself. His was a miserable, weak soul. They recognized this and on the basis of those qualities they made him first into a hero and finally into a martyr. Although the cowardly man always said "no" inwardly, he always said "yes" with his lips, even on the scaffold, when he died for the views of his party. Next to him stood one of his old comrades, who tyrannized him so by word and glance that he really did suffer death in the most seemly way, and has since been celebrated as a martyr and a man of great character.

## 74

*Everyday rule-of-thumb.* One will seldom go wrong to attribute extreme actions to vanity, moderate ones to habit, and petty ones to fear.

## 75

*Misunderstanding about virtue.* The man who has come to know vice in connection with pleasure, like the man who has a pleasure-seeking youth behind him, imagines that virtue must be associated with displeasure. On the other hand, the man who has been greatly plagued by his passions and vices longs to find peace and his soul's happiness in virtue. Thus it is possible that two virtuous people will not understand each other at all.

## 76

*The ascetic.* The ascetic makes a necessity[26] of virtue.

## 77

*The honor of the person applied to the cause.* We universally honor acts of love and sacrifice for the sake of one's neighbor, wherever we find them. In this way we heighten the *value of the things* loved in that way, or for which sacrifices are made, even though they are in themselves perhaps not worth much. A valiant army convinces us about the cause for which it is fighting.

## 78

*Ambition as a surrogate for moral sense.* Any character lacking in ambition must not be without a moral sense. Ambitious people make do without it, and have almost the same success. Thus the sons of humble families with no ambition will usually turn into complete cads very quickly, having once lost their moral sense.

## 79

*Vanity enriches.* How poor the human spirit would be without vanity! Instead it is like a warehouse, replete and forever replenishing its stock. It lures customers of every kind; they can find almost everything, have everything, assuming that they bring the right kind of coin (admiration) with them.

## 80

*The old man and death.* One may well ask why, aside from the demands of religion, it is more praiseworthy for a man grown old, who feels his powers decrease, to await his slow exhaustion and disintegration, rather than to put a term to his life with complete consciousness? In this case, suicide is quite natural, obvious, and should by rights awaken respect for the triumph of reason. This it did in those times when the leading Greek philosophers and the doughtiest Roman patriots used to die by suicide. Conversely, the compulsion to prolong life from day to day, anxiously consulting doctors and accepting the most painful, humiliating conditions, without the strength to come nearer the actual goal of one's life:

26. Nietzsche's pun in reversing this adage loses its real point in translation, for the German word *Not* (necessity) also means "misery."

this is far less worthy of respect. Religions provide abundant excuses to escape the need to kill oneself: this is how they insinuate
themselves with those who are in love with life.

# 81

*Misunderstanding between the sufferer and the perpetrator.* When
a rich man takes a possession from a poor man (for example, when
a prince robs a plebeian of his sweetheart), the poor man misun-
derstands. He thinks that the rich man must be a villain to take
from him the little he has. But the rich man does not feel the value
of a *particular* possession so deeply because he is accustomed to
having many. So he cannot put himself in the place of the poor
man, and he is by no means doing as great an injustice as the poor
man believes. Each has a false idea of the other. The injustice of
the mighty, which enrages us most in history, is by no means as
great as it appears. Simply the inherited feeling of being a higher
being, with higher pretensions, makes one rather cold, and leaves
the conscience at peace. Indeed, none of us feels anything like
injustice when there is a great difference between ourselves and
some other being, and we kill a gnat, for example, without any
twinge of conscience. So it is no sign of wickedness in Xerxes[27]
(whom even all the Greeks portray as exceptionally noble) when
he takes a son from his father and has him cut to pieces, because
the father had expressed an anxious and doubtful distrust of their
entire campaign. In this case the individual man is eliminated like
an unpleasant insect; he stands too low to be allowed to keep on
arousing bothersome feelings in a world ruler. Indeed, no cruel
man is cruel to the extent that the mistreated man believes. The
idea of pain is not the same as the suffering of it. It is the same
with an unjust judge, with a journalist who misleads public opinion by little dishonesties. In each of these cases, cause and effect
are experienced in quite different categories of thought and feeling; nevertheless, it is automatically assumed that the perpetrator
and sufferer think and feel the same, and the guilt of the one is
therefore measured by the pain of the other.

27. Xerxes: King of Persia from 486 to 465 B.C. In the seventh book of Hero-
dotus's *Histories,* Pythius, having witnessed an evil omen, pleads that his eldest
son be exempted from going on Xerxes' campaign. Xerxes orders the son cut in
half.

## 82

*The skin of the soul.* Just as the bones, flesh, intestines, and blood vessels are enclosed by skin, which makes the sight of a man bearable, so the stirrings and passions of the soul are covered up by vanity: it is the skin of the soul.

## 83

*Sleep of virtue.* When virtue has slept, it will arise refreshed.

## 84

*Refinement of shame.* Men are not ashamed to think something dirty, but they are ashamed when they imagine that others might believe them capable of these dirty thoughts.

## 85

*Malice is rare.* Most men are much too concerned with themselves to be malicious.

## 86

*Tipping the scales.* We praise or find fault, depending on which of the two provides more opportunity for our powers of judgment to shine.

## 87

*Luke 18:14,*[28] *improved.* He who humbleth himself wants to be exalted.

## 88

*Prevention of suicide.* There is a justice according to which we take a man's life, but no justice according to which we take his death: that is nothing but cruelty.

## 89

*Vanity.* We care about the good opinion of others first because it is profitable, and then because we want to give others joy (children want to give joy to their parents, pupils to their teachers, men of good will to all other men). Only when someone holds the

28. Luke 18:14. "He who humbleth himself shall be exalted."

good opinion of others to be important without regard to his interests or his wish to give joy, do we speak of vanity. In this case, the man wants to give joy to himself, but at the expense of his fellow men, in that he either misleads them to a false opinion about himself or aims at a degree of "good opinion" that would have to cause them all pain (by arousing their envy). Usually the individual wants to confirm the opinion he has of himself through the opinion of others and strengthen it in his own eyes; but the mighty habituation to authority (which is as old as man) also leads many to base their own belief in themselves upon authority, to accept it only from the hand of others. They trust other people's powers of judgment more than their own.

In the vain man, interest in himself, his wish to please himself, reaches such a peak that he misleads others to assess him wrongly, to overvalue him greatly, and then he adheres to their authority; that is, he brings about the error and then believes in it.

One must admit, then, that vain men want to please not only others, but also themselves, and that they go so far as to neglect their own interests thereby; for they are often concerned to make their fellow men ill-disposed, hostile, envious, and thus destructive toward them, only for the sake of having pleasure in themselves, self-enjoyment.

### 90

*Limit of human love.* Any man who has once declared the other man to be a fool, a bad fellow, is annoyed when that man ends by showing that he is not.

### 91

*Moralité larmoyante.*[29] How much pleasure we get from morality! Just think what a river of agreeable tears has flowed at tales of noble, generous actions. This one of life's delights would vanish away if the belief in complete irresponsibility were to get the upper hand.

29. Tearful morality: Nietzsche is playing with the phrase *comédie larmoyante,* a popular theatrical genre of the eighteenth century, introduced by the plays of Destouches (1680–1754) and later developed by Diderot (*Le Fils naturel,* 1757; *Le Père de famille,* 1758).

## 92

*Origin of justice.* Justice (fairness) originates among approximately *equal powers,* as Thucydides (in the horrifying conversation between the Athenian and Melian envoys)[30] rightly understood. When there is no clearly recognizable supreme power and
a battle would lead to fruitless and mutual injury, one begins to
think of reaching an understanding and negotiating the claims on
both sides: the initial character of justice is *barter.* Each satisfies
the other in that each gets what he values more than the other.
Each man gives the other what he wants, to keep henceforth, and
receives in turn that which he wishes. Thus, justice is requital
and exchange on the assumption of approximately equal positions
of strength. For this reason, revenge belongs initially to the realm
of justice: it is an exchange. Likewise gratitude.

Justice naturally goes back to the viewpoint of an insightful
self-preservation, that is, to the egoism of this consideration:
"Why should I uselessly injure myself and perhaps not reach my
goal anyway?"

So much about the *origin* of justice. Because men, in line with
their intellectual habits, have *forgotten* the original purpose of so-
called just, fair actions, and particularly because children have
been taught for centuries to admire and imitate such actions, it
has gradually come to appear that a just action is a selfless one.
The high esteem of these actions rests upon this appearance, an
esteem which, like all estimations, is also always in a state of
growth: for men strive after, imitate, and reproduce with their
own sacrifices that which is highly esteemed, and it grows because its worth is increased by the worth of the effort and exertion
made by each individual.

How slight the morality of the world would seem without forgetfulness! A poet could say that God had stationed forgetfulness
as a guardian at the door to the temple of human dignity.

## 93

*The right of the weaker.* If one party, a city under siege, for example, submits under certain conditions to a greater power, its reciprocal condition is that this first party can destroy itself, burn

---

30. In Bk. 5, 85–113, Thucydides recounts the surrender of Melos in 416
B.C.

the city, and thus make the power suffer a great loss. Thus there is a kind of *equalization,* on the basis of which rights can be established. Preservation is to the enemy's advantage.

Rights exist between slaves and masters to the same extent, exactly insofar as the possession of his slave is profitable and important to the master. The *right* originally extends *as far* as the one *appears* to the other to be valuable, essential, permanent, invincible, and the like. In this regard even the weaker of the two has rights, though they are more modest. Thus the famous dictum: "unusquisque tantum juris habet, quantum potentia valet"[31] (or, more exactly, "quantum potentia valere creditur").[32]

## 94

*The three phases of morality until now.* The first sign that an animal has become human is that his behavior is no longer directed to his momentary comfort, but rather to his enduring comfort, that is, when man becomes useful, *expedient:* then for the first time the free rule of reason bursts forth. A still higher state is reached when man acts according to the principle of *honor,* by means of which he finds his place in society, submitting to commonly held feelings; that raises him high above the phase in which he is guided only by personal usefulness. Now he shows— and wants to be shown—respect; that is, he understands his advantage as dependent on his opinion of others and their opinion of him. Finally, at the highest stage of morality *until now,* he acts according to *his* standard of things and men; he himself determines for himself and others what is honorable, what is profitable. He has become the lawgiver of opinions, in accordance with the ever more refined concept of usefulness and honor. Knowledge enables him to prefer what is most useful, that is, general usefulness to personal usefulness, and the respectful recognition of what has common, enduring value to things of momentary value. He lives and acts as a collective-individual.

## 95

*Morality of the mature individual.* Until now man has taken the true sign of a moral act to be its impersonal nature; and it has been

---

31. "Each has as much right as his power is worth." Spinoza, *Tractatus Politicus,* vol. 2, par. 8.

32. "as his power is assessed to be"

shown that in the beginning all impersonal acts were praised and distinguished in respect to the common good. Might not a significant transformation of these views be at hand, now when we see with ever greater clarity that precisely in the most *personal* respect the common good is also greatest; so that now it is precisely the strictly personal action which corresponds to the current concept of morality (as a common profit)? To make a whole *person* of oneself and keep in mind that person's *greatest good* in everything one does—this takes us further than any pitying impulses and actions for the sake of others. To be sure, we all still suffer from too slight a regard for our own personal needs; it has been poorly developed. Let us admit that our mind has instead been forcibly diverted from it and offered in sacrifice to the state, to science, to the needy, as if it were something bad which had to be sacrificed. Now too we wish to work for our fellow men, but only insofar as we find our own highest advantage in this work; no more, no less. It depends only on what ones understands by his *advantage*. The immature, undeveloped, crude individual will also understand it most crudely.

## 96

*Mores and morality.*[33] To be moral, correct, ethical means to obey an age-old law or tradition. Whether one submits to it gladly or with difficulty makes no difference; enough that one submits. We call "good" the man who does the moral thing as if by nature, after a long history of inheritance—that is, easily, and gladly, whatever it is (he will, for example, practice revenge when that is considered moral, as in the older Greek culture). He is called good because he is good "for" something. But because, as mores changed, goodwill, pity, and the like were always felt to be "good for" something, useful, it is primarily the man of goodwill, the helpful man, who is called "good." To be evil is to be "not moral" (immoral), to practice bad habits, go against tradition, however reasonable or stupid it may be. To harm one's fellow, however, has been felt primarily as injurious in all moral codes of different times, so that when we hear the word "bad" now, we think particularly of voluntary injury to one's fellow. When men determine between moral and immoral, good and evil, the basic opposition

33. *Sitte und Sittlichkeit.* See Introduction.

is not "egoism" and "selflessness," but rather adherence to a tradition or law, and release from it. The *origin* of the tradition makes no difference, at least concerning good and evil, or an immanent categorical imperative;[34] but is rather above all for the purpose of maintaining *a community,* a people. Every superstitious custom, originating in a coincidence that is interpreted falsely, forces a tradition that it is moral to follow. To release oneself from it is dangerous, even more injurious for the *community* than for the individual (because the divinity punishes the whole community for sacrilege and violation of its rights, and the individual only as a part of that community). Now, each tradition grows more venerable the farther its origin lies in the past, the more it is forgotten; the respect paid to the tradition accumulates from generation to generation; finally the origin becomes sacred and awakens awe; and thus the morality of piety is in any case much older than that morality which requires selfless acts.

# 97

*Pleasure in custom.* An important type of pleasure, and thus an important source of morality, grows out of habit. One does habitual things more easily, skillfully, gladly; one feels a pleasure at them, knowing from experience that the habit has stood the test and is useful. A morality one can live with has been proved salutary, effective, in contrast to all the as yet unproven new experiments. Accordingly, custom is the union of the pleasant and the useful; in addition, it requires no thought. As soon as man can exercise force, he exercises it to introduce and enforce his mores, for to him they represent proven wisdom. Likewise, a community will force each individual in it to the same mores. Here is the error: because one feels good with one custom, or at least because he lives his life by means of it, this custom is necessary, for he holds it to be the *only* possibility by which one can feel good; the enjoyment of life seems to grow out of it alone. This idea of habit as a condition of existence is carried right into the smallest details of custom: since lower peoples and cultures have only very slight insight into the real causality, they make sure, with superstitious fear, that everything take the same course; even where a custom is difficult, harsh, burdensome, it is preserved because it seems to be

34. See n. 25 to Section One.

highly useful. They do not know that the same degree of comfort can also exist with other customs and that even higher degrees of comfort can be attained. But they do perceive that all customs, even the harshest, become more pleasant and mild with time, and that even the severest way of life can become a habit and thus a pleasure.

## 98

*Pleasure and social instinct.* From his relationship to other men, man gains a new kind of pleasure, in addition to those pleasurable feelings which he gets from himself. In this way he widens significantly the scope of his pleasurable feelings. Perhaps some of these feelings have come down to him from the animals, who visibly feel pleasure when playing with each other, particularly mothers playing with their young. Next one might think of sexual relations, which make virtually every lass seem interesting to every lad (and vice versa) in view of potential pleasure. Pleasurable feeling based on human relations generally makes man better; shared joy, pleasure taken together, heightens this feeling; it gives the individual security, makes him better-natured, dissolves distrust and envy: one feels good oneself and can see the other man feel good in the same way. *Analogous expressions of pleasure* awaken the fantasy of empathy, the feeling of being alike. Shared sorrows do it, too: the same storms, dangers, enemies. Upon this basis man has built the oldest covenant, whose purpose is to eliminate and resist communally any threatening unpleasure, for the good of each individual. And thus social instinct grows out of pleasure.

## 99

*Innocence of so-called evil actions.* All "evil" actions are motivated by the drive for preservation, or, more exactly, by the individual's intention to gain pleasure and avoid unpleasure; thus they are motivated, but they are not evil. "Giving pain in and of itself" *does not exist,* except in the brain of philosophers, nor does "giving pleasure in and of itself" (pity, in the Schopenhauerian sense). In conditions *preceding* organized states, we kill any being, be it ape or man, that wants to take a fruit off a tree before we do, just when we are hungry and running up to the tree. We would treat the animal the same way today, if we were hiking through inhospitable territory.

Those evil actions which outrage us most today are based on the error that that man who harms us has free will, that is, that he had the *choice* not to do this bad thing to us. This belief in his choice arouses hatred, thirst for revenge, spite, the whole deterioration of our imagination; whereas we get much less angry at an animal because we consider it irresponsible. To do harm not out of a drive for preservation, but for requital—that is the result of an erroneous judgment, and is therefore likewise innocent. The individual can, in conditions preceding the organized state, treat others harshly and cruelly to *intimidate* them, to secure his existence through such intimidating demonstrations of his power. This is how the brutal, powerful man acts, the original founder of a state, who subjects to himself those who are weaker. He has the right to do it, just as the state now takes the right. Or rather, there is no right that can prevent it. The ground for all morality can only be prepared when a greater individual or collective-individual, as, for example, society or the state, subjects the individuals in it, that is, when it draws them out of their isolatedness and integrates them into a union. *Force* precedes morality; indeed, for a time morality itself is force, to which others acquiesce to avoid unpleasure. Later it becomes custom, and still later free obedience, and finally almost instinct: then it is coupled to pleasure, like all habitual and natural things, and is now called *virtue*.

### 100

*Shame.* Shame exists wherever there is a "mysterium"; this is a religious concept that was widely prevalent in the older period of human culture. Everywhere there were circumscribed areas, to which divine right forbade entrance, except under certain conditions: at first these were spatial areas, in that certain places were not to be trodden upon by the foot of the unconsecrated, who would feel horror and fear in their vicinity. This feeling was frequently carried over to other relationships, to sexual relationships, for example, which were to be removed from the eyes of youth (for its own good), as a privilege and sacred mystery of the more mature. Many gods were thought to be active in protecting and furthering the observance of these relationships, watching over them as guardians in the nuptial chamber. (This is why this chamber is called Harem, "sanctuary," in Turkish, which is the

same word commonly used for the vestibules of mosques.)[35]
Likewise kingship, as a center radiating power and splendor, is to
the humble subject a mysterium full of secrecy and shame; it has
many aftereffects, which can still be felt in peoples who are otherwise in no way ashamed. In the same way, that whole world of
inner states, the so-called "soul," is still a mysterium to all non-
philosophers since from time immemorial it was thought worthy
of divine origin, divine intercourse: thus it is a sacred mystery and
awakens shame.

## 101

*Judge not.*[36] When we consider earlier periods, we must be
careful not to fall into unjust abuse. The injustice of slavery, the
cruelty in subjugating persons and peoples, cannot be measured
by our standards. For the instinct for justice was not so widely
developed then. Who has the right to reproach Calvin of Geneva
for burning Dr. Servet?[37] His was a consistent act, flowing out of
his convictions, and the Inquisition likewise had its reasons; it is
just that the views dominant then were wrong and resulted in a
consistency that we find harsh, because we now find those views
so alien. Besides, what is the burning of one man compared to the
eternal pains of hell for nearly everyone! And yet this much more
terrible idea used to dominate the whole world without doing any
essential damage to the idea of a god. In our own time, we treat
political heretics harshly and cruelly, but because we have learned
to believe in the necessity of the state we are not as sensitive to
this cruelty as we are to that cruelty whose justification we reject.
Cruelty to animals, by children and Italians, stems from ignorance; namely, in the interests of its teachings, the church has
placed the animal too far beneath man.

Likewise, in history much that is frightful and inhuman, which
one would almost like not to believe, is mitigated by the observation that the commander and the executor are different people: the
former does not witness his cruelty and therefore has no strong
impression of it in his imagination; the latter is obeying a superior

35. Nietzsche's Turkish is correct.
36. Matthew 7:1.
37. Michel Servet, actually Miguel Serveto (1511–53), Spanish doctor and
theologian, was burned in Geneva at the order of Calvin because of his heretical
views on the Trinity.

and feels no responsibility. Because of a lack of imagination, most
princes and military leaders can easily appear to be harsh and
cruel, without being so.

*Egoism is not evil,* for the idea of one's "neighbor" (the word has
a Christian origin[38] and does not reflect the truth) is very weak in
us; and we feel toward him almost as free and irresponsible as
toward plants and stones. That the other suffers *must be learned;*
and it can never be learned completely.

## 102

*"Man always acts for the good."*[39] We don't accuse nature of
immorality when it sends us a thunderstorm, and makes us wet:
why do we call the injurious man immoral? Because in the first
case, we assume necessity, and in the second a voluntarily governing free will. But this distinction is in error. Furthermore, even
intentional injury is not called immoral in all circumstances: without hesitating, we intentionally kill a gnat, for example, simply
because we do not like its buzz; we intentionally punish the criminal and do him harm, to protect ourselves and society. In the first
case it is the individual who does harm intentionally, for self-preservation or simply to avoid discomfort; in the second case the state
does the harm. All morality allows the intentional infliction of
harm *for self-defense;* that is, when it is a matter of *self-preservation!* But these two points of view are *sufficient* to explain all evil
acts which men practice against other men; man wants to get
pleasure or resist unpleasure; in some sense it is always a matter of
self-preservation. Socrates and Plato are right: whatever man
does, he always acts for the good; that is, in a way that seems to
him good (useful) according to the degree of his intellect, the
prevailing measure of his rationality.

## 103

*Harmlessness of malice.* Malice does not aim at the suffering of
the other in and of itself, but rather at our own enjoyment, for
example, a feeling of revenge or a strong nervous excitement.
Every instance of teasing shows that it gives us pleasure to release

38. Nietzsche is probably referring to Luke 10:25–37, the parable of the
Good Samaritan.

39. Cf. Plato, *The Gorgias,* 468.

our power on the other person and experience an enjoyable feeling of superiority. Is the *immoral* thing about it, then, to have *pleasure on the basis of other people's unpleasure?* Is *Schadenfreude*[40] devilish, as Schopenhauer says? Now, in nature, we take pleasure in breaking up twigs, loosening stones, fighting with wild animals, in order to gain awareness of our own strength. Is the *knowledge,* then, that another person is suffering because of us supposed to make immoral the same thing about which we otherwise feel no responsibility? But if one did not have this knowledge, one would not have that pleasure in his own superiority, which can *be discovered* only in the suffering of the other, in teasing, for example. All joy in oneself is neither good nor bad; where should the determination come from that to have pleasure in oneself one may not cause unpleasure in others? Solely from the point of view of advantage, that is, from consideration of the *consequences,* of possible unpleasure, when the injured party or the state representing him leads us to expect requital and revenge; this alone can have been the original basis for denying oneself these actions.

Pity does not aim at the pleasure of others any more than malice (as we said above) aims at the pain of others, per se. For in pity at least two (maybe many more) elements of personal pleasure are contained, and it is to that extent self-enjoyment: first of all, it is the pleasure of the emotion (the kind of pity we find in tragedy) and second, when it drives us to act, it is the pleasure of our satisfaction in the exercise of power. If, in addition, a suffering person is very close to us, we reduce our own suffering by our acts of pity.

Aside from a few philosophers, men have always placed pity rather low in the hierarchy of moral feelings—and rightly so.

## 104

*Self-defense.* If we accept self-defense as moral, then we must also accept nearly all expressions of so-called immoral egoism; we inflict harm, rob or kill, to preserve or protect ourselves, to prevent personal disaster; where cunning and dissimulation are the correct means of self-preservation, we lie. *To do injury intentionally,* when it is a matter of our existence or security (preserva-

40. Malicious pleasure in another's misfortune.

tion of our well-being) is conceded to be moral; the state itself injures from this point of view when it imposes punishment. Of course, there can be no immorality in unintentional injury; there coincidence governs. Can there be a kind of intentional injury where it is *not* a matter of our existence, the preservation of our well-being? Can there be an injury out of pure *malice,* in cruelty, for example? If one does not know how painful an action is, it cannot be malicious; thus the child is not malicious or evil to an animal: he examines and destroys it like a toy. But do we ever completely *know* how painful an action is to the other person? As far as our nervous system extends, we protect ourselves from pain; if it extended further, right into our fellow men, we would not do harm to anyone (except in such cases where we do it to ourselves, that is, where we cut ourselves in order to cure ourselves, exert and strain ourselves to be healthy). We *conclude* by analogy that something hurts another, and through our memory and power of imagination we ourselves can feel ill at such a thought. But what difference remains between a toothache and the ache (pity) evoked by the sight of a toothache? That is, when we injure out of so-called malice, the *degree* of pain produced is in any case unknown to us; but in that we feel *pleasure* in the action (feeling of our own power, our own strong excitement) the action takes place to preserve the well-being of the individual and thus falls within a point of view similar to that of self-defense or a white lie. No life without pleasure; the struggle for pleasure is the struggle for life. Whether the individual fights this battle in ways such that men call him *good* or such that they call him *evil* is determined by the measure and makeup of his intellect.

## 105

*A rewarding justice.* The man who has fully understood the theory of complete irresponsibility can no longer include the so-called justice that punishes and rewards within the concept of justice, if that consists in giving each his due. For the man who is punished does not deserve the punishment: he is only being used as the means to frighten others away from certain future actions; likewise, the man who is rewarded does not deserve this reward; he could not act other than as he did. Thus a reward means only an encouragement, for him and others, to provide a motive for subsequent actions: praise is shouted to the runner on the track, not to the one who has reached the finish line. Neither punish-ment nor reward are due to anyone as *his;* they are given to him because it is useful, without his justly having any claims on them. One must say, "The wise man rewards not because men have acted rightly," just as it was said, "The wise man punishes not because men have acted badly, but so they will not act badly." If we were to dispense with punishment and reward, we would lose the strongest motives driving men away from certain actions and toward other actions; the advantage of man requires that they continue; and in that punishment and reward, blame and praise affect vanity most acutely, the same advantage also requires that vanity continue.

## 106

*At the waterfall.* When we see a waterfall, we think we see free-dom of will and choice in the innumerable turnings, windings, breakings of the waves; but everything is necessary; each move-ment can be calculated mathematically. Thus it is with human actions; if one were omniscient, one would be able to calculate each individual action in advance, each step in the progress of knowledge, each error, each act of malice. To be sure, the acting man is caught in his illusion of volition; if the wheel of the world were to stand still for a moment and an omniscient, calculating mind were there to take advantage of this interruption, he would be able to tell into the farthest future of each being and describe every rut that wheel will roll upon. The acting man's delusion about himself, his assumption that free will exists, is also part of the calculable mechanism.

## 107

*Irresponsibility and innocence.* Man's complete lack of responsi-bility, for his behavior and for his nature, is the bitterest drop which the man of knowledge must swallow, if he had been in the habit of seeing responsibility and duty as humanity's claim to no-bility. All his judgments, distinctions, dislikes have thereby be-come worthless and wrong: the deepest feeling he had offered a victim or a hero was misdirected; he may no longer praise, no longer blame, for it is nonsensical to praise and blame nature and necessity. Just as he loves a good work of art, but does not praise it, because it can do nothing about itself, just as he regards a plant, so he must regard the actions of men and his own actions. He can admire their strength, beauty, abundance, but he may not find any earned merit in them: chemical processes, and the clash of elements, the agony of the sick man who yearns for recovery, these have no more earned merit than do those inner struggles and crises in which a man is torn back and forth by various motives until he finally decides for the most powerful—as is said (in truth until the most powerful motive decides about us). But all these motives, whatever great names we give them, have grown out of the same roots which are thought to hold the evil poisons. Between good and evil actions there is no difference in type; at most, a difference in degree. Good actions are sublimated evil actions; evil actions are good actions become coarse and stupid. The individual's only demand, for self-enjoyment (along with the fear of losing it), is satisfied in all circumstances: man may act as he can, that is, as he must, whether in deeds of vanity, revenge, pleasure, usefulness, malice, cunning, or in deeds of sacrifice, pity, knowledge. His powers of judgment determine where a man will let this demand for self-enjoyment take him. In each society, in each individual, a hierarchy of the good is always present, by which man determines his own actions and judges other people's actions. But this standard is continually in flux; many actions are called evil, and are only stupid, because the degree of intelligence which chose them was very low. Indeed, in a certain sense *all* actions are stupid even now, for the highest degree of human intelligence which can now be attained will surely be surpassed. And then, in hindsight, all *our* behavior and judgments will appear as inadequate and rash as the behavior and judgments of backward savage tribes now seem to us inadequate and rash.

To understand all this can cause great pain, but afterwards there is consolation. These pains are birth pangs. The butterfly wants to break through his cocoon; he tears at it, he rends it: then he is blinded and confused by the unknown light, the realm of freedom. Men who are *capable* of that sorrow (how few they will be!) will make the first attempt to see if mankind *can transform itself* from a *moral* into a *wise* mankind. In those individuals, the sun of a new gospel is casting its first ray onto the highest mountaintop of the soul; the fog is condensing more thickly than ever, and the brightest light and cloudiest dusk lie next to each other. Everything is necessity: this is the new knowledge, and this knowledge itself is necessity. Everything is innocence: and knowledge is the way to insight into this innocence. If pleasure, egoism, vanity are *necessary* for the generation of moral phenomena and their greatest flower, the sense for true and just knowledge; if error and confusion of imagination were the only means by which mankind could raise itself gradually to this degree of self-illumination and self-redemption—who could scorn those means? Who could be sad when he perceives the goal to which those paths lead? Everything in the sphere of morality has evolved; changeable, fluctuating, everything is fluid, it is true: but *everything is also streaming onward*—to one goal. Even if the inherited habit of erroneous esteeming, loving, hating continues to govern us, it will grow weaker under the influence of growing knowledge: a new habit, that of understanding, non-loving, non-hating, surveying is gradually being implanted in us on the same ground, and in thousands of years will be powerful enough perhaps to give mankind the strength to produce wise, innocent (conscious of their innocence)[41] men as regularly as it now produces unwise, unfair men, conscious of their guilt[42]—*these men are the necessary first stage, but not the opposite of those to come.*

41. *unschuld-bewussten*
42. *schuldbewussten*

# SECTION THREE
## Religious Life

### 108

*The twofold struggle against misfortune.* When a misfortune strikes us, we can overcome it either by removing its cause or else by changing the effect it has on our feelings, that is, by reinterpreting the misfortune as a good, whose benefit may only later become clear. Religion and art (as well as metaphysical philosophy) strive to effect a change in our feeling, in part by changing the way we judge experiences (for example, with the aid of the tenet, "Whom the Lord loves, he chastens")[1] and in part by awakening a pleasure in pain, in emotion generally (which is where tragic art has its starting point). The more a person tends to reinterpret and justify, the less will he confront the causes of the misfortune and eliminate them; a momentary palliation and narcotization (as used, for example, for a toothache) is also enough for him in more serious suffering. The more the rule of religions and all narcotic arts decreases, the more squarely do men confront the real elimination of the misfortune—of course, this is bad for the tragic poets (there being less and less material for tragedy, because the realm of inexorable, invincible fate grows ever smaller) but it is even worse for the priests (for until now they fed on the narcotization of human misfortunes).

### 109

*Sorrow is knowledge.* How gladly one would exchange the false claims of priests—that there is a God who demands the Good from us, who is guardian and witness of each act, each moment,

---

1. "Whom the Lord loveth, he chasteneth, and scourgeth every son whom he receiveth" (Hebrews 12:6).

each thought, who loves us and wants the best for us in every misfortune—how gladly one would exchange these claims for truths which would be just as salutary, calming, and soothing as those errors! But there are no such truths; at the most, philosophy can oppose those errors with other metaphysical fictions (basically also untruths). But the tragic thing is that we can no longer *believe* those dogmas of religion and metaphysics, once we have the rigorous method of truth in our hearts and heads, and yet on the other hand, the development of mankind has made us so delicate, sensitive, and ailing that we need the most potent kind of cures and comforts—hence arises the danger that man might bleed to death from the truth he has recognized. Byron expressed this in his immortal lines:

> Sorrow is knowledge: they who know the most
> must mourn the deepest o'er the fatal truth,
> the tree of knowledge is not that of life.[2]

There is no better cure for such cares than to conjure up the festive frivolity of Horace, at least for the worst hours and eclipses of the soul, and with him to say to yourself:

> quid aeternis minorem
> consiliis animum fatigas?
> cur non sub alta vel platano vel hac
> pinu jacentes—[3]

Of course, any degree of frivolity or melancholy is better than a romantic regression and desertion, an approach to Christianity in any form; for one can simply not engage in Christianity, given the present state of knowledge, without hopelessly soiling his *intellectual conscience* and abandoning it to himself and to others. Those pains may be distressing enough, but without pains one cannot become a leader and educator of mankind; and woe to him who would try to lead and no longer had that clean conscience![4]

2. *Manfred,* act 1, sc. 1, lines 10–12.

3. Horace, *Odes* 2.11.13–14: "Why do you torture your poor reason for insight into the riddle of eternity? Why do we not simply lie down under the high plantane? or here under this pine tree?" Also quoted in Schopenhauer, *Parerga and Paralipomena,* trans. E. F. J. Payne, vol. 1 (Oxford: Clarendon Press, 1974) p. 412.

4. This paragraph responds in particular to Wagner's *Parsifal.*

110

*Truth in religion.* During the Enlightenment, people did not do justice to the significance of religion, there is no doubt of that. But it is just as certain that in the subsequent opposition to the Enlightenment they went a good piece beyond justice, by treating religions with love or even infatuation, and adjudging them to have, for example, a deeper, even the very deepest understanding of the world. It was for science to divest this understanding of its dogmatic trappings in order to possess the "truth" in unmythical form. Thus all opponents of the Enlightenment claimed that the religions stated *sensu allegorico,*[5] so the masses would understand, that age-old wisdom which is wisdom in and of itself, inasmuch as all true modern science has always led to it instead of away from it. In this way, a harmony, even identity of views, would obtain between mankind's oldest sages and all later ones, and the progress of knowledge (should one wish to speak of such a thing) would refer not to its substance but rather to its communication. This whole view of religion and science is erroneous through and through; and no one would dare to profess it still today, had not Schopenhauer used his eloquence to take it under his protection, this eloquence which rings out so loudly, and yet reaches its listeners only after a generation. As surely as one can gain much for the understanding of Christianity and other religions from Schopenhauer's religious and moral interpretation of men and the world, so surely was he in error about the *value of religion for knowledge.* In this regard he himself was simply the too tractable student of the scientific teachers of his time, who all cherished romanticism and had renounced the spirit of the Enlightenment; born into our present age, he would have found it impossible to speak of the *sensus allegoricus* of religion; rather, he would have done honor to truth, as was his wont, with the words: *"Never, neither indirectly nor directly, neither as a dogma nor as an allegory, has religion yet held any truth."* For out of fear and need each religion is born, creeping into existence on the byways of reason. Perhaps at one time, when endangered by science, it included some fabricated philosophical theory in its system, so that it could be found there later; but this is a theologian's trick from the period when a religion is already doubting itself. These tricks

5. in the allegorical representation or sense

of theology, which of course were practiced very early on in Christianity, the religion of a scholarly age, steeped in philosophy, led to that superstition about a *sensus allegoricus*. Even more, they led to the habit of philosophers (particularly those half-men, the poetic philosophers and the philosophizing artists) of treating all feelings which they found in *themselves* as if they were essential to man in general, and thus to the habit of granting their own religious feelings a significant influence on the conceptual structure of their systems. Because philosophers often philosophized in traditional religious habits, or at least under the old inherited power of that "metaphysical need," they arrived at dogmas that in fact greatly resembled Jewish or Christian or Indian religious doctrines, resembled them in the way children tend to resemble their mothers. In this case, however, the fathers weren't sure of the maternity (as can happen) but rather, in the innocence of their amazement, told tales of a family resemblance of all religions and sciences. In reality there is no relationship nor friendship nor even enmity between religion and real science: they live on different stars. Any philosophy that allows a religious comet to trail off ablaze into the darkness of its last prospects makes suspicious everything about itself that it presents as science; presumably all this too is religion, although decked out as science.

Incidentally, if all peoples were to agree about certain religious things, the existence of a god for example (which, by the way, is not so in this case), then this would only be a *counterargument* to those things that were maintained, the existence of a god for example: the *consensus gentium* and *hominum*[6] in general can in fairness only pertain to foolishness. Conversely there is no *consensus omnium sapientium*[7] regarding a single thing, with the exception spoken of in Goethe's lines:

Alle die Weisesten aller der Zeiten
lächeln und winken und stimmen mit ein:
Thöricht, auf Bess'rung der Thoren zu harren!
Kinder der Klugheit, o habet die Narren
eben zum Narren auch, wie sich's gehört![8]

6. the consensus of peoples and men
7. the consensus of all wise men
8. "Kophtisches Lied": All of the wise men in all of the ages, /Smile and nod and agree one and all: /It is foolish to wait for fools to be better,/Children of

Saying it without rhythm or rhyme, and applying it to our case: it is the *consensus sapientium* that any *consensus gentium* is foolishness.

### I I I

*Origin of religious worship.* If we imagine ourselves back in the times when religious life was in fullest flower, we find a fundamental conviction which we no longer share, and because of which we see the gates to the religious life closed to us once and for all: it concerns nature and our interaction with it. People in those times do not yet know anything of natural laws; neither for the earth nor for the heavens is there a "must": a season, the sunshine, the rain can come, or also fail to appear. There is no concept whatsoever of *natural* causality. When one rows, it is not the rowing that moves the ship; rather rowing is simply a magical ceremony by which one compels a demon to move it. All illnesses, death itself, are the result of magical influences. There is never anything natural about becoming ill or dying; the whole idea of a "natural development" is lacking (it first begins to dawn on the older Greeks, that is, in a very late phase of mankind, with the conception of a *moira*[9] which reigned over the gods). When someone shoots with bow and arrow, an irrational hand and strength is always at work; if springs suddenly dry up, one thinks first of subterranean demons and their mischief; it has to be the arrow of a god whose invisible influence causes a man to drop suddenly. In India (according to Lubbock),[10] a carpenter makes sacrifices to his hammer, his axe, and his other tools; in the same way does a Brahman handle the pencil with which he writes, a soldier his weapons of battle, a mason his trowel, a worker his plow. In the mind of religious men, all nature is the sum of the actions of conscious and intentioned beings, an enormous complex of *arbitrary acts.* There is nothing outside ourselves about which we are allowed to conclude that it *will* become thus and so, *must* be thus and so: we ourselves are what is more or less certain, calculable. Man is the *rule,* nature *without rule:* in this tenet lies the basic conviction that governs primitive, religiously productive ancient

---

cleverness, make dupes of / The stupid, too, as is their due.

9. fate

10. Sir John Lubbock (1834–1913), English historian of prehistory.

cultures. We present-day men experience precisely the reverse: the richer a man feels inwardly, the more polyphonic he is as a subject, the more powerfully nature's symmetry affects him. With Goethe, we all recognize in nature the great means of soothing the modern soul;[11] we hear the stroke of the greatest clock with a longing to rest, to become settled and still, as if we could drink this symmetry into ourselves, and thus come finally to an enjoyment of our own selves. Formerly it was the reverse: if we think back to primitive, early tribal states, or if we closely observe present-day savages, we find them most strongly directed by *law, tradition:* the individual is almost automatically bound to it, and moves with the uniformity of a pendulum. To him nature—uncomprehended, frightful, mysterious nature—must seem to be the *realm of freedom,* of choice, of a higher power, a seemingly superhuman level of existence, a god. Now, every individual in those times and conditions feels that his existence, his happiness, that of his family, the state, the success of all enterprises, depends on those arbitrary acts of nature: some natural events must take place at the right time, others must fail to take place. How can one exercise an influence on these terrible unknowns? How can one bind the realm of freedom? The individual wonders and asks himself anxiously: "Is there no means, through tradition and law, to make those powers as governed by rule as you are yourself?"

The thinking of men who believe in magic and miracles is bent on *imposing a law on nature;* and in short, religious worship is the result of this thinking. The problem that those men set themselves is most closely related to this one: how can the *weaker* tribe nevertheless dictate laws to the *stronger,* direct it, and guide its actions (as they relate to the weaker tribe)? At first one will be reminded of the most harmless kind of pressure, that pressure one exerts when one has courted someone's *affections*. By entreaties and prayers, by submissiveness, by committing oneself to regular tributes and gifts, by flattering glorifications, it is also possible to exert pressure on the forces of nature, by making them favorably inclined: love binds and is bound. Then one can seal *contracts,* by which one commits oneself reciprocally to certain behavior, puts up pledges and exchanges vows. But much more important is a

11. See, for example, his poem "Adler und Taube": "Allgegenwärtiger Balsam / Allheilender Natur" (the omnipresent balsam of all-healing nature).

kind of more powerful pressure through magic. Just as man knows how to use the help of a magician to hurt a stronger enemy and keep him afraid, just as love spells are effective from afar, so the weaker man believes he can also direct the more powerful spirits of nature. The main means of all magic is to gain power over something that belongs to the other, hair, nails, some food from his table, even his picture or his name. With such apparatus one can then proceed to do magic, for the basic assumption is that there is something physical to everything spiritual; with its help one can bind the spirit, harm it, destroy it. The physical furnishes the ways and means by which to catch the spiritual. Just as man now directs man, so he also directs some one spirit of nature; for the spirit too has its physical aspect, by which it can be caught. The tree and, compared with it, the seed from which it sprang: this puzzling juxtaposition seems to prove that one and the same spirit is embedded in both forms, now little, now big. A stone that starts to roll suddenly is the body in which a spirit acts; if there is a block of stone lying on a lonely heath, it seems impossible that human strength should have brought it there; thus the stone must have moved itself there, that is, it must be housing a spirit. Everything that has a body is accessible to magic, including spirits of nature. If a god is virtually bound to his image, then one can also exert direct pressure against him (by refusing him sacrificial nourishment, by flagellation, enchainment and the like). To exact the wanting favor of their god, who has left them in the lurch, the humble people in China entwine his image with rope, tear it down, drag it in the streets through heaps of mud and dung: "You dog of a spirit," they say, "we let you dwell in a splendid temple, we covered you prettily in gold, fed you well, sacrificed to you, and yet you are so ungrateful." In Catholic lands, similar violent measures have also been taken during this century against images of saints or of the Virgin Mary when during plagues or droughts, for example, they did not want to do their duty.

All these magical relationships to nature have called into being countless ceremonies; finally when the confusion of them has grown too great, one tries to order them, systematize them, so that one thinks he is guaranteeing the favorable course of the whole process of nature, particularly the great cycle of the seasons, by a parallel course of a system of proceedings. The meaning of religious worship is to direct nature, and cast a spell on her to human advantage, that is, *to impose a lawfulness on her, which she does not have at the start;* whereas in present times, man wishes to *understand* the lawfulness of nature in order to submit to it. In short, religious worship is based on ideas of magic between man and man; and the magician is older than the priest. But it is *likewise* based on other and more noble ideas; it presumes a sympathetic relationship of man to man, the existence of goodwill, gratitude, hearing supplicants, of contracts between enemies, of bestowal of pledges, of demand for protection of property. Even in very primitive stages of culture, man does not confront nature as a powerless slave, he is *not* necessarily her involuntary servant: in the Greek stage of religion, especially in the relationship to the Olympian gods, there is the thought of a coexistence of two castes, one nobler and more powerful, the other less noble; but according to their origin both belong together somehow and are of *one* kind; they need not be ashamed before one another. That is the noble element in Greek religiosity.

### 112

*On viewing certain ancient sacrificial utensils.* The combination of farce, even obscenity, with religious feeling, shows us how some feelings are disappearing: the sensibility that this is a possible mixture is vanishing; we understand only historically that it once existed, in festivals of Demeter and Dionysos, at Christian passion plays and mystery plays. But even we are still familiar with the sublime in league with the burlesque, for example, the sentimental blended with the ludicrous—and this a later age will perhaps no longer understand.

### 113

*Christianity as antiquity.* When we hear the old bells ringing out on a Sunday morning, we ask ourselves: can it be possible? This is for a Jew, crucified two thousand years ago, who said he was the son of God. The proof for such a claim is wanting.

Within our times the Christian religion is surely an antiquity jutting out from a far-distant olden time; and the fact that people believe such a claim (while they are otherwise so strict in testing assertions) is perhaps the oldest part of this heritage. A god who conceives children with a mortal woman; a wise man who calls upon us to work no more, to judge no more, but to heed the signs of the imminent apocalypse; a justice that accepts the innocent man as a proxy sacrifice; someone who has his disciples drink his blood; prayers for miraculous interventions; sins against a god, atoned for by a god; fear of the afterlife, to which death is the gate; the figure of the cross as a symbol, in a time that no longer knows the purpose and shame of the cross—how horridly all this wafts over us, as from the grave of the ancient past! Are we to believe that such things are still believed?

### 114

*What is un-Greek in Christianity.* The Greeks did not see the Homeric gods above them as masters and themselves below them as servants, as did the Jews. They saw, as it were, only the reflection of the most successful specimens of their own caste, that is, an ideal, not a contrast to their own nature. They felt related to them, there was a reciprocal interest, a kind of *symmachia.*[12] Man thinks of himself as noble when he gives himself such gods, and puts himself into a relationship similar to that of the lesser nobility to the higher. Whereas the Italic peoples have a regular peasant religion, with continual fearfulness about evil and capricious powers and tormentors. Where the Olympian gods retreated, there Greek life too grew gloomier and more fearful.

Christianity, on the other hand, crushed and shattered man completely, and submerged him as if in deep mire. Then, all at once, into his feeling of complete confusion, it allowed the light of divine compassion to shine, so that the surprised man, stunned by mercy, let out a cry of rapture, and thought for a moment that he carried all of heaven within him. All psychological inventions[13] of Christianity work toward this sick excess of feeling, toward the deep corruption of head and heart necessary for it. Christianity wants to destroy, shatter, stun, intoxicate: there is only one thing it does not want: *moderation,* and for this reason, it is in its deepest meaning barbaric, Asiatic, ignoble, un-Greek.

### 115

*Being religious to one's advantage.* There are sober and efficient men on whom religion is embroidered like the hem of a higher

---

12. alliance
13. *Erfindungen.* In some editions *Empfindungen* (sentiments).

humanity. These men do well to remain religious: it beautifies them.

All men who have no expertise with any weapon (mouth and pen counting as weapons) become servile: for such men, religion is very useful, for here servility takes on the appearance of a Christian virtue and is surprisingly beautified.

People who think their daily lives too empty and monotonous easily become religious: this is understandable and forgivable; however, they have no right to demand religiosity from those whose daily life does not pass in emptiness and monotony.

## 116

*The everyday Christian.* If Christianity were right in its tenets of a vengeful god, general sinfulness, predestination, and the danger of an eternal damnation, it would be a sign of stupidity and lack of character *not* to become a priest, apostle, or hermit, and, with fear and trembling, work exclusively on one's own salvation. It would be nonsensical to lose sight of one's eternal advantage for temporary comfort. Assuming that he *believes* at all, the everyday Christian is a pitiful figure, a man who really cannot count up to three, and who besides, precisely because of his mental incompetence, would not deserve such a punishment as Christianity promises him.

## 117

*On the shrewdness of Christianity.* It is a trick of Christianity to teach the utter worthlessness, sinfulness, and despicableness of man in general so loudly that disdain for one's fellow men becomes impossible. "Let him sin as he will, he is essentially no different from me; I am the one who is in all ways unworthy and despicable," the Christian tells himself. But this feeling too has lost its sharpest sting because the Christian does not believe in his individual despicableness: he is wicked simply because he is a man, and calms himself a bit with the tenet: we are all of one kind.

## 118

*Change of roles.* As soon as a religion comes to prevail, it has as its enemies all those who would have been its first disciples.

## 119

*Fate of Christianity.* Christianity came into existence in order to lighten the heart; but now it has to burden the heart first, in order to be able to lighten it afterward. Consequently it will perish.

## 120

*The proof by pleasure.* An agreeable opinion is accepted as true: this is the proof by pleasure (or, as the church says, the proof by strength), that all religions are so proud of, whereas they ought to be ashamed. If the belief did not make us happy, it would not be believed: how little must it then be worth!

## 121

*Dangerous game.* Whoever allows room in himself again for religious feeling these days must also allow it to grow: he cannot do otherwise. Then his nature gradually changes: it favors that which is dependent on or near to the religious element; the whole range of his judgment and feeling is befogged, overcast with religious shadows. Feeling cannot stand still: be on your guard!

## 122

*Blind disciples.* As long as one knows very well the strengths and weaknesses of his teaching, his art, or his religion, its power is still slight. The disciple and apostle who has no eye for the weakness of the teaching, the religion, etc., blinded by the stature of his master and his own piety towards him, for that reason generally has more power than his master. Without blind disciples, no man or his work has ever gained great influence. Sometimes, to promote the triumph of a form of knowledge means only that one weds it to stupidity, so that the weight of the stupidity also forces the triumph of the knowledge.

## 123

*Demolition of churches.* There is not enough religion in the world even to destroy religions.

## 124

*Sinlessness of man.* Once man has grasped "how sin came into the world" (which is to say, through errors of reason, due to

which men take each other—and the individual takes himself—
for much blacker and more wicked than is actually the case), then
his whole mood is greatly improved, and men and world seem at
times to be in such a halo of harmlessness as to make him utterly
contented. Amid nature, man is always the child per se. This
child might once dream an oppressive, terrifying dream, but
when he opens his eyes, he always finds himself in paradise again.

## 125

*Irreligiosity of artists.* Homer is so at home among his gods, and
takes such delight in them as a poet that he surely must have been
deeply irreligious. He took what popular belief offered him (a pal-
try, crude, in part horrible superstition) and dealt as freely as a
sculptor with his clay, that is, with the same openness Aeschylus
and Aristophanes possessed, and which in more recent times has
distinguished the great artists of the Renaissance, as well as
Shakespeare and Goethe.

## 126

*Art and strength of false interpretation.* All the visions, horrors,
exhaustions and raptures of the saint are familiar states of illness,
which, based on deep-rooted religious and psychological errors,
he simply *interprets* otherwise, that is, not as illnesses.

Thus Socrates' *Daimonion*[14] likewise is perhaps a disease of the
ear, which he *explains* in accordance with his prevailing moral
thinking, but other than how it would be explained today. It is no
different with the madness and ravings of prophets and oracular
priests: it is always the degree of knowledge, imagination, ambition, morality in the head and heart of the *interpreters* that has
*made* so much out of them. One of the greatest effects of men
whom we call geniuses and saints is that they exact interpreters
who *misunderstand* them, to the good of mankind.

## 127

*Reverence for madness.* Because it was observed that an excited
state would often clear the mind and produce happy ideas, it was
thought that through the states of greatest excitement one would

14. The divine warning inner voice Socrates claimed to hear. For an earlier—
and different—evaluation see *The Birth of Tragedy,* sec. 13.

partake of the happiest ideas and inspirations. And so the madman was revered as the wise man and oracle giver. This is based
on a false conclusion.

## 128

*Promises of science.* Modern science has as its goal the least pain
and the longest life possible—that is, a kind of eternal happiness:
to be sure, a very modest kind in comparison with the promises of
religions.

## 129

*Forbidden generosity.* There is not enough love and kindness in
the world to permit us to give any of it away to imaginary beings.

## 130

*Religious worship lives on within.* The Catholic Church, and
before it all ancient worship, commanded the whole range of
means by which man is set into unusual moods and torn away
from the cold calculation of his advantage, or pure, rational thinking. A church reverberating with deep sounds; muted, regular,
restrained invocations of a priestly host that instantaneously
transmits its tension to the congregation so that it listens almost
fearfully, as if a miracle were in the making; the atmosphere of the
architecture that, as the dwelling of a divinity, extends into the
indefinite and makes one fear the movings of the divinity in all its
dark spaces—who would want to return such goings-on to man,
once the assumptions for them are no longer believed? Nevertheless, the results of all that have not been lost: the inner world of
sublime, tender, intuitive, deeply contrite, blissfully hopeful
moods was begotten in man primarily through worship; what
now exists of it in the soul was raised at the time of its sprouting,
growing, and flowering.

## 131

*Religious after-effects.* However much one thinks he has lost the
habit of religion, he has not lost it to the degree that he would not
enjoy encountering religious feelings and moods without any conceptual content as, for example, in music. And if a philosophy
shows us the justification of metaphysical hopes, of a deep peace
of the soul to be attained therefrom, and, for example, speaks of

the "whole, certain gospel in the glance of Raphael's madonnas,"[15] then we approach such statements and explanations with an especially warm disposition. Here it is easier for the philosopher to make his proofs; what he wants to give accords with a heart that gladly takes. We notice here how less careful free thinkers actually object only to the dogmas, but know very well the magic of religious feeling; it hurts them to let the latter go, for the sake of the former.

Scientific philosophy has to be very careful about smuggling in errors on the basis of that need (an acquired and, consequently, also transitory need). Even logicians[16] speak of "intuitions" of truth in morality and art (for example, the intuition "that the essence of things is one"), which should be forbidden them. Between painstakingly deduced truths and such "intuited" things there remains the unbridgeable gap that the former are due to the intellect, the latter to need. Hunger does not prove that any food to satisfy it *exists,* but it wishes the food. "To intuit" does not mean to recognize the existence of a thing to any extent, but rather to hold it to be possible, in that one wishes or fears it. "Intuition" takes us not one step farther into the land of certainty.

We believe instinctively that the religiously tinged sections of a philosophy are better proved than the others. But basically it is the reverse; we simply have the inner wish that it might be so— that is, that what gladdens might be also true. This wish misleads us into buying bad reasons as good ones.

## 132

*On the Christian need for redemption.* If we reflect carefully, it ought to be possible to arrive at an explanation for the process in a Christian's soul that is called the need for redemption, an explanation that is free of mythology, that is, a purely psychological one. Of course, until now psychological explanations of religious states and processes have been in some disrepute, in that a theology that calls itself free has been up to its bootless mischief in this area; for from the start, as the spirit of its founder Schleiermacher[17] allows us to assume, "free theology" was aiming at the preservation of the

15. Cf. Schopenhauer, *Parerga and Paralipomena,* 1:478.

16. Another reference to Afrikan Spir (see n. 21 to Section One).

17. Friedrich Schleiermacher (1768–1830), romantic religious philosopher.

Christian religion and the continuance of Christian theologists,[18] who were to gain a new anchor, and above all a new occupation, in the psychological analysis of religious "facts." Undeterred by such predecessors, we venture to present the following interpretation of the phenomenon in question. Man is conscious of certain actions that rank low in the customary hierarachy of actions; in fact, he discovers within himself a tendency to these kinds of actions, a tendency that seems to him almost as unchangeable as his whole nature. How he would like to try his luck in that other category of actions, those that are generally esteemed to be the topmost and highest; how he would like to feel full of a good consciousness, which is said to follow a selfless way of thinking! But unfortunately it does not go beyond this wish: the dissatisfaction about being unable to satisfy the wish is added to all the other kinds of dissatisfaction that his lot in life generally, or the consequences of those actions, termed evil, have aroused in him. Thus he develops a deep discontent and searches for a doctor who might be able to put an end to this discontent and all its causes.

This condition would not be felt so bitterly if man would only compare himself dispassionately to other men; then he would have no reason to be dissatisfied with himself to any special degree; he would only be sharing the common burden of human dissatisfaction and imperfection. But he compares himself to a being who is solely capable of those actions called selfless and who lives in the continual consciousness of a selfless way of thinking: God. Because he is looking into this bright mirror, his own nature appears so clouded, so abnormally distorted. Next, the thought of this other being makes him fearful, in that it hovers in his imagination as a punishing justice; in every possible experience, large or small, he thinks he recognizes its anger, its menace, and he even thinks he has a presentiment of the whiplashes it will deliver as judge and executioner. Who helps him in this danger, which by its prospect of an immeasurable duration of punishment, surpasses in horror all other terrors of the imagination?

### 133

Before we present the further consequences of this condition, we want to avow that man has arrived at this condition not

18. *Theologen.* In some editions *Theologie* (theology).

through his "guilt" and "sin," but rather through a series of errors of reason, that if his nature seemed dark and hateful to him to that degree, it was the fault of the mirror, and that that mirror was *his* creation, the very imperfect creation of human imagination and powers of judgment. First, any being who would be capable of purely selfless actions only is more fabulous than the phoenix. It cannot even be imagined clearly because from the start the whole concept of "selfless action," if carefully examined, evaporates into the air. Never has a man done anything that was only for others and without any personal motivation. Indeed, how *could* he do anything that had no reference to himself, that is, with no inner compulsion (which would have to be based on a personal need)? How could the ego act without ego?

A God who conversely is *all* love, as is occasionally assumed, would not be capable of one single selfless action, which should remind us of a thought of Lichtenberg's, taken, to be sure, from a more common sphere: "It is impossible for us to *feel* for others, as the saying goes. We feel only for ourselves. The principle sounds harsh, but it is not, if it is only understood correctly. We love neither father nor mother nor wife nor child, but rather the agreeable feelings that they give us."[19] Or, as La Rochefoucauld says, "Si on croit aimer sa maîtresse pour l'amour d'elle, on est bien trompé."[20] For the explanation of why actions of love are *esteemed* higher than others, namely because of their usefulness rather than their essence, see the above-mentioned investigations *On the Origin of Moral Feelings*.[21] But if a man should want to embody Love, quite like that God, to do everything for others, nothing for himself, it is already impossible from the start, because he has to do *a great deal* for himself in order to be able to do anything at all for the sake of others. Next, it assumes the other person is egoist enough to accept those sacrifices, that life for his sake, over and over again: so men of love and self-sacrifice have an interest in the continued existence of loveless egoists incapable of self-sacrifice, and the highest morality, in order to endure, would have virtually to *exact* the existence of immorality (by which, to be sure, it would cancel itself out).

19. Cf. *Vermischte Schriften* (Göttingen, 1867), vol. 1, 83.
20. "If one thinks he loves his mistress for love of her, he is quite mistaken."
21. Paul Rée's work of 1877 (cf. n. 5 to Section Two).

Furthermore, the idea of a God disturbs and humiliates as long as it is believed, but given the present state of comparative ethnology, *its origin* can no longer be in doubt; and with insight into that origin, the belief disappears. The Christian who compares his nature to God is like Don Quixote, who underestimates his own bravery because he is preoccupied with the miraculous deeds of heroes out of chivalric novels; in both cases, the standard of measure being used belongs to the realm of fable. But if the idea of God disappears, so too does the feeling of "sin" as a transgression against divine precepts, as a stain on a creature consecrated to God. Then what probably remains is that discontent which is very intimately bound up with and related to the fear of punishment by a secular justice, or the fear of men's disrespect; but discontent from the pangs of conscience, the sharpest sting in the feeling of guilt, has been stopped short when one perceives that through one's actions one may have transgressed against human tradition, human statutes and regulations, but that one has not yet jeopardized the "eternal salvation of the soul" and its relation to the divinity. If in the end man succeeds in convincing himself philosophically that all actions are unconditionally necessary and completely irresponsible, and if he takes this conviction into his flesh and blood, those vestiges of the pangs of conscience disappear, too.

## 134

If the Christian has, as we said, come to feel self-contempt through certain errors, through a false, unscientific interpretation of his actions and feelings, he must notice with the greatest astonishment how that condition of contempt, of remorse, of displeasure generally, does not last; how occasionally there are hours when it is all blown away from his soul and he feels free and courageous again. In truth, pleasure in oneself and contentment with one's own strength, in league with the inevitable weakening of any great excitation, have gained the victory: man loves himself again; he feels it—but this very love, this new self-esteem, seems unbelievable to him; he can see in it only the wholly undeserved downpouring of a merciful light from above. If he previously thought he saw warnings, threats, punishments, and every kind of sign of divine anger in all occurrences, so now he *reads* divine goodness *into* his experiences: one event seems to be loving, another seems to be a helpful hint, a third, and particularly his whole joyful mood, seems to be proof that God is merciful. As previously, in a state of discontent, he interpreted his actions wrongly, so now he misinterprets his experiences. He understands his mood as the consoling effect of a power governing outside himself; the love with which he fundamentally loves himself, appears as divine love; that which he calls mercy and a prelude to redemption is in truth self-pardon, self-redemption.

## 135

Thus a certain false psychology, a certain kind of fantasy in interpreting motives and experiences, is the necessary prerequisite for becoming a Christian and experiencing the need for redemption. With the insight into this aberration of reason and imagination, one ceases to be a Christian.

## 136

*On Christian asceticism and saintliness.* However much individual thinkers have tried to represent the rare manifestations of morality that tend to be called asceticism and saintliness as something miraculous, which to examine in the light of a rational explanation would be almost sacrilege and profanation, so strong, on the other hand, is the temptation to this sacrilege. Throughout history, a powerful impulse of *nature* has led men to protest generally against those manifestations; science to the extent it is, as we have said, an imitation of nature, permits itself to protest at least against the claim of their inexplicability, even inaccessibility. To be sure, it has not yet been successful; those manifestations are still unexplained, to the great delight of the above-mentioned admirers of the morally miraculous. For in general, the unexplained should be thoroughly inexplicable, the inexplicable thoroughly unnatural, supernatural, miraculous—so goes the demand in the souls of all religious men and metaphysicians (artists, too, if they are also thinkers). Whereas the scientific man sees in this demand the "evil principle."

The general, first probability one arrives at when considering asceticism and saintliness is that their nature is complicated: for almost everywhere, within both the physical and the moral world, the ostensibly miraculous has been successfully traced back to complicated and multiply-conditioned causes. Let us venture first to isolate certain impulses in the souls of saints and ascetics, and in conclusion to imagine them entwined.

## 137

There exists a *defiance against oneself* that includes among its most sublime expressions various forms of asceticism. For some men have such an intense need to exercise their strength and love of power that, lacking other objects or because they have always otherwise failed, it finally occurs to them to tyrannize certain parts of their own being, as if they were sections or stages of their selves. Thus some thinkers will confess to views that clearly do not serve to increase or improve their reputation; some virtually beg to be despised by others, whereas it would be easy for them to retain respect by being silent. Others retract earlier opinions and are not afraid to be called inconsistent thereafter; on the contrary, that is what they try for, behaving like high-spirited horsemen who like their horse best only when it has become wild, skittish, covered with sweat. Thus man climbs on dangerous paths into the highest mountains in order to mock his own fearfulness and his shaking knees; thus the philosopher confesses to views of asceticism, humility and saintliness, by which light his own image is most grievously made ugly. This shattering of oneself, this scorn for one's own nature, this *spernere se sperni,*[22] which religions have made so much out of, is actually a very high degree of vanity. The whole morality of the Sermon on the Mount belongs here; man takes a truly voluptuous pleasure in violating himself by exaggerated demands and then deifying this something in his soul that is so tyrannically taxing. In each ascetic morality, man prays to one part of himself as a god and also finds it necessary to diabolify the rest.

## 138

Man is not equally moral at all times—this is well known. If one judges his morality by his capacity for great sacrificial resolve and self-denial (which, when it has become constant and habitual, is saintliness), man is most moral in *affect;* greater excitation offers him new motives, which he, when sober and cool as usual, per-

22. "despise that one is despised" (after Hildebert of Lavardius [1056–1132], *Carmina Miscellanea,* 124).

haps did not think himself capable of. How can this be? Probably because of the relatedness of everything great and highly exciting: once man has been brought into a state of extraordinary tension, he can decide as easily to take frightful revenge as to make a frightful break with his need for revenge. Under the influence of the powerful emotion, he wants in any event what is great, powerful, enormous, and if he notices by chance that to sacrifice his own self satisfies as well or better than to sacrifice the other person, then he chooses that. Actually, all he cares about is the release of his emotion; to relieve his tension, he may gather together his enemies' spears and bury them in his own breast. Mankind had to be educated through long habituation to the idea that there is something great in self-denial, and not only in revenge; a divinity that sacrifices itself was the strongest and most effective symbol of this kind of greatness. The triumph over the enemy hardest to conquer, the sudden mastery of an emotion: this is what such a denial *appears* to be; and to this extent it counts as the height of morality. In truth, it has to do with the exchange of one idea for another, while the heart remains at the same pitch, the same volume. Men who have sobered up and are resting from an emotion no longer understand the morality of those moments, but the admiration of all who witnessed in them supports these men; pride consoles them, when the emotion and the understanding for their deed have faded. Thus those acts of self-denial are basically not moral either, insofar as they are not done strictly with regard for other people; rather the other person simply offers the tense heart an opportunity to relieve itself, by that self-denial.

## 139

In some respects, the ascetic too is trying to make life easy for himself, usually by completely subordinating himself to the will of another or to a comprehensive law and ritual, rather in the way the Brahman leaves absolutely nothing to his own determination, but determines himself at each minute by a holy precept. This subordination is a powerful means of becoming master of oneself; one is occupied, that is, free of boredom, and yet has no willful or passionate impulse; after a deed is completed, there is no feeling of responsibility, and therefore no agony of regret. One has renounced his own will once and for all, and this is easier than to renounce it only occasionally, just as it is easier to give up a desire entirely than to moderate it. If we remember man's present attitude towards the state, we find there too that an unqualified obedience is more convenient than a qualified one. The saint, then, makes his life easier by that complete abandonment of his personality, and a man is fooling himself when he admires that phenomenon as the most heroic feat of morality. In any event, it is harder to assert one's personality without vacillation or confusion than to free oneself from it in the manner described; it also takes much more intellect and thought.

## 140

After having discovered in many of the more inexplicable actions, expressions of that pleasure in *emotion per se,* I would also discern in self-contempt (which is one of the signs of saintliness) and likewise in self-tormenting behavior (starvation and scourges, dislocation of limbs, simulated madness) a means by which those natures combat the general exhaustion of their life-force (of their nerves): they use the most painful stimulants and horrors in order to emerge, for a time at least, from that dullness and boredom into which their great spiritual indolence and that subordination to a foreign will described above have so often let them sink.

## 141

The most common means that the ascetic and saint uses in order to make his life more bearable and entertaining consists in occasionally waging war and alternating victory and defeat. To do this he needs an opponent, and finds him in the so-called "inner enemy." He exploits particularly his tendency to vanity, ambition, and love of power, as well as his sensual desires, to allow himself to see his life as a continuing battle and himself as the battlefield on which good and evil spirits struggle, with alternating results. It is well known that regularity of sexual intercourse moderates the sensual imagination, even almost suppresses it and, conversely, that it is unleashed and made dissolute by abstinence or irregularity in intercourse. Many Christian saints' imaginations were exceedingly dirty; thanks to their theory that these desires were real demons who raged in them, they did not feel very responsible; to this feeling of irresponsibility, we owe the so instructive honesty of their confessions. It was in their interest that the battle always be entertained to some degree, for, as we said, their bleak life was entertained by it. But in order that the battle appear important enough to arouse continuing interest and admiration in the nonsaints, sensuality had to be more and more calumniated and branded; indeed, the danger of eternal damnation became so closely linked to these things that quite probably for whole generations, Christians conceived children with a bad conscience, indubitably doing great harm to mankind. And yet truth is standing on its head here, which is especially unseemly for truth. To be sure, Christianity had said that each man is conceived and born in sin, and in the insufferable superlative Christianity of Calderón this thought had been knotted together and tangled up once again, so that he ventured the craziest paradox there can be, in the well-known lines:

> the greatest guilt of man
> is that he was born.[23]

In all pessimistic religions, the act of procreation is felt to be bad per se, but this feeling is by no means a general, human one; not even the judgment of all pessimists is the same on this point. Empedocles, for example, knows nothing of shame, devil, sin in all things erotic; rather, on the great meadow of calamity, he sees one single salutary and hopeful apparition: Aphrodite. For him she is the guarantee that strife will not prevail indefinitely, but will eventually give the scepter to a gentler daemon.[24] Practicing Christian pessimists, as we said, had an interest in seeing a different opinion in power; for the loneliness and spiritual desolation of their lives, they needed an ever-active and generally recognized enemy, by opposing and conquering whom they again and again portrayed themselves to the unsaintly as half-incomprehensible, supernatural beings. When finally, as a consequence of their way of life and their destroyed health, this enemy took flight forever, they knew at once how to *see* their inner self populated by new demons. The scales of arrogance and humility, in vacillation up and down, entertained their brooding minds as finely as the alternation of desire and serenity. At that time psychology served not only to throw suspicion on everything human, but also to revile it,

23. Calderón de la Barca (1600–81), *La Vida es Sueño,* act 1, sc. 3: "Pues el delito mayor / del hombre es haber nacido." Often quoted by Schopenhauer, as in *The World as Will and Idea,* bk. 3, par. 51.

24. Empedocles: *On Nature,* 35.

to scourge it, to crucify it; man *wanted* to consider himself as bad and evil as possible; he sought out fear for the salvation of his soul, despair about his own strength. Everything natural, to which man attaches the idea of badness, sinfulness (as is still his habit in regard to the erotic, for example) burdens him, clouds his imagination, makes his glance timid, lets him quarrel with himself and makes him unsure, lacking confidence; even his dreams acquire the flavor of his troubled conscience. And yet this suffering about the natural is in the reality of things totally unfounded; it is only the consequence of opinions *about* things. It is easy to see how men become worse by labeling the unavoidably natural as bad and later feeling it to be so constituted. It is the device of religion, and of those metaphysicians who want to think of man as evil and sinful by nature, to have him cast suspicion on nature and to *make* himself bad; for he learns thus to experience himself as bad, since he cannot take off the dress of nature. Gradually, after a long life of nature, he feels so oppressed by such a burden of sins that supernatural powers become necessary to lift this burden; and with that, the need for redemption, which we have already discussed, enters the scene, corresponding to no real sinfulness but rather only to an imagined one. If one goes through the individual moral statements of the documents of Christianity, one will find everywhere that the demands have been exaggerated so that man *cannot* satisfy them; the intention is not that he *become* more moral, but rather that he feel *as sinful as possible*. If man had not found this feeling *agreeable,* why should he have produced such an idea and been attached to it for so long? As in the ancient world an immeasurable strength of spirit and inventiveness was employed to increase joy in life through ceremonial worship, so in the age of Christianity an equally immeasurable amount of spirit has been offered up to a different striving: man was to feel sinful in all ways and excited, animated, inspired thereby. Excite, animate, inspire at all costs—is that not the watchword of an enervated, overripe, overcultivated age? The circle of all natural feelings had been run through a hundred times, the soul had grown tired of them; then the saint and ascetic invented a new category of life-stimuli. They presented themselves to everyone, not actually for the many to imitate, but rather as a frightening and yet delightful spectacle, which was performed on that border between this world and the afterworld, where everyone used to think he perceived, now heavenly gleams of light, now eerie tongues of flame glowing up from the depths. The eye of the saint, focused on the meaning of a short earthly life, frightful in every way, focused on the imminence of the final decision about an endless new life to come, this burnt-out eye, in a half-wasted body, made men of the old world tremble to their depths. To look at, to look away from with a shudder, to sense again the fascination of the spectacle, to yield to it, have one's fill of it, until the feverish soul shivers aglow and chilled— this was the last *pleasure which the ancient world invented,* after it had itself grown indifferent even to the sight of animal and human contests.

### 142

To sum up what we have said: that disposition which the saint, or evolving saint, enjoys is constituted of elements that we all know quite well. However, under the influence of other than religious ideas, they show themselves in different colors and then tend to suffer men's censure as intensely as, when decorated by religion and the ultimate questions of existence, they can count on admiration, even worship—or at least they could count on it in earlier times. Sometimes the saint exercises a defiance against himself, which is a close relative of the love of power, and which gives even the most solitary man a feeling of power; sometimes his bloated sensibility leaps from the longing to give his passions free rein to the longing to make them collapse like wild stallions, powerfully driven by a proud soul. Sometimes he wants the complete cessation of all bothersome, tormenting, irritating feelings, a waking sleep, a continuing repose in the lap of a dull, animal-like or vegetative indolence; sometimes he seeks out battle and provokes it in himself, because boredom holds its yawning visage up to him. He scourges his self-deification with self-contempt and cruelty; he takes pleasure in the wild uprising of his desires, and in the sharp pain of sin, even in the idea of being lost; he knows how to set a trap for his emotions, for his most extreme love of power, for example, so that it changes over into the emotion of the most extreme humiliation, and his agitated soul is pulled to pieces by this contrast. And finally, when he yearns for visions, conversations with the dead, or with divine beings, it is basically a rare form of voluptuousness that he desires, perhaps that voluptuousness in which all others are wound together in one knot.

Novalis, by experience and instinct one of the authorities in questions of saintliness, pronounces the whole secret with naive joy: "It is a wonder indeed that the association of voluptuousness, religion and cruelty has not long ago made men take notice of their intimate relationship and common intention."[25]

## 143

Not that which the saint is, but that which *he signifies* in the minds of nonsaints, gives him his value in world history. Because people were mistaken about him, interpreting his inner states incorrectly and divorcing him from themselves as radically as possible as something completely beyond compare and strangely superhuman, he acquired the extraordinary strength with which he could control the imagination of whole peoples, whole ages. He himself did not know himself; he himself understood the script of his moods, inclinations, actions by an interpretive art which was as exaggerated and artificial as the pneumatic interpretation of the Bible. The queer, sick elements in his nature, coupled as they were with spiritual poverty, inadequate knowledge, ruined health, overstimulated nerves, were as hidden fom his eye as from the eye of the onlooker. He was not an especially good man, and even less an especially wise man. But he *signified* something that was to surpass human proportions in goodness and wisdom. Belief in him supported the belief in the divine and the miraculous, in a religious meaning of all existence, in an imminent Judgment Day. By the evening light of the apocalyptic sun that shone over the Christian peoples, the shadowy figure of the saint grew to enormous size, indeed to such a height that even in our time, which no longer believes in God, there are still plenty of thinkers who believe in the saint.

## 144

It is self-evident that this portrait of the saint, which is sketched according to the average member of the whole type, can be opposed by other portraits that might result in a more favorable impression. Isolated exceptions to this type stand out, whether by their great gentleness and benevolence, or by the magic of their

25. "Fragmente und Studien," 1799–1800, *Schriften,* vol. 3 (Stuttgart: Kohlhammer, 1968), p. 568.

unusual energy; others are attractive in the highest degree because certain delusions diffuse streams of light over their whole
being, as for example is the case with the famous founder of Christianity, who thought he was God's only begotten son, and therefore without sin; so that through a fantasy (which one should not
judge too harshly, because the whole ancient world is aswarm
with sons of gods) he reached the same goal: the feeling of utter
sinlessness, utter freedom from responsibility—a feeling that
everyone can now attain through science.

I have also left out the Indian holy men, who are an intermediate stage between the Christian saint and the Greek philosopher,
and to that extent do not represent a pure type. Buddhists demanded knowledge, science (as far as there was one), superiority
to other men by logical discipline and training of thought as a
sign of saintliness, as much as the same qualities are rejected and
calumniated as a sign of nonsaintliness in the Christian world.

# SECTION FOUR
## From the Soul of
## Artists and Writers

### 145

*Perfection said not to have evolved.* When something is perfect, we tend to neglect to ask about its evolution, delighting rather in what is present, as if it had risen from the ground by magic. In this regard we are probably still under the influence of an ancient mythological sentiment. We still feel (in a Greek temple like the one at Paestum, for example) *almost* as if a god, playing one morning, had built his residence out of these enormous masses; at other times as if a soul had all of a sudden magically entered into a stone and now wished to use it to speak. The artist knows that his work has its full effect only when it arouses belief in an improvisation, in a wondrous instantaneousness of origin; and so he encourages this illusion and introduces into art elements of inspired unrest, of blindly groping disorder, of expectantly attentive dreaming when creation begins, as deceptions that dispose the soul of the viewer or listener to believe in the sudden emergence of perfection.

As is self-evident, the science of art must oppose this illusion most firmly, and point out the false conclusions and self-indulgences of the intellect that drive it into the artist's trap.

### 146

*The artist's feeling for truth.* When it comes to recognizing truths, the artist has a weaker morality than the thinker; on no account does he want his brilliant, profound interpretations of life to be taken from him, and he defends himself against sober, plain methods and results. Ostensibly, he is fighting for the higher dignity and meaning of man; in truth, he does not want to give up the *most effective* presuppositions for his art, that is the fantastic, the mythic, uncertain, extreme, feeling for the symbolic, over-estimation of the individual, belief in something miraculous about genius: thus he thinks the continuation of his manner of creating is more important than a scientific dedication to truth in every form, however plain it may appear.

## 147

*Art as conjuror of the dead.* Art incidentally performs the task of preserving, even touching up extinct, faded ideas; when it accomplishes this task it weaves a band around various eras, and causes their spirits to return. Only a semblance of life, as over graves, or the return of dead loved ones in dreams, results from this, of course, but for moments at least, the old feeling revives and the heart beats to an otherwise forgotten rhythm. Because art has this general benefit, one must excuse the artist himself if he does not stand in the front ranks of the enlightenment, of mankind's progressive *maturation.* He has remained his whole life long a child or youth, and has stood still at the point where his artistic drive came upon him; but feelings from the first stages of life are admittedly closer to feelings of earlier eras then to those of the present century. His unwitting task becomes the juvenescence of mankind: this is his glory and his limitation.

## 148

*How poets ease life.* Poets, insofar as they too wish to ease men's lives, either avert their glance from the arduous present, or else help the present acquire new colors by making a light shine in from the past. To be able to do this, they themselves must in some respects be creatures facing backwards, so that they can be used as bridges to quite distant times and ideas, to religions and cultures dying out or dead. Actually, they are always and necessarily *epigones.* Of course, some unfavorable things can be said about their ways of easing life: they soothe and heal only temporarily, only for the moment; they even prevent men from working on a true improvement of their conditions, by suspending and, like a palliative, relieving the very passion of the dissatisfied, who are impelled to act.

## 149

*The slow arrow of beauty.* The most noble kind of beauty is that which does not carry us away suddenly, whose attacks are not violent or intoxicating (this kind easily awakens disgust), but rather the kind of beauty which infiltrates slowly, which we carry along with us almost unnoticed, and meet up with again in dreams; finally, after it has for a long time lain modestly in our heart, it takes complete possession of us, filling our eyes with tears, our hearts with longing.

What do we long for when we see beauty? To be beautiful. We think much happiness must be connected with it. But that is an error.

### 150

*Infusion of soul into art.* Art raises its head where religions decline. It takes over a number of feelings and moods produced by religion, clasps them to its heart, and then becomes itself deeper, more soulful, so that it is able to communicate exaltation and enthusiasm, which it could not yet do before. The wealth of religious feeling, swollen to a river, breaks out again and again, and seeks to conquer new realms: but growing enlightenment has shaken the dogmas of religion and generated a thorough mistrust of it; therefore, feeling, forced out of the religious sphere by enlightenment, throws itself into art; in certain instances, into political life, too, indeed even directly into science. Wherever one perceives a loftier, darker coloration to human endeavors, one may assume that the fear of spirits, the smell of incense, and the shadow of churches have remained attached to them.

### 151

*How meter beautifies.* Meter lays a gauze over reality; it occasions some artificiality of speech and impurity of thinking; through the shadow that it throws over thought, it sometimes conceals, sometimes emphasizes. As shadow is necessary to beautify, so "muffling" is necessary in order to make clearer.

Art renders the sight of life bearable by laying over it the gauze of impure thinking.

### 152

*Art of the ugly soul.* One is limiting art much too severely when one demands that only the composed soul, suspended in moral balance, may express itself there. As in the plastic arts, there is in music and poetry an art of the ugly soul, as well as an art of the beautiful soul; and in achieving art's mightiest effects—breaking souls,[1] moving stones, and humanizing animals—perhaps that very art has been most successful.

## 153

*Art weighs down the thinker's heart.* We can understand how strong the metaphysical need[2] is, and how even nature in the end makes it hard to leave it, from the way, even in a free spirit who has rid himself of everything metaphysical, the highest effects of art easily produce a reverberation of a long-silenced, or even broken metaphysical string. At a certain place in Beethoven's Ninth Symphony, for example, he might feel that he is floating above the earth in a starry dome, with the dream of *immortality* in his heart; all the stars seem to glimmer around him, and the earth seems to sink ever deeper downwards.

If he becomes aware of this condition, he may feel a deep stab in his heart and sigh for the man who will lead back to him the lost beloved, be she called religion or metaphysics. In such moments, his intellectual character is being tested.

## 154

*Playing with life.* The lightness and looseness[3] of the Homeric imagination was necessary to soothe and temporarily suspend the Greeks' inordinately passionate heart and oversharp mind. When their reason speaks, how bitter and horrible life then appears! They do not deceive themselves, but they deliberately play over life with lies. Simonides[4] advised his countrymen to take life as a game; they were all too familiar with seriousness in the form of pain (indeed, man's misery is the theme that the gods so love to hear sung about), and they knew that only through art could even misery become a pleasure. As punishment for this insight, however, they were so plagued by the wish to invent tales that in everyday life it became hard for them to keep free of falsehood and deceit, just as all poetic people have this delight in lying, and, what is more, an innocence in it. That must sometimes have driven their neighboring nations to despair.

1. *das Seelenbrechen*
2. See n. 26 to Section One.
3. *Die Leichtigkeit und Leichtfertigkeit*
4. Greek poet (c. 556–467 B.C.) from Ceos, cf. his *Theon, Progymnasmata.*

## 155

*Belief in inspiration.* Artists have an interest in others' believing in sudden ideas, so-called inspirations; as if the idea of a work of art, of poetry, the fundamental thought of a philosophy shines down like a merciful light from heaven. In truth, the good artist's or thinker's imagination is continually producing things good, mediocre, and bad, but his *power of judgment,* highly sharpened and practiced, rejects, selects, joins together; thus we now see from Beethoven's notebooks that he gradually assembled the most glorious melodies and, to a degree, selected them out of disparate beginnings. The artist who separates less rigorously, liking to rely on his imitative memory, can in some circumstances become a great improviser; but artistic improvisation stands low in relation to artistic thoughts earnestly and laboriously chosen. All great men were great workers, untiring not only in invention but also in rejecting, sifting, reforming, arranging.

## 156

*Once again inspiration.* When productive energy has been dammed up for a while and has been hindered in its outflow by an obstacle, there is finally a sudden outpouring, as if a direct inspiration with no previous inner working out, as if a miracle were taking place. This constitutes the well-known illusion which all artists, as we have said, have somewhat too great an interest in preserving. The capital has simply *piled up;* it did not fall suddenly from heaven. Incidentally, such apparent inspiration also exists elsewhere, for example, in the domain of goodness, virtue, vice.

## 157

*The genius's[5] sorrows and their value.* The artistic genius wants to give pleasure, but if his work is on a very high level, he may easily lack people to appreciate it; he offers them food, but no one wants it. That gives him a sometimes ludicrously touching pathos; for basically he has no right to force pleasure on men. His pipe sounds, but no one wants to dance. Can that be tragic?

5. Genius: Nietzsche uses the more archaic form *der Genius* interchangeably with the more modern term *das Genie* (as is clear in Aph. 164, where he uses both in the same aphorism); *der Genius,* strictly speaking, refers more to the disembodied, creative spirit, while *das Genie* refers to a person, a great man of genius.

Perhaps it can. Ultimately, he has as compensation for this privation more pleasure in creating than other men have in all other kinds of activity. One feels his sorrows excessively, because the sound of his lament is louder, his tongue more eloquent. And *sometimes* his sorrows really are very great, but only because his ambition, his envy, are so great. The learned genius,[6] like Kepler and Spinoza, is usually not so desirous, and raises no such fuss about his really greater sorrows and privations. He can count with greater certainty on posterity and dismiss the present while an artist who does this is always playing a desperate game, at which his heart must ache. In very rare cases—when the genius of skill and understanding merges with the moral genius in the same individual—we have, in addition to the above-mentioned pains, those pains that must be seen as the exceptions in the world: the extra-personal, transpersonal feelings, in sympathy with a people, mankind, all civilization, or all suffering existence; these feelings acquire their value through association with especially difficult and remote perceptions (pity per se is not worth much).

But what measure, what scale is there for their authenticity? Is it not almost imperative to be distrustful of anyone who *speaks* about having feelings of this kind?

## 158

*Fate of greatness.* Every great phenomenon is followed by degeneration, particularly in the realm of art. The model of the great man stimulates vainer natures to imitate him outwardly or to surpass him; in addition, all great talents have the fateful quality of stifling many weaker forces and seeds, and seem to devastate the nature around them. The most fortunate instance in the development of an art is when several geniuses reciprocally keep each other in check; in this kind of a struggle, weaker and gentler natures are generally also allowed air and light.

## 159

*Art dangerous for the artist.* When art seizes an individual powerfully, it draws him back to the views of those times when art flowered most vigorously; then its effect is to form by retrogression. The artist comes more and more to revere sudden excite-

6. *Der wissende Genius.*

ments, believes in gods and demons, imbues nature with a soul, hates science, becomes unchangeable in his moods like the men of antiquity, and desires an overthrow of all conditions that are not favorable to art, and this with the vehemence and unreasonableness of a child. Now, the artist in and of himself is already a laggard creature because he still plays a game that belongs to youth and childhood; in addition, he is gradually being formed by retrogression into former times. Thus between him and the other men of his period who are the same age a vehement antagonism is finally generated, and a sad end—just as, according to the tales of the ancients, both Homer and Aeschylus finally lived and died in melancholy.

## 160

*Created people.* When one says that the dramatist (and the artist in general) *creates* real characters, this is a beautiful illusion and exaggeration, in whose existence and dissemination art celebrates one of its unintentional, almost superfluous triumphs. In fact, we don't understand much about real, living people, and generalize very superficially when we attribute to them this character or that; the poet is reflecting this, our *very incomplete* view of man, when he turns into people (in this sense "creates") those sketches which are just as superficial as our knowledge of people. There is much deception in these characters created by artists; they are by no means examples of nature incarnate, but rather, like painted people, rather too thin; they cannot stand up to close examination. Moreover, it is quite false to say that whereas the character of the average living man often contradicts itself, that created by a dramatist is the original model which nature had in mind. A real man is something completely *necessary* (even in those so-called contradictions), but we do not always recognize this necessity. The invented man, the phantasm, claims to signify something necessary, but only for those who would also understand a real person only in terms of a rough, unnatural simplification, so that a few prominent, often recurring traits, with a great deal of light on them and a great deal of shadow and semidarkness about, completely satisfy their demands. They are ready to treat the phantasm as a real, necessary person, because in the case of a real person they are accustomed to taking a phantasm, a silhouette, a deliberate abbreviation as the whole.

That the painter and sculptor express at all the "idea" of man is nothing but a vain fantasy and deception of the senses; one is being tyrannized by the eye when one says such a thing, since, of the human body itself, the eye sees only the surface, the skin; the inner body, however, is as much part of the idea. Plastic art wants to make characters visible on the skin; the spoken arts use the word for the same purpose, portraying character in sound. Art proceeds from man's natural *ignorance* about his interior (in body and character): it is not for physicists and philosophers.

## 161

*Self overestimation in the faith in artists and philosophers.* We all think that the goodness of a work of art or an artist is proven when it seizes and profoundly moves us. And yet our own *goodness* in judging and feeling would first have to be proven—which is not the case. Who in the realm of plastic art has moved and delighted us more than Bernini?[7] Who has had a more powerful effect than that post-Demosthenian orator[8] who introduced the Asianic style and brought it to dominate during two centuries? This dominance over whole centuries proves nothing about the goodness and enduring validity of a style; one should therefore not be too sure of his good faith in any artist; after all, such faith is not only faith in the reality of our feeling but also in the infallibility of our judgment; whereas judgment or feeling, or both, can themselves be too crude or too refined, too extreme or rough. The blessings and raptures of a philosophy or a religion likewise prove nothing about their truth—as little as the happiness which the madman enjoys from his idée fixe proves anything about the rationality of his idea.

## 162

*Worshipping the genius out of vanity.* Because we think well of ourselves, but in no way expect that we could ever make the sketch to a painting by Raphael or a scene like one in a play by Shakespeare, we convince ourselves that the ability to do so is

7. Gian Lorenzo Bernini (1608–1680).

8. Hegesias of Magnesia (250 B.C.) introduced a popular, witty, bombastic style of oration, contrasting with the Classical Attic style.

quite excessively wonderful, a quite uncommon accident, or, if we still have a religious sensibility, a grace from above. Thus our vanity, our self-love, furthers the worship of the genius, for it does not hurt only if we think of it as very remote from ourselves, as a miracle (even Goethe, who was without envy, called Shakespeare his star of the farthest height, recalling to us that line, "Die Sterne, die begehrt man nicht"—one does not covet the stars).[9] But those insinuations of our vanity aside, the activity of the genius seems in no way fundamentally different from the activity of a mechanical inventor, a scholar of astronomy or history, a master tactician. All these activities are explained when one imagines men whose thinking is active in one particular direction; who use everything to that end; who always observe eagerly their inner life and that of other people; who see models, stimulation everywhere; who do not tire of rearranging their material. The genius, too, does nothing other than first learn to place stones, then to build, always seeking material, always forming and reforming it. Every human activity is amazingly complicated, not only that of the genius: but none is a "miracle."

From where, then, the belief that there is genius only in the artist, orator, or philosopher? That only they have "intuition" (thus attributing to them a kind of magical eye glass, by which they can see directly into "being")?[10] It is evident that men speak of genius only where they find the effects of the great intellect most agreeable and, on the other hand, where they do not want to feel envy. To call someone "divine" means "Here we do not have to compete." Furthermore, everything that is complete and perfect is admired; everything evolving is underestimated. Now, no one can see in an artist's work how it *evolved:* that is its advantage, for wherever we can see the evolution, we grow somewhat cooler. The complete art of representation wards off all thought of its evolution; it tyrannizes as present perfection. Therefore representative artists especially are credited with genius, but not scientific men. In truth, to esteem the former and underestimate the latter is only a childish use of reason.

9. The quotation (from "Trost in Tränen") continues: "man freut sich ihrer Pracht" (one rejoices in their splendor).

10. A reference to Schopenhauer.

## 163

*The seriousness of craft.* Speak not of gifts, or innate talents! One can name all kinds of great men who were not very gifted. But they *acquired* greatness, became "geniuses" (as we say) through qualities about whose lack no man aware of them likes to speak; all of them had that diligent seriousness of a craftsman, learning first to form the parts perfectly before daring to make a great whole. They took time for it, because they had more pleasure in making well something little or less important, than in the effect of a dazzling whole. For example, it is easy to prescribe how to become a good short story writer, but to do it presumes qualities which are habitually overlooked when one says, "I don't have enough talent." Let a person make a hundred or more drafts of short stories, none longer than two pages, yet each of a clarity such that each word in it is necessary; let him write down anecdotes each day until he learns how to find their most concise, effective form; let him be inexhaustible in collecting and depicting human types and characters; let him above all tell tales as often as possible, and listen to tales, with a sharp eye and ear for the effect on the audience; let him travel like a landscape painter and costume designer; let him excerpt from the various sciences everything that has an artistic effect if well portrayed; finally, let him contemplate the motives for human behavior, and disdain no hint of information about them, and be a collector of such things day and night. In this diverse exercise, let some ten years pass: and then what is created in the workshop may also be brought before the public eye.

But how do most people do it? They begin not with the part but with the whole. Perhaps they once make a good choice, excite notice, and thereafter make ever worse choices for good, natural reasons.

Sometimes when reason and character are lacking to plan this kind of artistic life, fate and necessity take over their function, and lead the future master step by step through all the requisites of his craft.

## 164

*Danger and benefit of worshipping the genius.*[11] The belief in great, superior, fertile minds is not necessarily, yet very often con-

11. This aphorism is in reference to Richard Wagner.

nected to the religious or half-religious superstition that those minds are of superhuman origin and possess certain miraculous capabilities, which enable them to acquire their knowledge in a way quite different from that of other men. They are credited with a direct view into the essence of the world, as through a hole in the cloak of appearance, and thought able, without the toil or rigor of science, thanks to this miraculous seer's glance, to communicate something ultimate and decisive about man and the world. As long as anyone still believes in miracles in the realm of knowledge, one can admit perhaps that the believers themselves gain an advantage thereby, in that by unconditionally subordinating themselves to great minds, they provide the best discipline and schooling for their own mind during its development. On the other hand, it is at least questionable whether, when it takes root in him, superstition about the genius, about his privileges and special capabilities, is advantageous to the genius himself. At any rate, it is a dangerous sign when a man is overtaken by awe of himself, be it the famous awe of Caesar, or (as in this case) awe of the genius, when the aroma of a sacrifice, which by rights is offered only to a god, penetrates the genius's brain, so that he begins to waver, and to take himself for something superhuman. The eventual results are a feeling of irresponsibility, of exceptional rights, the belief that he blesses merely through his company, and mad rage at the attempt to compare him to others, or, indeed, to judge him lower and reveal what is unsuccessful in his work. By ceasing to criticize himself, the pinions finally begin, one after the other, to fall out of his plumage; superstition digs at the roots of his strength and may even make him a hypocrite after his strength has left him. It is probably more useful for great minds to gain insight into their power and its origin, to grasp what purely human traits have flowed together in them, what fortunate circumstances played a part: persistent energy first of all, resolute attention to particular goals, great personal courage; and then the good fortune of an education that early on offered the best teachers, models, methods. To be sure, if their goal is to have the greatest possible *effect,* then vagueness about themselves, and an added gift of a semimadness have always helped a lot, for they have at all times been admired and envied for their very power to make men weak-willed, and to sway them to the delusion that they were being led by supernatural guides. Indeed, it uplifts and inspires

men to believe someone in possession of supernatural powers; to
that extent, madness, as Plato says, has brought the greatest
blessings upon men.[12]

In isolated, rare cases this portion of madness may well have
been the means which held such an excessively scattered nature
firmly together: in the lives of individuals, too, delusions often
have the value of curatives, which are actually poisons. Yet in the
case of every "genius" who believes in his divinity, the poison at
last becomes apparent, to the degree that the "genius" grows old.
One may recall Napoleon, for example: surely through that very
belief in himself and his star, and through a scorn for men that
flowed from him, his nature coalesced into the mighty unity that
distinguishes him from all modern men, until finally this same
belief turned into an almost mad fatalism, robbed him of his
quick, penetrating eye, and became the cause of his downfall.

## 165

*The genius and emptiness.* Among artists, it is precisely the
original minds, creating out of themselves, who can in certain
circumstances produce what is wholly empty and insipid; while
more dependent natures, so-called talents, remain full of memo-
ries of everything at all good, and produce something tolerable
even in their weak condition. But if the original ones are deserted
by their own selves, memory gives them no help: they become
empty.

## 166

*The public.* The people actually desire nothing more from tragedy than to be moved, to be able to cry their hearts out; an artist
who sees a new tragedy, however, has his joy in its ingenious
technical inventions and devices, in its manipulation and appor-
tionment of the material, in its new use of old motifs, old thoughts.
His is the aesthetic attitude towards a work of art, that of the
creator; the attitude described first, which considers only content,
is that of the people. There is nothing to be said about the man in
the middle: he is neither "people" nor artist, and does not know
what he wants. Thus his pleasure, too, is vague and slight.

12. Cf. *Phaedrus*, 244.

## 167

*Artistic education of the public.* If the same motif is not treated a hundredfold by different masters, the public does not learn to get beyond its interest in the content; but the public will itself ultimately grasp and enjoy the nuances, the delicate new inventions in the treatment of a motif, if it has long known it in many adaptations and no longer experiences the charm of novelty or suspense.

## 168

*Artist and his followers must keep step.* The progress from one level of style to the next must be so slow that not only the artists, but also the listeners and spectators participate in it and know exactly what is taking place. Otherwise, a great gap suddenly forms between the artist, who creates his works on remote heights, and the public, which can no longer climb up to those heights, and finally climbs farther downhill again, disgruntled. For when the artist no longer lifts his public, it sinks quickly downward and falls, in fact, the deeper and more dangerously the higher a genius had carried it; like the eagle, from whose talons the turtle, carried up into the clouds, drops to disaster.[13]

## 169

*Origin of the comic.* If one considers that for some hundred thousand years man was an animal susceptible to fright in the highest degree, and that anything sudden or unexpected meant that he was ready to do battle, perhaps to die; indeed, that even later in social relations, all security rested on the expected, on tradition in meaning and activity; then one cannot be surprised that at every sudden, unexpected word or deed, if it comes without danger or harm, man is released and experiences instead the opposite of fright. The cringing creature, trembling in fear, springs up, expands wide: man laughs. This transition from momentary fear to short-lived exuberance is called the *comic.* Conversely, in the phenomenon of the tragic, man quickly goes from great, enduring exuberance to great fear; however, since among mortals great enduring exuberance is much less common than the occasion for fear, there is much more of the comic than of the tragic in the world; man laughs much more often than he is devastated.

13. A reference to Aesop's fable of the tortoise and the eagle.

## 170

*Artistic ambition.* The Greek artists, the tragedians, for example, wrote in order to triumph; their whole art cannot be imagined without competition. Ambition, Hesiod's good Eris,[14] gave wings to their genius. Now, this ambition demanded above all that their work maintain the highest excellence *in their own eyes,* as *they* understood excellence, without consideration for a prevailing taste or the general opinion about excellence in a work of art. And so, for a long time, Aeschylus and Euripides remained unsuccessful until they finally *educated* critics of art who esteemed their work by the standards that they themselves applied. Thus they strive for victory over their rivals according to their own estimation, before their own tribunal; they really want *to be* more excellent; then they demand that others outside agree with their own estimation, confirm their judgment. In this case, to strive for honor means "to make oneself superior and wish that that also be publicly evident." If the first is lacking and the second nevertheless desired, one speaks of *vanity.* If the latter is lacking, and not missed, one speaks of *pride.*

## 171

*Necessity in a work of art.* Those who talk so much about necessity in a work of art, exaggerate, if they are artists, *in majorem artis gloriam,*[15] or, if they are laymen, out of ignorance. The forms of a work of art, which express its ideas and are thus its way of speaking, always have something inessential, like every sort of language. The sculptor can add many little details or leave them out; so can the representative artist, be he an actor, or a musical virtuoso or conductor. Today these many small details and refinements please him, tomorrow they do not; they are more for the sake of the artist than of the art, for with the rigorous self-discipline demanded of him in portraying the main idea, he, too, occasionally needs sweets and toys in order not to grow surly.

---

14. In his *Works and Days* (1. 1–13), Hesiod (750–720 B.C.) distinguishes between the "terrible Eris," goddess of war, and the "good Eris," who calls forth peaceable competition among men, and particularly artists. This goddess of struggle is one anticipation of Nietzsche's theory of the will to power.

15. to the greater glory of art

## 172

*Making the audience forget the master.* The pianist who performs the work of a master will have played best if he has made the audience forget the master, and if it has seemed that he were telling a tale from his own life, or experiencing something at that very moment. To be sure, if he himself *is* nothing significant, everyone will curse his loquacity in telling about his life. So he must understand how to capture the listener's imagination for himself. On the other hand, this also explains all the weaknesses and follies of "virtuosity."

## 173

*Corriger la fortune.*[16] In the lives of great artists, there are unfortunate contingencies which, for example, force the painter to sketch his most significant picture as only a fleeting thought, or which forced Beethoven to leave us only the unsatisfying piano reduction of a symphony in certain great piano sonatas (the great B flat major).[17] In such cases, the artist coming after should try to correct the great men's lives after the fact; for example, a master of all orchestral effects would do so by restoring to life the symphony that had suffered an apparent pianistic death.

## 174

*Reduction.* Some things, events, or people do not tolerate being treated on a small scale. One cannot reduce the Laocoön group to a knick-knack: it needs size.[18] But it is even more uncommon for something small by nature to tolerate magnification; that is why biographers will always have more success in portraying a great man small than a small man great.

## 175

*Sensuality in contemporary art.* Artists often miscalculate when they aim at a sensual effect for their works of art; for their viewers or listeners no longer have all their senses about them, and, quite against the artist's intention, arrive by means of his work of art at a "sanctity" of feeling that is closely related to boredom.

16. to correct fortune, in the sense of "to deceive."
17. Opus 106, the "Hammerklavier."
18. The Laocoön group: large Hellenistic statue of the first century B.C.

Perhaps their sensuality begins where the artist's has just ended; at the most, then, they meet at one point.

## 176

*Shakespeare the moralist.* Shakespeare reflected a great deal on
passions, and by temperament probably had very easy access to
many of them (dramatists in general are rather wicked people).
But, unlike Montaigne, he was not able to talk about them; rather
he laid his observations *about* passions in the mouths of his passionate characters. Of course, this is unnatural, but it makes his
dramas so full of thought that all other dramas seem empty and
easily inspire a general aversion.

Schiller's maxims (which are almost always based on false or
insignificant ideas) are theatrical maxims, and as such have a
powerful effect, while Shakespeare's maxims do honor to his
model Montaigne,[19] and contain quite serious thoughts in an elegant form, but are therefore too distant and too fine for the eyes of
the theater-going public, and thus ineffective.

## 177

*Making oneself heard.* One must know not only how to play
well but also how to make oneself heard. A violin in the hand of
the greatest master emits only a squeak if the hall is too big; there
the master can be confused with any bungler.

## 178

*The incomplete as the effective.* As figures in relief sometimes
strike the imagination so powerfully because they seem to be on
the point of stepping out of the wall and, hindered by something,
suddenly come to a stop; so the relieflike, incomplete representation of a thought, or of a whole philosophy, is sometimes more
effective than its exhaustive realization. More is left to the effort of
the viewer; he is incited to continue developing what comes so
intensely lit and shaded into relief before him, to think it through,
and to overcome himself the obstacle that hindered until then its
complete emergence.

19. Michel de Montaigne (1533–92). He was translated into English in 1603,
thus during Shakespeare's lifetime (1564–1616).

## 179

*Against originals.* When art is dressed in the most threadbare cloth, we recognize it most clearly as art.

## 180

*Collective mind.* A good writer possesses not only his own mind but also the mind of his friends.

## 181

*Two kinds of mistaking.* The misfortune of clear and acute writers is that one takes them for shallow, and therefore expends no effort on them. And the good fortune of unclear writers is that the reader takes trouble with them, giving credit to them for his pleasure at his own zeal.

## 182

*Relationship to science.* Those people have no real interest in a science who start to get excited only when they themselves have made discoveries in it.

## 183

*The key.* For a significant man, the one thought he values greatly, to the laughter and scorn of insignificant men, is a key to hidden treasure chambers; for those others, it is nothing but a piece of old iron.

## 184

*Untranslatable.* It is neither the best nor the worst of a book that is untranslatable.

## 185

*The paradoxes of an author.* The so-called paradoxes of an author, which a reader objects to, are often not at all in the author's book but rather in the reader's head.

## 186

*Wit.* The wittiest authors raise the very slightest of smiles.

## 187

*The antithesis.* The antithesis is the narrow gate through which error prefers to worm its way to truth.

## 188

*Thinkers as stylists.* Most thinkers write badly because they tell us not only their thoughts but also the thinking of the thoughts.

## 189

*Thoughts in poetry.* The poet presents his thoughts in splendor, on the wagon of rhythm—usually because they cannot go on foot.

## 190

*Sin against the mind of the reader.* When an author denies his talent, merely to make himself the equal of his reader, he commits the only deadly sin that the reader will never forgive him for (if he should notice it). Otherwise, we can say anything bad about a man, but we must know how to restore his vanity in the *way* we say it.

## 191

*Limit of honesty.* Even the most honest writer lets slip a word too many when he wants to round off a period.

## 192

*The best author.* The best author will be the one who is ashamed to become a writer.[20]

## 193

*Draconian law[21] against writers.* One should regard a writer as a criminal who deserves acquittal or clemency only in the rarest cases: that would be a way to keep books from getting out of hand.

20. *Schriftsteller* (writer) can have a nuance of mechanical, trivial writing, as opposed to the word for a loftier kind of writer, *Dichter.*
21. Draconian law, after the early Greek lawgiver, Dracon, refers to overly strict laws.

## 194

*The fools of modern culture.* Our feuilleton writers are like medieval court fools: it is the same category of people. Half-rational, witty, excessive, silly, they are sometimes there only to soften the atmosphere of pathos with whimsy and chatter, and to drown out with their shouting the all too ponderous, solemn tintinnabulation of great events. Formerly they were in the service of princes and nobles; now they serve political parties, for a good part of the people's old submissiveness in dealing with their prince still lives on in party feeling and party discipline. However, the whole class of modern men of letters is not far removed from the feuilleton writers; they are the "fools of modern culture," who are judged more mildly if they are taken as not quite accountable. To think of writing as one's life's profession should by rights be considered a kind of madness.

## 195

*Following the Greeks.* Knowledge today is greatly hindered by the fact that all words have become hazy and inflated through centuries of exaggerated feeling. The higher stage of culture, which places itself under the rule of knowledge (though not under its tyranny), requires a much greater sobriety of feeling and a stronger concentration of words—in this the Greeks in the age of Demosthenes preceded us. Extravagance characterizes all modern writings; even if they are written simply, the words in them are still *felt* too eccentrically. Rigorous reflection, compression, coldness, plainness (even taken intentionally to the limits)—in short, restraint of feeling and taciturnity: that alone can help.

Such a cold way of writing and feeling, incidentally, is now very attractive by its contrast; and therein, of course, lies a new danger. For bitter cold can be as good a stimulant as a high degree of heat.

## 196

*Good narrators bad explainers.* Good narrators can display in the actions of their characters an admirable psychological certainty and consistency, which often stands in downright ludicrous contrast to their lack of skill in thinking psychologically. Thus their culture appears at one moment as excellently high as in the next it appears regrettably low. Too often it even happens that they are obviously explaining the actions and natures of their own heroes *incorrectly*—there is no doubt about it, as improbable as it sounds. The greatest pianist may have thought only a little about technical requirements and the special virtue, vice, use and educability of each finger (dactyl-ethics), and make crude errors when he speaks about such things.

## 197

*The writings of acquaintances and their readers.* We read the writings of acquaintances (friends and enemies) doubly, inasmuch as our knowledge keeps whispering alongside, "That is by him, a sign of his inner nature, his experience, his gift;" and, on the other hand, a different kind of knowledge tries to ascertain what the yield of the work itself is, what esteem it deserves aside from its author, what enrichment of learning it brings with it. As is self evident, these two kinds of reading and weighing interfere with one another. Even a conversation with a friend will produce good fruits of knowledge only when both people finally think solely of the matter at hand and forget that they are friends.

## 198

*Rhythmical sacrifices.* Good writers change the rhythm of some sentences simply because they do not credit the ordinary reader with the ability to grasp the meter of the sentence in its first version. So they simplify it for the reader, by choosing better-known rhythms.

Such consideration for the contemporary reader's lack of rhythmical ability has already elicited some sighs, for much has already been sacrificed to it. Do good musicians experience the same thing?

## 199

*Incompleteness as an artistic stimulation.* Incompleteness is often more effective than completeness, especially in eulogies. For such purposes, one needs precisely a stimulating incompleteness as an irrational element that simulates a sea for the listener's imagination, and, like fog, hides its opposite shore, that is, the limitation of the subject being praised. If one mentions the well-known merits of a man, and is exhaustive and expansive in doing so, it always gives rise to the suspicion that these are his only merits. He who praises completely places himself above the man being praised; he seems to *take him in at a glance*. For that reason, completeness has a weakening effect.

## 200

*Caution in writing and teaching.* Whoever has once begun to write and felt the passion of writing in himself, learns from almost everything he does or experiences only what is communicable for a writer. He no longer thinks of himself but rather of the writer and his public. He wants insight, but not for his own use. Whoever is a teacher is usually incapable of doing anything of his own for his own good. He always thinks of the good of his pupils, and all new knowledge gladdens him only to the extent that he can teach it. Ultimately he regards himself as a thoroughfare of learning, and in general as a tool, so that he has lost seriousness about himself.

## 201

*Bad writers necessary.* There will always have to be bad writers, for they reflect the taste of undeveloped, immature age groups, who have needs as much as the mature do. If human life were longer, there would be more of the individuals who have matured than of the immature, or at least as many. But as it is, the great majority die too young, which means there are always many more undeveloped intellects with bad taste. Moreover, these people demand satisfaction of their needs with the greater vehemence of youth, and they *force* the existence of bad authors.

## 202

*Too near and too far.* Often reader and author do not understand each other because the author knows his theme too well and finds it almost boring, so that he leaves out the examples he knows by the hundred; but the reader is strange to the matter and finds it poorly substantiated if the examples are withheld from him.

## 203

*One vanished preparation for art.* Of all the things the Gymnasium[22] did, the most valuable was its training in Latin style, for

---

22. *Gymnasium:* academic high school.

this was an *artistic exercise,* while all other occupations were aimed solely at learning. To put the German essay first is barbarism, for we have no classical German style developed by a tradition of public eloquence; but if one wants to use the German essay to further the practice of thinking, it is certainly better if one ignores the style entirely for the time being, thus distinguishing between exercise in thinking and in describing. The latter should be concerned with multiple versions of a given content, and not with independent invention of the content. Description only, with the content given, was the assignment of Latin style, for which the old teachers possessed a long-since-lost refinement of hearing. Anyone who in the past learned to write well in a modern language owed it to this exercise (now one is obliged to go to school under the older French teachers); and still further: he gained a concept of the majesty and difficulty of form, and was prepared for art in general in the only possible right way: through practice.

## 204

*Darkness and excessive brightness juxtaposed.* Writers who do not know how to express their thoughts clearly in general, will in particular prefer to select the strongest, most exaggerated terms and superlatives: this produces an effect as of torchlights along confusing forest paths.

## 205

*Writerly painting.*[23] When portraying important objects, one will do best to take the colors for the painting from the object itself, as would a chemist, and then to use them as would an artist, allowing the design to develop out of the distinctions and blendings of the colors. In this way, the painting acquires something of the thrilling innate quality that makes the object itself significant.

## 206

*Books that teach us to dance.* There are writers who, by portraying the impossible as possible, and by speaking of morality and genius as if both were merely a mood or a whim, elicit a feeling of

23. Writerly painting: Nietzsche is reversing the famous dictum of Horace, *ut pictura poesis* (poetry is like a picture) (*De Arte Poetica,* 361).

high-spirited freedom, as if man were rising up on tiptoe and simply had to dance out of inner pleasure.[24]

## 207

*Unfinished thoughts.* Just as youth and childhood have value *in
and of themselves* (as much as the prime of life) and are not to be
considered a mere transition or bridge, so too do unfinished
thoughts have their own value. Thus we must not pester a poet
with subtle interpretations, but should take pleasure in the uncertainty of his horizon, as if the road to various other thoughts were
still open. We stand on the threshold; we wait as if a treasure were
being dug up; it is as if a lucky trove of profundity were about to
be found. The poet anticipates something of the thinker's pleasure
in finding a central thought and in doing so makes us covetous, so
that we snatch at it. But it flutters past over our heads, showing
the loveliest butterfly wings—and yet it slips away from us.

## 208

*The book become almost human.* Every writer is surprised anew
when a book, as soon as it has separated from him, begins to take
on a life of its own. He feels as if one part of an insect had been
severed and were going its own way. Perhaps he almost forgets
the book; perhaps he rises above the views set down in it; perhaps
he no longer understands it and has lost those wings on which he
soared when he devised that book. Meanwhile, it goes about finding its readers, kindles life, pleases, horrifies, fathers new works,
becomes the soul of others' resolutions and behavior. In short, it
lives like a being fitted out with mind and soul—yet it is nevertheless not human.

The most fortunate author is one who is able to say as an old
man that all he had of life-giving, invigorating, uplifting, en-
lightening thoughts and feelings still lives on in his writings, and
that he himself is only the gray ash, while the fire has been rescued and carried forth everywhere.

If one considers, then, that a man's every action, not only his
books, in some way becomes the occasion for other actions, decisions, and thoughts; that everything which is happening is inex-

24. Nietzsche was thinking of Christoph Martin Wieland (1733–1813).

tricably tied to everything which will happen; then one understands the real *immortality,* that of movement: what once has moved others is like an insect in amber, enclosed and immortalized in the general intertwining of all that exists.

### 209

*Joy in old age.* The thinker or artist whose better self has fled into his works feels an almost malicious joy when he sees his body and spirit slowly broken into and destroyed by time; it is as if he were in a corner, watching a thief at work on his safe, all the while knowing that it is empty and that all his treasures have been rescued.

### 210

*Quiet fruitfulness.* The born aristocrats of the spirit are not overeager; their creations blossom and fall from the trees on a quiet autumn evening, being neither rashly desired, not hastened on, nor supplanted by new things. The wish to create incessantly is vulgar, betraying jealousy, envy, and ambition. If one is something, one does not actually need to do anything—and nevertheless does a great deal. There is a type higher than the "productive" man.

### 211

*Achilles and Homer.* One is always reminded of the difference between Achilles and Homer: one has the experience, the feeling; the other *describes* it. A real writer merely gives words to the emotion and experience of others. He is an artist to be able to guess a great deal from the little he has felt. Artists are by no means people of great passion, but they often *pretend* to be, in the unconscious feeling that others will believe more in the passion they depict if their own lives speak for their experience in this regard. One has only to let himself go, not control himself, give free rein to his anger and desires, and at once the whole world cries: "How passionate he is!" But that deep, raging passion that gnaws at and often swallows up the individual is something all its own. He who experiences it certainly does not describe it in dramas, music, or novels. Artists are often *licentious* individuals, insofar as they are not artists—but that is something else.

## 212

*Old doubts about the effect of art.* Are pity and fear really discharged through tragedy, as Aristotle claims,[25] so that the spectator goes home cooler and quieter? Do ghost stories make us less fearful and superstitious? It is true that in certain physical processes—the act of love, for example—the gratification of a need brings with it an alleviation and temporary abatement of the drive. But fear and pity are not the requirements of particular organs in this sense; they do not need to be relieved. And, in the long run, a drive is actually *strengthened* by gratifying it, despite periodic alleviations. It might be that pity and fear are assuaged and discharged by tragedy in each individual case; nevertheless they might even increase as a whole, due to the tragic effect, and Plato would be right, after all, when he claims that tragedy makes us on the whole more anxious and sentimental. The tragic poet himself would, of necessity, acquire a gloomy, fearful world view and a weak, susceptible, lachrymose soul; it would agree with Plato's view if tragic poets, and likewise the whole community which took delight in them especially, were to degenerate to ever greater extravagance and licentiousness.[26]

But what right does our age have to give an answer to Plato's great question about the moral influence of art? Even if we had the art—where do we see the influence, *any* influence of art?

## 213

*Joy in nonsense.* How can men take joy in nonsense? They do so, wherever there is laughter—in fact, one can almost say that wherever there is happiness there is joy in nonsense. It gives us pleasure to turn experience into its opposite, to turn purposefulness into purposelessness, necessity into arbitrariness, in such a way that the process does no harm and is performed simply out of high spirits. For it frees us momentarily from the forces of necessity, purposefulness, and experience, in which we usually see our merciless masters. We can laugh and play when the expected (which usually frightens us and makes us tense) is discharged without doing harm. It is the slaves' joy at the Saturnalia.

25. *Poetics* 1449b, 28.
26. Cf. Plato's *Republic,* 10.1–8.

214

*The ennobling of reality.* Because men once took the aphrodisiacal drive to be a godhead, showing worshipful gratitude when they felt its effect, that emotion has in the course of time been permeated with higher kinds of ideas, and thus in fact greatly ennobled. By virtue of this idealizing art, some peoples have turned diseases into great beneficial forces of culture—the Greeks, for example, who in earlier centuries suffered from widespread nervous epidemics (similar to epilepsy and the St. Vitus Dance) and created the glorious prototype of the bacchante from them. For the health of the Greeks was not at all robust; their secret was to honor illness like a god, too, if only it were *powerful.*

215

*Music.* In and of itself, music is not so full of meaning for our inner life, so profoundly moving, that it can claim to be a *direct* language of emotion. Rather, it is its ancient connection to poetry that has invested rhythmical movement, loudness and softness of tone, with so much symbolism that we now *believe* music is speaking directly *to* the inner life and that it comes *out* of it. Dramatic music is possible only when the art of music has already conquered an enormous realm of symbolic techniques through song, opera, and hundreds of attempts at tone painting. "Absolute music" is either pure form, in the raw state of music, where sounds in rhythm and at various volumes are enough to give joy; or else it is the symbolism of forms that, without poetry, can speak to our understanding (since, after the two arts had undergone a long development together, musical form was finally woven through and through with threads of concepts and feelings). Men who have lagged behind in the development of music can experience a particular piece of music in a purely formal way, while the more advanced will understand the whole thing symbolically. No music is in itself deep and full of meaning. It does not speak of the "will" or the "thing in itself." Only in an age that had conquered the entire sphere of inner life for musical symbolism could the intellect entertain this idea. The intellect itself has *projected* this meaning into the sound, as it has also read into the relationship of lines and masses in architecture a meaning that is, however, actually quite foreign to mechanical laws.

## 216

*Gesture and language.* Imitation of gesture is older than language, and goes on involuntarily even now, when the language of gesture is universally suppressed, and the educated are taught to control their muscles. The imitation of gesture is so strong that we cannot watch a face in movement without the innervation of our own face (one can observe that feigned yawning will evoke natural yawning in the man who observes it). The imitated gesture led the imitator back to the sensation expressed by the gesture in the body or face of the one being imitated. This is how we learned to understand one another; this is how the child still learns to understand its mother. In general, painful sensations were probably also expressed by a gesture that in its turn caused pain (for example, tearing the hair, beating the breast, violent distortion and tensing of the facial muscles). Conversely, gestures of pleasure were themselves pleasurable and were therefore easily suited to the communication of understanding (laughing as a sign of being tickled, which is pleasurable, then served to express other pleasurable sensations).

As soon as men understood each other in gesture, a *symbolism* of gesture could evolve. I mean, one could agree on a language of tonal signs, in such a way that at first both tone and gesture (which were joined by tone symbolically) were produced, and later only the tone. It seems that in earlier times, something must often have occurred much like what is now going on before our eyes and ears in the development of music; namely of dramatic music: while music without explanatory dance and miming (language of gesture) is at first empty noise, long habituation to that juxtaposition of music and gesture teaches the ear an immediate understanding of the tonal figures. Finally, the ear reaches a level of rapid understanding such that it no longer requires visible movement, and *understands* the composer without it. Then we are talking about absolute music, that is, music in which everything can be understood symbolically, without further aids.

## 217

*The desensualization of higher art.* Because the artistic development of modern music has forced the intellect to undergo an extraordinary training, our ears have become increasingly intellectual. Thus we can now endure much greater volume, much greater "noise," because we are much better trained than our forefathers were to listen for the *reason in it.* All our senses have in fact become somewhat dulled because we always inquire after the reason, what "it means" and no longer what "it is." Such a dullness is betrayed, for example, by the unqualified rule of tempered notes. For now those ears still able to make the finer distinctions, say, between C-sharp and D-flat are exceptions. In this regard, our ear has become coarsened. Furthermore, the ugly side of the world, originally inimical to the senses, has been won over for music. Its area of power to express the sublime, the frightful, and the mysterious, has thus been astonishingly extended. Our music makes things speak that before had no tongue. Similarly, some painters have made the eye more intellectual, and have gone far beyond what was previously called a joy in form and color. Here, too, that side of the world originally considered ugly has been conquered by artistic understanding.

What is the consequence of all this? The more the eye and ear are capable of thought, the more they reach that boundary line where they become asensual. Joy is transferred to the brain; the sense organs themselves become dull and weak. More and more, the symbolic replaces that which exists—and so, as surely as on any other path, we arrive along this one at barbarism. For the present, it is still said that the world is uglier than ever, but it *means* a more beautiful world than ever existed. But the more the perfumed fragrance of meaning is dispersed and evaporated, the rarer will be those who can still perceive it. And the rest will stay put at ugliness, seeking to enjoy it directly; such an attempt is bound to fail. Thus we have in Germany a twofold trend in musical development: on the one side, a group of ten thousand with ever higher, more delicate pretensions, ever more attuned to "what it means"; and on the other side, the vast majority, which each year is becoming ever more incapable of understanding meaning, even in the form of sensual ugliness, and is therefore learning to reach out with increasing pleasure for that which is intrinsically ugly and repulsive, that is, the basely sensual.

## 218

*The stone is more stone than before.* In general we no longer understand architecture, at least by far not in the way we under-

stand music. We have outgrown the symbolism of lines and figures, as we have grown unaccustomed to the tonal effects of rhetoric, no longer having sucked in this kind of cultural mother's
milk from the first moment of life. Originally everything about a
Greek or Christian building meant something, and in reference to
a higher order of things. This atmosphere of inexhaustible mean-
ingfulness hung about the building like a magic veil. Beauty entered the system only secondarily, impairing the basic feeling of
uncanny sublimity, of sanctification by magic or the gods' near-
ness. At the most, beauty tempered the *dread*—but this dread was
the prerequisite everywhere.

What does the beauty of a building mean to us now? The same
as the beautiful face of a mindless woman: something masklike.

## 219

*Religious origin of modern music.* Soulful music originates in
the Catholicism that was reestablished following the Council of
Trent, through Palestrina,[27] who helped the newly awakened,
ardent, deeply moved spirit to ring out; with Bach, it also originates later, in Protestantism, insofar as it had been deepened by
the Pietists[28] and released from its originally dogmatic nature.
For both origins, a prerequisite and necessary preliminary stage
was the involvement with music as it existed in the Renaissance
and the pre-Renaissance, especially that scholarly occupation with
music, a fundamentally scientific pleasure in harmonic feats and
polyphony. On the other side, soulful music also had to be preceded by opera, in which the layman made known his protest
against cold and overly-learned music, and tried to restore a soul
to Polyhymnia.[29]

Without that deeply religious change of heart, without the fading sound of a most inwardly agitated soul, music would have
remained learned or operatic; the spirit of the Counter-Reformation is the spirit of modern music (for the Pietism in Bach's music

27. Giovanni Palestrina (1525–94), Italian composer who wrote masses to
promote the greater glory of the Catholic church, following the Council of Trent
(1545–63).

28. Pietists: Christian sect, begun by Philipp Jakob Spener (1635–1705) and
A. H. Francke (1663–1727), stressing the individual soul's heartfelt experience of
the divine.

29. Polyhymnia: the muse of song.

is also a kind of Counter-Reformation). This is how deeply we are indebted to religious life.

Music was the Counter-Renaissance in the domain of art; the later painting of Murillo[30] belongs to it, perhaps the Baroque style, too (more so in any event than architecture of the Renaissance or of antiquity). And even now we might ask, whether our modern music, if it could move stones, would assemble them into an ancient architecture? I doubt it very much. For what governs in this music—emotion, pleasure in heightened, all-embracing moods, a wish to come alive at any cost, rapid change of feeling, a strong relief-effect of light and shade, juxtaposition of ecstasy and naiveté—all that ruled the plastic arts once before, and created new principles of style; but this was neither in antiquity nor in the time of the Renaissance.

### 220

*Transcendence in art.* Not without deep sorrow do we admit to ourselves that artists of all times, at their most inspired, have transported to a heavenly transfiguration precisely those ideas that we now know to be false: artists glorify mankind's religious and philosophical errors, and they could not have done so without believing in their absolute truth. Now, if belief in such truth declines at all, if the rainbow colors around the outer edges of human knowledge and imagination fade; then art like *The Divine Comedy,* Raphael's paintings, Michelangelo's frescoes, Gothic cathedrals, art that presumes not only a cosmic but also a metaphysical meaning in the art object, can never blossom again. There will some day be a moving legend that such an art, such an artistic faith, once existed.

### 221

*The revolution in poetry.* The severe constraint which the French dramatists imposed upon themselves with respect to unity of action, place, and time, to style, versification and sentence structure, selection of words and of themes, was as important a training as counterpoint and the fugue in the development of modern music, or the Gorgian figures[31] in Greek rhetoric. To

30. Bartolomé Murillo (1618–82). Spanish painter.
31. Gorgian figures: the figures of the orator-philosopher Gorgias of Leontini (480?–370 B.C.), using parallelisms and antitheses, often rhyming, in a highly ornate form of Attic diction.

restrict oneself so may appear absurd; nevertheless there is no way to get beyond realism other than to limit oneself at first most severely (perhaps most arbitrarily). In that way one gradually learns to step with grace, even on the small bridges that span dizzying abysses, and one takes as profit the greatest suppleness of movement, as everyone now alive can attest from the history of music. Here one sees how the shackles become looser with every step until they finally can seem quite thrown off: this *seeming* is the highest result of a necessary development in art. In modern poetry, there was no such happy gradual development out of the self-imposed shackles. Lessing made French form, the only modern art form, into an object of ridicule in Germany, and pointed instead to Shakespeare;[32] so the continuity of the unshackling process was lost and one leapt instead into naturalism, which is to say, back into the beginnings of art. Goethe tried to save himself from naturalism by restricting himself again and again in different ways; but once the thread of development has been broken off, even the most gifted artist can achieve only a continual experimentation. Schiller owes the relative sureness of his form to the model of French tragedy, which he instinctively respected, even though he spurned it, and kept rather independent of Lessing (whose dramatic efforts he rejected, as everyone knows). After Voltaire, the French themselves suddenly lacked great talents who might have led the development of tragedy out of constraint to the illusion of freedom; later they followed the German example, making the leap into a kind of Rousseauistic state of nature in art, and experimented. One should read Voltaire's *Mahomet* from time to time, in order fully to take to heart what has been lost forever to European culture through that rupture with tradition. Voltaire was the last of the great dramatists to restrict with Greek moderation his polymorphic soul, equal to even the greatest tragic tempests. (He achieved what no German has, because the Frenchman's nature is much more closely related to the Greek's than is the German's.) Also, in the treatment of prose speech, he was the last great writer to have a Greek ear, Greek artistic conscience, and Greek plainness and grace. Indeed, he was one of the last people to unite in himself, without being inconsistent or cow-

32. Cf. Lessing's *Briefe, die neueste Literatur betreffend* (1759–65).

ardly, the highest freedom of spirit and a positively unrevolution-
ary frame of mind.[33]

Since then, the modern spirit has come to rule in all areas, with
its unrest, its hatred of moderation and limitation, at first unleashed by the fever of revolution, and then, when attacked by
fear and dread of itself, applying the reins to itself again—but the
reins of logic, no longer of artistic moderation. True, through this
unshackling we enjoy for a time the poetry of all peoples,[34] everything that has grown up in hidden places, elemental, blooming
wildly, strangely beautiful and gigantically irregular, from the
folk song right up to the "great barbarian,"[35] Shakespeare. We
taste the joys of local color and period costume, which were alien
to all artistic peoples heretofore; we reap in rich measure the "barbaric advantages" of our time, on which Goethe insisted against
Schiller,[36] in order to put the formlessness of his *Faust* in the most
favorable light. But for how long can we do it? The oncoming
flood of poetry of every people, in every style, *must* eventually
sweep away the ground on which a quiet, hidden growth might
still have been possible. All poets *must* become experimenting
imitators, daredevil copyists, however great their strength may be
in the beginning. Finally, the public that has forgotten how to see
the real artistic act in the *restriction* of its energy to represent, in
the organizing mastery of all artistic means, *must* learn increasingly to appreciate power for the sake of power, color for the
sake of color, thought for the sake of thought, even inspiration for
the sake of inspiration; accordingly it will not enjoy the elements
and requirements of a work of art unless they are *isolated,* and
lastly, it will make the natural demand that the artist *must* represent them in isolation. Yes, we have thrown off the "unreasonable" shackles of Franco-Hellenic art, but without knowing it, we
have gotten used to finding all shackles, all limitation unreasonable. And so art moves towards its dissolution, and touches in the
process (which is to be sure highly instructive) all phases of its

33. The foregoing passage serves to justify Nietzsche's dedicating *Human, All
Too Human* to Voltaire.

34. *die Poesien aller Völker:* a reference to Herder's anthology *Stimmen der Völker in Liedern* (1807). (The Voices of Peoples in Songs).

35. Voltaire's judgment about Shakespeare.

36. Cf. Goethe, *Anmerkungen über Personen und Gegenstände,* and letter to
Schiller, June 27, 1797.

beginnings, its childhood, its imperfection, its former risks and extravagances. It interprets its origin, its evolution, as it is perishing.

Lord Byron, a great man whose instinct we can trust and whose theory lacked nothing but thirty years *more* of practice, once stated: "As to poetry, in general, the more I think about it, the more I am firm in the conviction that we are all on the wrong path, each and every one. We are all following a revolutionary system that is inherently false. Our generation or the next will come to the same conclusion."[37] This is the same Byron who said, "I look upon Shakespeare to be the worst of models, though the most extraordinary of poets."[38] And in the second half of his life, does not Goethe, with his matured artistic insight, basically say exactly the same thing? His insight gained him so great a head start over a succession of generations that by and large one can claim that Goethe's effect has not yet been fully realized, and that his time is yet to come. Precisely because, for a long time, his nature held him in the path of poetic revolution, precisely because he enjoyed thoroughly whatever in the way of new discoveries, prospects, and aids had been found indirectly and dug up, so to speak, from under the ruins of art by that rupture with tradition—for those reasons, his later reversal and conversion carries such weight. It means that he felt the deepest longing to regain the tradition of art, and, if the arm should prove far too weak to build where destruction has already required such enormous powers, to attribute with the eye's imagination at least the old perfection and completeness to the remaining ruins and porticos of the temple. So he lived in art as in the memory of true art: his poetry was an aid to his memory, to his understanding of old, long since vanished art periods. Considering the strength of the new era, his demands, of course, could not be satisfied; but his pain

37. Byron, *Letters and Journals,* vol. 4, 1816–1820, ed. Rowland E. Prothero (New York: Scribner, 1903–22), pp. 169–170. Letter of September 15, 1817. The exact quotation reads: "With regard to poetry in general, I am convinced, the more I think of it, that he (Moore) and all of us—Scott, Southey, Wordsworth, Moore, Campbell, I—are all in the wrong, one as much as another; that we are upon a wrong revolutionary poetical system, or systems, not worth a damn in itself, and from which none but Rogers and Crabbe are free; and that the present and next generations will finally be of this opinion."

38. Ibid., 5:323, July 14, 1821: "Shakespeare's the worst model, if a great poet."

about it was richly balanced by his joy that such demands were fulfilled once, and that we too can still share in that fulfillment. Not individuals, but more or less ideal masks; not reality but an allegorical generality; historical characters and local color made mythical and moderated almost to invisibility; contemporary feeling and the problems of contemporary society compressed to the simplest forms, stripped of their stimulating, suspenseful, pathological qualities, made *ineffective* in all but the artistic sense; no new subjects and characters, but rather the old long-familiar ones, in ever enduring reanimation and reformation: that is art as Goethe later *understood* it, as the Greeks and even the French *practiced* it.

## 222

*What remains of art.* It is true that with certain metaphysical assumptions, art has a much greater value—if it is believed, for example, that one's character is unchangeable and that the essence of the world is continually expressed in all characters and actions. Then the artist's work becomes the image of what *endures eternally*. In our way of thinking, however, the artist can give his image validity only for a time, because man as a whole has evolved and is changeable, and not even an individual is fixed or enduring.

The same is true of another metaphysical assumption: were our visible world only appearance, as metaphysicians assume, then art would come rather close to the real world; for there would be much similarity between the world of appearance and the artist's world of dream images; the remaining difference would actually enhance the meaning of art rather than the meaning of nature, because art would portray the symmetry, the types and models of nature.

But such assumptions are wrong: what place remains for art, then, after this knowledge? Above all, for thousands of years, it has taught us to see every form of life with interest and joy, and to develop our sensibility so that we finally call out, "However it may be, life is good."[39] This teaching of art—to have joy in existence and to regard human life as a part of nature, without being moved too violently, as something that developed through laws—this

39. Goethe: "Der Bräutigam".

teaching has taken root in us; it now comes to light again as an all-powerful need for knowledge. We could give art up, but in doing so we would not forfeit what it has taught us to do. Similarly, we have given up religion, but not the emotional intensification and exaltation it led to. As plastic art and music are the standard for the wealth of feeling really earned and won through religion, so the intense and manifold joy in life, which art implants in us, would still demand satisfaction were art to disappear. The scientific man is a further development of the artistic man.

## 223

*Sunset of art.* As in old age one remembers his youth and celebrates its memory, so mankind will soon relate to art as to a touching memory of youthful joys. Perhaps never before has art been grasped so fully and soulfully as now, when the magic of death seems to play about it. Think of that Greek city in Southern Italy[40] which one day a year still celebrates Greek festivals, amid melancholy and tears that foreign barbarism has triumphed more and more over its inherited customs. Never has the Hellenic been enjoyed so much, nowhere this golden nectar drunk with such intense relish, as among these disappearing Hellenes. Soon the artist will be regarded as a wondrous relic, on whose strength and beauty the happiness of earlier times depended; honors will be shown him, such as we cannot grant to our own equals. The best in us has perhaps been inherited from the feelings of former times, feelings which today can hardly be approached on direct paths; the sun has already set, but our life's sky glows and shines with it still, although we no longer see it.

40. Paestum (cf. *Selected Table Talk* of Aristoxenos [350 B.C.]). This reference to Paestum recalls Aphorism 145, the first aphorism of this section.

# SECTION FIVE
## Signs of Higher and Lower Culture

### 224

*Ennoblement through degeneration.* History teaches us that that part of a people maintains itself best whose members generally share a vital public spirit, due to the similarity of their long-standing, incontrovertible principles, that is, of their common faith. In their case, good, sound custom strengthens them; they are taught to subordinate the individual, and their character is given solidity, at first innately and later through education. The danger in these strong communities, founded on similar, steadfast individual members, is an increasing, inherited stupidity, which follows all stability like a shadow. In such communities, *spiritual progress* depends on those individuals who are less bound, much less certain, and morally weaker; they are men who try new things, and many different things. Because of their weakness, countless such men are destroyed without having much visible effect; but in general, especially if they have descendants, they loosen things up, and, from time to time, deliver a wound to the stable element of a community. Precisely at this wounded, weakened place, the common body is *inoculated,* so to speak, with something new; however, the community's overall strength has to be great enough to take this new thing into its bloodstream and assimilate it. Wherever progress is to ensue, deviating natures are of greatest importance. Every progress of the whole must be preceded by a partial weakening. The strongest natures *retain* the type, the weaker ones help to *advance* it.

Something similar also happens in the individual. There is rarely a degeneration, a truncation, or even a vice or any physical or moral loss without an advantage somewhere else. In a warlike and restless clan, for example, the sicklier man may have occasion to be alone, and may therefore become quieter and wiser; the one-eyed man will have *one* eye the stronger; the blind man will see deeper inwardly, and certainly hear better. To this extent, the famous theory of the survival of the fittest[1] does not seem to me to be the only viewpoint from which to explain the progress of strengthening of a man or of a race. Rather, two things must coincide: first of all, stable power must increase through minds bound in faith and communal feeling; and secondly, it must be possible to attain higher goals when degenerating natures partially weaken or wound the stable power; it is precisely the weaker nature, as the more delicate and free, that makes progress possible at all. If a people starts to crumble and grow weak at some one place, but is still strong and healthy in general, it can accept being infected with something new, and can incorporate it to its advantage. The task of education is to make the individual so firm and sure that, as a whole being, he can no longer be diverted from his path. But then the educator must wound him, or use the wounds that fate delivers; when pain and need have come about in this way, something new and noble can also be inoculated into the wounded places. His whole nature will take it in, and show the ennoblement later in its fruits.

Regarding the state, Machiavelli[2] says that "the form of governments is of very slight importance, although semi-educated people think otherwise. The great goal of politics should be *permanence,* which outweighs anything else, being much more valuable than freedom." Only when permanence is securely established and guaranteed is there any possibility of constant development and ennobling inoculation, which, to be sure, will usually be opposed by the dangerous companion of all permanence: authority.

## 225

*The free spirit*[3] *a relative concept.* A man is called a free spirit if he thinks otherwise than would be expected, based on his origin, environment, class, and position, or based on prevailing contemporary views. He is the exception: bound spirits are the rule; the latter reproach him that his free principles have their origin either in a need to be noticed, or else may even lead one to suspect him

1. Darwin's *Origin of Species* (1859).
2. Niccolò Machiavelli (1469–1527).
3. *Freigeist.* See Introduction.

of free actions, that is, actions that are irreconcilable with bound morality. Sometimes it is also said that certain free principles derive from perverseness and eccentricity; but this is only the voice of malice, which does not, itself, believe what it says, but only wants to hurt: for the free spirit generally has proof of his greater kindness and sharp intellect written so legibly on his face that bound spirits understand it well enough. But the two other derivations of free-thinking are meant honestly; and many free spirits do indeed come into being in one or the other of these ways. But the tenets they arrive at thereby could still be more true and reliable than the tenets of bound spirits. In the knowledge of truth, what matters is *having* it, not what made one seek it, or how one found it. If the free spirits are right, the bound spirits are wrong, whether or not the former came to truth out of immorality and the others have kept clinging to untruth out of morality.

Incidentally, it is not part of the nature of the free spirit that his views are more correct, but rather that he has released himself from tradition, be it successfully or unsuccessfully. Usually, however, he has truth, or at least the spirit of the search for truth, on his side: he demands reasons, while others demand faith.

## 226

*Origin of faith.* The bound spirit assumes a position, not for reasons, but out of habit; he is a Christian, for example, not because he had insight into the various religions and chose among them; he is an Englishman not because he decided for England; but rather, Christianity and England were givens, and he accepted them without having reasons, as someone who was born in wine country becomes a wine drinker. Later, when he was a Christian and an Englishman, he may also have devised some reasons in favor of his habit; even if these reasons are overthrown, he, in his whole position, is not. Ask a bound spirit for his reasons against bigamy, for example, and you will learn whether his holy zeal for monogamy is based on reasons or on habit. The habit of intellectual principles without reasons is called faith.

## 227

*Reason or unreason deduced from the consequences.* All states and social arrangements—class, marriage, education, law—acquire strength and permanence solely because of the faith of bound spirits in them; they exist, then, in the absence of reasons, or at least in the resistance to asking for reasons. That is something bound spirits do not want to admit, and they probably feel that it is a *pudendum*.[4] Christianity, which was very innocent in its intellectual ideas, perceived nothing of this *pudendum;* it demanded faith and nothing but faith, and passionately rejected the desire for reasons; it pointed to the successful result of faith: "You'll soon discover the advantage of faith," it suggested, "you'll be blessed because of it." The state, in fact, does the same thing, and each father raises his son in the same way: "Just take this to be true," he says, "you'll discover how good it feels." But this means that the *truth* of an opinion should be proved by its personal *benefit;* the usefulness of a teaching should guarantee its intellectual certainty and substantiation. This is as if the defendant were to say in court: "My defender is telling the whole truth, for just see what happens as a result of his plea: I am acquitted."

Because bound spirits hold principles for the sake of their usefulness, they also assume that the free spirit is likewise seeking his benefit with his views, holding for true only that which benefits him. But since he seems to find useful the opposite of what his countrymen or people of his class do, they assume that his principles are dangerous to them; they say or feel, "He must not be right, for he is harmful to us."

## 228

*The strong, good character.* Bound views, when habit has made them instinctive, lead to what is called strength of character. If someone acts from a few motives which are always the same, his actions take on great energy; if these actions are in harmony with the principles of bound spirits, they are acknowledged, and also produce in the one performing them the feeling of a good conscience. Few motives, energetic action, and a good conscience constitute what is called strength of character. The man of strong character lacks knowledge of the many possibilities and directions of action: his intellect is unfree, bound, because it shows him in any given case perhaps only two possibilities; between these he must necessarily choose, in accordance with his whole nature, and he does so easily and quickly because he doesn't have to choose

4. source of shame

among fifty possibilities. The educating environment wants to make each man unfree by always presenting him with the smallest number of possibilities. His educators treat the individual as if he were something new, to be sure, but as if he ought to become a *repetition*. If man first appears to be something unknown, never before existing, he should be made into something known, preexisting. What is called good character in a child is the manifestation of its being bound by the preexisting. By placing itself on the side of bound spirits, the child first demonstrates its awakening public spirit. On the basis of this public spirit, it will later be useful to its state or class.

### 229

*Bound spirit's measure of things.* Bound spirits say that four sorts of things are in the right: first, all things having permanence are in the right; second, all things that are no burden to us are in the right; third, all things that benefit us are in the right; fourth, all things for which we have made sacrifices are in the right. The last explains, for example, why, just as soon as sacrifices are made, people continue with enthusiasm a war that was begun against their wishes.

Free spirits, pleading their cause before the tribunal of bound spirits, have to prove that there have always been free spirits and that freethinking therefore has permanence; then, that they do not want to be a burden; and finally, that on the whole they are beneficial to bound spirits. But because they cannot convince the bound spirits of this last point, it does not help them to have proved the first and second.

### 230

*Esprit fort.*[5] Compared with the man who has tradition on his side and needs no reasons for his actions, the free spirit is always weak, especially in his actions. For he knows too many motives and standpoints, and is therefore uncertain, awkward. By what means, then, can he be made *relatively strong,* so that he can at least assert himself effectively and not perish, having acted ineffectually? How does a strong spirit (*esprit fort*) come into being? In

5. *Esprit fort:* strong spirit, synonymous with "free spirit" or "free thinker," used originally by La Bruyère, in the last section of his *Caractères* (1688).

one particular case, this is the question of how the genius is engendered. Where does the energy come from, the unbending strength, the endurance, with which one person, against all tradition, endeavors to acquire a quite individual understanding of the world?

## 231

*Genesis of the genius.* The prisoner's wits, which he uses to seek means to free himself by employing each little advantage in the most calculated and exhaustive way, can teach us the tools nature sometimes uses to produce a genius (a word that I ask be understood without any mythological or religious nuance). Nature traps the genius into a prison, and piques to the utmost his desire to free himself.

Or, to use another image, someone who has completely lost his way in a forest, but strives with uncommon energy to get out of it in whatever direction, sometimes discovers a new, unknown way: this is how geniuses come into being, who are then praised for their originality.

We have already mentioned that mutilation, crippling, or serious lack of an organ often causes another organ to develop unusually well because it has to carry out both its own function and another besides. From this we can divine the origin of many a splendid talent.

One should apply these general comments about the origin of the genius to the special case, the genesis of the perfect free spirit.

## 232

*Conjectures about the origin of freethinking.*[6] Just as glaciers increase when the sun burns down on the seas in equatorial zones with greater heat than before, so a very strong and spreading freethinking may testify to the fact that somewhere emotional heat has extraordinarily increased.

## 233

*The voice of history.* In general history *seems* to teach the following lesson about the engendering of the genius: "Mistreat and torment men," history calls to the passions Envy, Hatred, and

6. *Freigeisterei*

Competition, "drive them to extremes; pit them one against the other, people against people, and this for centuries; then perhaps, as from a stray spark of the terrible energy thus ignited, the light of genius will blaze up suddenly. The will, driven wild like a stallion spurred by its rider, will break out and leap over to a different spot."

A man who was aware of how geniuses are engendered and also wanted to proceed practically, as nature usually does, would have to be just as evil and inconsiderate as nature.

But perhaps we have heard wrong.

### 234

*Value of the middle of the path.* Perhaps the engendering of genius is reserved to only a limited period of humanity. For one cannot expect the future of humanity to hold at the same time everything that only very particular conditions in some past time could produce—the amazing effects of religious feeling, for example. This has had its time, and many very good things can never grow again because they could grow from it alone. Thus there will never again be a religiously defined horizon to life and culture. Perhaps even the type of the saint is possible only along with a certain intellectual narrowness, which is apparently gone forever. And so, perhaps, has the highest level of intelligence been reserved for one single era of humanity; it came forth (and is coming forth, for we still live in this era) when, by way of exception, an extraordinary, long-accumulated energy of the will was diverted through inheritance to *intellectual* goals. This highest level will end when such wildness and energy are no longer cultivated. Perhaps mankind, in the middle of its path, the middle period of its existence, is nearer to its actual goal than it will be at the end. The energies that condition art, for example, could very well die out; pleasure in lying, in vagueness, in symbolism, in intoxication, in ecstasy, could come into disrepute. Indeed, once life is structured in a perfect state, then the present will no longer offer any theme for poetry whatsoever, and only backward people would still demand poetic unreality. They would then look back longingly to the times of the imperfect state, the half-barbaric society, to *our* times.

## 235

*Genius and ideal state in contradiction.* Socialists desire to produce a good life for the greatest number. If the enduring homeland of this good life, the perfect state, were really achieved, it would destroy the earth from which a man of great intellect, or any powerful individual grows: I mean great energy. When this state is achieved, mankind would have become too feeble to produce genius any longer. Should we not therefore wish that life retain its violent character, and that wild strengths and energies be called forth over and over again? Now, a warm, sympathetic heart desires precisely the *elimination* of that violent and wild character, and the warmest heart one can imagine would yearn for it most passionately; though this same passion would have had its fire, its warmth, even its existence from that wild and violent character of life. The warmest heart, then, desires the elimination of its rationale and its own destruction; that is, it wants something illogical; it is not intelligent. The highest intelligence and the warmest heart cannot coexist in one person, and a wise man who passes judgment on life also places himself above kindness, considering it only as something to be evaluated along with everything else in the sum of life. The wise man must oppose the extravagant wishes of unintelligent kindness, because he cares about the survival of his type, and the eventual genesis of the highest intellect. At least he will not further the establishment of the "perfect state," if there is room there only for feeble individuals. Christ, on the other hand, whom we like to imagine as having the warmest of hearts, furthered men's stupidity, took the side of the intellectually weak, and kept the greatest intellect from being produced: and this was consistent. We can predict that his opposite, the absolute wise man, will just as necessarily prevent the production of a Christ.

The state is a clever institution for protecting individuals from one another; if one goes too far in ennobling it, the individual is ultimately weakened by it, even dissolved—and thus the original purpose of the state is most thoroughly thwarted.

## 236

*The zones of culture.* For the sake of comparison, one can say that cultural eras correspond to various climactic belts, only that the former follow one another and do not, like the geographical zones, lie next to one another. In comparison with the temperate cultural zone, which it is our duty to enter, the past gives, on the whole, the impression of a *tropical* climate. Violent contrasts; abrupt alternation of day and night; heat and magnificent colors; reverence for everything sudden, mysterious, frightful; rapid onset of oncoming storms; everywhere the wasteful overflowing of nature's horns of plenty; and on the other hand, in our culture, a light, though not brilliant sky; pure, rather unchanging air; briskness, even cold occasionally: thus the two zones contrast with one another. When we see how the most raging passions are overcome and broken with uncanny power by metaphysical ideas, we feel as if wild tigers in the tropics were being crushed before our eyes in the coils of monstrous snakes. Such things do not happen in our spiritual climate; our fantasy is temperate; even in dreams, we do not experience what earlier peoples saw when awake. But may we not be happy about this change, even admitting that artists are seriously impaired by the disappearance of tropical culture and find us nonartists a bit too sober? To this extent, artists are probably right in denying "progress," for it can indeed at least be doubted that the last three thousand years show a course of progress in the arts; likewise, a metaphysical philosopher like Schopenhauer will have no cause to acknowledge progress, if he surveys the last four thousand years with reference to metaphysical philosophy and religion.

But for us, the very *existence* of the temperate cultural zone counts as progress.

## 237

*Renaissance and Reformation.* The Italian Renaissance contained within itself all the positive forces to which we owe modern culture: namely, liberation of thought, disdain for authority, the triumph of education over the arrogance of lineage, enthusiasm for science and men's scientific past, the unshackling of the individual, an ardor for veracity and aversion to appearance and mere effect (which ardor blazed forth in a whole abundance of artistic natures who, with the highest moral purity, demanded perfection in their works and nothing but perfection). Yes, the Renaissance had positive forces which *up to now* have not yet again become so powerful in our modern culture. Despite all its flaws and vices, it was the Golden Age of this millennium. By contrast, the German Reformation stands out as an energetic protest of backward minds who had not yet had their fill of the medieval world view and perceived the signs of its dissolution—the extraordinary shallowness and externalization of religious life—not with appropriate rejoicing, but with deep displeasure. With their northern strength and obstinacy, they set men back, forced the Counter-Reformation, that is, a defensive Catholic Christianity, with the violence of a state of siege, delaying the complete awakening and rule of the sciences for two or three centuries, as well as making impossible, perhaps forever, the complete fusion of the ancient and modern spirit. The great task of the Renaissance could not be carried to its completion; this was hindered by the protest of the now backward German character (which in the Middle Ages had had enough sense to redeem itself by climbing over the Alps again and again). The fact that Luther survived at that time, and that his protest gathered strength, lay in the coincidence of an extraordinary political configuration: the Emperor protected him in order to use his innovation to apply pressure against the Pope, and likewise the Pope secretly favored him, in order to use the imperial Protestant princes as a counterweight against the Emperor. Without this strange concert of intent, Luther would have been burned like Huss[7]—and the dawn of the Enlightenment would have risen a bit earlier, perhaps, and with a splendor more beautiful than we can now imagine.

## 238

*Justice towards the evolving God.* If the whole history of culture looks like a confusion of ideas, evil and noble, true and false, and one gets almost seasick at the sight of these waves, then one understands what comfort lies in the idea of an *evolving God;* he reveals himself more and more in the metamorphoses and destinies of mankind; all is not blind mechanism, senseless, purposeless interplay of forces. The deification of evolution is a metaphysical outlook—as from a lighthouse along the sea of history—which gave comfort to a generation of scholars who had historicized too much. One must not become angry about it, however erroneous their idea may be. Only someone who, like Schopen-

7. John Huss (1369?–1415), Bohemian religious reformer and martyr.

hauer, denies development also feels nothing of the misery of those historical waves; and because he neither knows nor feels anything of that evolving God or the need to accept him, he can fairly let out his scorn.

## 239

*Fruits according to the season.* Every better future that one wishes for mankind is also necessarily a worse future in some respects, for it is fanatical to believe that a new, higher stage of mankind would unite all the merits of earlier stages and would, for example, also have to produce the highest form of art. Rather, each season has its own merits and charms, and excludes those of the other seasons. Whatever has grown out of religion, and near it, cannot grow again, once religion has been destroyed. At the most, late stray shoots can mislead us to delusions about it, as does the intermittent memory of the old art; a condition that may well betray the feeling of loss and privation, but is no proof of any force from which a new art could be born.

## 240

*The world's increasing gravity.* The higher the culture of a man rises, the greater the number of topics are removed from joking or mockery. Voltaire was heartily grateful to heaven for inventing marriage and the church, for taking such good care for our merriment. But he and his time, and the sixteenth century before him, mocked these topics to their limit; any joke about them today comes too late and especially much too cheap to tempt buyers. Now we inquire after causes; this is the age of seriousness. Who still cares to see the lighter side of the differences between reality and pretentious appearance, between that which man is and that which he wants to present? We feel these contrasts very differently when we seek their reasons. The more thoroughly a person understands life, the less he will mock, though in the end he might still mock the "thoroughness of his understanding."

## 241

*Genius of culture.* If one were to dream up a genius of culture, what would be his nature? He uses lies, power, the most inconsiderate self-interest so confidently as his tools that he could only be called an evil, demonic creature; but his goals, which shine through here and there, are great and good. He is a centaur, half animal, half human, and even has angel's wings at his head.

## 242

*Education as a miracle.* Interest in education will gain great strength only at the moment when belief in a God and his loving care is given up, just as the art of healing could blossom only when belief in miraculous cures had ceased. But to date, all the world still believes in education as a miracle: one saw the most productive, mightiest men grow out of great disorder, confused goals, unfavorable circumstances: how could this properly happen?

Now we will look more closely, test more carefully, in these cases, too. No one will ever discover miracles. Under equal condition, many men continually perish, but in return, the single saved individual is usually the stronger, because he endured these unfavorable circumstances thanks to his indestructible innate strength, which he developed and augmented: this explains the miracle. An education that no longer believes in miracles will have to pay attention to three things: first, how much energy is inherited? Second, how can other new energy still be kindled? Third, how can the individual be adapted to those very diverse demands of culture, without their disturbing him and dissipating his uniqueness? In short, how can the individual be integrated into the counterpoint of private and public culture; how can he both sing the melody and simultaneously make it the accompaniment?

## 243

*The future of the doctor.* There is no profession today that would permit such high aspirations as that of the doctor, particularly since spiritual doctors, the so-called spiritual advisers, may no longer practice their conjuring arts to public applause, and a cultured man avoids them. A doctor's highest intellectual development is no longer reached when he knows the best new methods, and is well practiced in them, able to make those swift deductions from effects to causes, for which diagnosticians are famed; he must in addition have an eloquence adaptable to each individual and capable of drawing the heart out of his body; a masculinity at whose sight even despondency (the worm-eaten spot in all ill people) is dispelled; a diplomat's smoothness in mediating between those who need joy for their cure and those who must (and can) create joy for reasons of health; the subtlety of a police agent or lawyer in understanding the secrets of a soul without betraying them—in short, a good doctor today needs all the tricks and privileges of all the other professions; thus armed, he is then in a position to become a benefactor to all of society, by increasing good works, spiritual joy and productivity; by warding off bad thoughts or intentions, and villainy (whose repulsive source is so often the belly); by producing a spiritual-physical aristocracy (as marriage broker and marriage censor); by well-meaning amputation of all so-called spiritual torments and pangs of conscience. Thus from a "medicine man" he will become a savior, and yet need neither to work miracles nor to be crucified.

### 244

*In the neighborhood of madness.* The sum of feelings, knowledge, experiences, that is, the whole burden of culture, has grown so great that the general danger is an overstimulation of nervous and mental powers; the cultivated classes of European countries are altogether neurotic, and almost every one of their great families has, in one of its branches, moved close to madness. It is true that we can now approach health in all kinds of ways, but in the main we still need a decrease of emotional tension, of the oppressive cultural burden, a decrease that, even if it must be bought with serious losses, does give us room for the great hope of a *new Renaissance.* We owe to Christianity, to the philosophers, poets, and musicians, a superabundance of deeply agitated feelings; to keep these from engulfing us, we must conjure up the spirit of science, which makes us somewhat colder and more skeptical, on the whole, and cools down particularly the hot flow of belief in ultimate truths, which Christianity, especially, has made so wild.

### 245

*Casting the bell of culture.* Culture came into being like a bell inside a mold of cruder, more common material, a mold of untruth, violence, an unbounded aggrandizement of all distinct egos, and all distinct peoples. Is it now time to remove this mold? Has the fluid solidified? Have the good, useful drives, the habits of nobler hearts, become so sure and universal that there is no longer any need to depend on metaphysics and the errors of re-

ligion, on harsh and violent acts, as the most powerful bond between man and man, people and people?

No sign from a god can help us any longer to answer this question: our own insight must decide. The earthly government of
man as a whole must be taken into man's own hands; his "omnis-
cience" must watch with a sharp eye over the future fate of culture.

## 246

*The Cyclopses of culture.* Seeing the furrowed hollows in which
glaciers have lain, one hardly thinks it possible that a time will
come when a valley of meadows, forests, and brooks will move
onto the same spot. It is the same in the history of mankind: the
wildest forces break the way, destroying at first, but yet their activity was necessary, so that later a gentler civilization might set
up its house there. Frightful energies—that which is called evil—
are the Cyclopean architects and pathmakers of humanity.

## 247

*Cycle of the human race.* Perhaps the whole human race is only
a temporally limited, developmental phase of a certain species of
animal, so that man evolved from the ape and will evolve back to
the ape again, while no one will be there to take any interest in
this strange end of the comedy. Just as with the fall of Roman
culture, and its most important cause, the spread of Christianity,
there was a general increase of loathsomeness in man within the
Roman empire, so the eventual fall of the general world culture
might also cause men to be much more loathsome and finally ani-
malistic, to the point of being apelike.

Precisely because we are able to keep this perspective in mind,
we may be in a position to protect the future from such an end.

## 248

*Consolation of a desperate progress.* Our age gives the impression of being an interim; the old views on life, the old cultures are
still evident in part, the new ones not yet sure and habitual, and
therefore lacking in unity and consistency. It looks as if everything were becoming chaotic, the old dying out, the new not
worth much and growing ever weaker. But this is what happens
to the soldier who learns to march; for a time he is more uncertain

and clumsy than ever because his muscles move, now to the old system, now to the new, and neither has yet decisively claimed the victory. We waver, but we must not become anxious about it, or surrender what has been newly won. Besides, we *cannot* go back to the old system; we *have* burned our bridges behind us. All that remains is to be brave, whatever may result.

*Let us* step forward, let's get going! Perhaps our behavior will indeed look like *progress;* but if it does not, may we take consolation in the words of Frederick the Great: "Ah, mon cher Sulzer, vous ne connaissez pas assez cette race maudite, à laquelle nous appartenons."[8]

### 249

*Suffering from culture's past.* Whoever has clearly understood the problem of culture suffers from a feeling similar to that of a man who has inherited riches that were acquired through illegal means, or a prince who rules because of his forefathers' atrocities. He thinks of his origin with sadness, and is often ashamed, often irritable. The whole sum of the strength, will to life, and joy that he expends on his estate is often balanced by a deep weariness: he cannot forget his origin. He regards the future with melancholy: he knows in advance that his descendants will suffer from the past as he does.

### 250

*Manners.* Good manners disappear proportionately as the influence of the court and a self-contained aristocracy declines. This decrease can be observed clearly from decade to decade, if one has an eye for public events, which visibly become more and more vulgar. No one today understands how to pay homage or flatter with wit; this leads to the ludicrous fact that in cases where one *must* do homage (to a great statesman or artist, for example), one borrows the language of deepest feeling, of loyal and honorable decency—out of embarrassment and a lack of wit and grace. So men's public, ceremonious encounters seem ever more clumsy, but more tender and honorable, without being so.

But will manners keep going downhill? I think, rather, that

8. "My dear Sulzer, you know too little this accursed race to which we belong."

manners are going in a deep curve, and that we are nearing its low point. Now we inherit manners shaped by earlier conditions, and they are passed on and learned ever less thoroughly. But once society has become more certain of its intentions and principles, these will have a shaping effect, and there will be social manners, gestures, and expressions that must appear as necessary and simply natural as these intentions and principles are. Better division of time and labor; gymnastic exercise become the companion of every pleasant leisure hour; increased and more rigorous contemplation, which gives cleverness and suppleness even to the body—all this will come with it.

As this point one might, of course, think, somewhat scornfully, of our scholars: do they, who claim to be antecedents of the new culture, distinguish themselves by superior manners? Such is not the case, though their spirit may be willing enough: their flesh is weak.[9] The past is still too strong in their muscles; they still stand in an unfree position, half secular clergymen, half the dependent educators of the upper classes; in addition, the pedantry of science and out-of-date, mindless methods have made them crippled and lifeless. Thus they are, bodily at least, and often three-quarters spiritually, too, still courtiers of an old, even senile culture, and, as such, senile themselves; the new spirit, which occasionally rumbles about in these old shells, serves for the meanwhile only to make them more uncertain and anxious. They are haunted by ghosts of the past, as well as ghosts of the future; no wonder that they neither look their best, nor act in the most obliging way.

### 251

*Future of science.* To the man who works and searches in it, science gives much pleasure; to the man who *learns* its results, very little. But since all important scientific truths must eventually become everyday and commonplace, even this small amount of pleasure ceases; just as we have long ago ceased to enjoy learning the admirable multiplication tables. Now, if science produces ever less joy in itself and takes ever greater joy in casting suspicion on the comforts of metaphysics, religion, and art, then the greatest source of pleasure, to which mankind owes almost its whole humanity, is impoverished. Therefore a higher culture must give

9. Matthew 26:41.

man a double brain, two brain chambers, as it were, one to experience science, and one to experience nonscience. Lying next to one another, without confusion, separable, self-contained: our health demands this. In the one domain lies the source of strength, in the other the regulator. Illusions, biases, passions must give heat; with the help of scientific knowledge, the pernicious and dangerous consequences of overheating must be prevented.

If this demand made by higher culture is not satisfied, we can almost certainly predict the further course of human development: interest in truth will cease, the less it gives pleasure; illusion, error, and fantasies, because they are linked with pleasure, will reconquer their former territory step by step; the ruin of the sciences and relapse into barbarism follow next. Mankind will have to begin to weave its cloth from the beginning again, after having, like Penelope, destroyed it in the night. But who will guarantee that we will keep finding the strength to do so?

## 252

*Pleasure in knowing.* Why is knowledge, the element of researchers and philosophers, linked to pleasure? First and foremost, because by it we gain awareness of our power—the same reason that gymnastic exercises are pleasurable even without spectators. Second, because, as we gain knowledge, we surpass older ideas and their representatives, become victors, or at least believe ourselves to be. Third, because any new knowledge, however small, makes us feel superior to *everyone* and unique in understanding this matter correctly. These three reasons for pleasure are the most important, but depending on the nature of the knower, there are still many secondary reasons.

At one unlikely place, my expostulation about Schopenhauer[10] gives a not inconsiderable catalogue of these reasons, a tabulation to satisfy every experienced servant of knowledge, even if he would want to wish away the hint of irony that seems to lie on the pages. For if it is true that "a number of very human drives and urges have to be mixed together" for a scholar to come into being, that he is, to be sure, of a very noble metal, but not a pure one, and "consists of a complicated weave of very different impulses

10. "Schopenhauer as Educator" (1874), the third of Nietzsche's *Untimely Meditations*.

and stimulations," then the same is also true of the origin and nature of the artist, philosopher, or moral genius—and whatever glorified great names there are in that essay. With regard to *origin, everything* human deserves ironic reflection: that is why there is such an *excess* of irony in the world.

### 253

*Fidelity as proof of soundness.* It is a perfect sign that a theory is good if, for *forty* years, its creator never comes to distrust it; but I contend that there has never been a philosopher who did not finally look down on the philosophy he invented in his youth with disdain, or at least suspicion.

But perhaps he did not speak about his change of mind publicly, for reasons of ambition or (as is more probable in nobler natures) out of sensitive consideration for his adherents.

### 254

*Increase of what is interesting.* In the course of a man's higher education, everything becomes interesting; he knows how to find the instructive side of a matter quickly, and to indicate the point where it can fill up a hole in his thinking, or confirm an idea. In the process, boredom vanishes more and more, as does excessive emotional excitability. Ultimately, he goes among men like a natural scientist among plants, and perceives his own self simply as a phenomenon that intensely stimulates his drive for knowledge.

### 255

*Superstition in simultaneity.*[11] Simultaneous things are thought to be connected. Our relative dies far away, at the same time we dream about him—there you are! But countless relatives die without our dreaming about them. It is as with shipwrecked people who make vows: later, in the temple, one does not see the votive tablets of those who perished.

A man dies; an owl screeches; a clock stops; all in one nocturnal hour: shouldn't there be a connection there? This idea presumes a kind of intimacy with nature that flatters man.

Such superstition is found again in refined form in historians and painters of culture. They tend to have a kind of hydrophobia

11. Cf. Schopenhauer's essay "On the Apparent Design in the Fate of the Individual."

towards all senseless juxtapositions, even though these are so abundant in the life of individuals, and of peoples.

## 256

*Ability, not knowledge, cultivated through science.* The value of having for a time rigorously pursued a *rigorous science* does not rest especially in its results: for in relation to the sea of worthy knowledge, these will be but a negligible little drop. But it brings forth an increase of energy, of deductive ability, of persistence; one has learned to gain one's *purpose purposefully.* To this extent, in respect to all one does later, it is very valuable to have once been a scientific man.

## 257

*Youthful charm of science.* The search for truth still has the charm of always contrasting strongly with gray and boring Error; this charm is progressively disappearing. It is true that we still live in the youth of science, and tend to pursue truth like a pretty girl; but what will happen when she has one day turned into an elderly, scowling woman? In almost all the sciences, the basic insight has either just been found or else is still being sought; how different is this appeal from the appeal when everything essential has been found and all that is left for the researcher is a scanty autumn gleaning (a feeling one can come to know in certain historical disciplines).

## 258

*The statue of humanity.* The cultural genius acts like Cellini,[12] when he made the cast of his statue of Perseus: the fluid mass threatened not to suffice, but it *had* to; so he threw in bowls and dishes and whatever else came into his hands. And in just the same way does the cultural genius throw in errors, vices, hopes, delusions, and other things of baser as well as nobler metal, for the statue of humanity must emerge and be finished. What does it matter if, here and there, an inferior material was used?

## 259

*A male culture.* Greek culture of the Classical era is a male culture. As for women, Pericles, in his funeral oration, says every-

---

12. Benvenuto Cellini (1500–71), Italian sculptor.

thing with the words: "They are best when men speak about them as little as possible."[13]

The erotic relationship of men to youths was, on a level which we cannot grasp, the necessary, sole prerequisite of all male education (more or less in the way love affairs and marriage were for a long time the only way to bring about the higher education of women); the whole idealism of strength of the Greek character was thrown into that relationship, and the treatment of young people has probably never again been so aware, loving, so thoroughly geared to their excellence (*virtus*), as it was in the sixth and fifth centuries—in accordance with Hölderlin's beautiful line, "denn liebend giebt der Sterbliche vom Besten" (for loving the mortal gives of his best).[14] The more important this relationship was considered, the lower sank interaction with women: the perspective of procreation and lust—nothing further came into consideration; there was no spiritual intercourse with them, not even a real romance. If one considers further that woman herself was excluded from all kinds of competitions and spectacles, then the sole higher entertainment remaining to her was religious worship.

To be sure, when Electra and Antigone were portrayed in tragedies, the Greeks *tolerated* it in art, although they did not like it in life; just as we now do not tolerate anything with pathos in *life,* but like to see it in art.

Women had no task other than to produce beautiful, powerful bodies, in which the character of the father lived on as intact as possible, and thus to counteract the increasing overstimulation of nerves in such a highly developed culture. This kept Greek culture young for such a relatively long time. For in Greek mothers, the Greek genius returned again and again to nature.

## 260

*Prejudice in favor of size.* Men clearly overestimate everything large and obtrusive. This comes from their conscious or unconscious insight that it is very useful if someone throws all his

13. "That woman is most praiseworthy whose name is least bandied about on men's lips, whether for praise or dispraise," Thucydides, 1.2.35:46. The funeral oration celebrates the Athenians who had fallen in the Peloponnesian War (431 B.C.).

14. *Der Tod des Empedokles,* first version, act 2, sc. 4.

strength into one area, and makes of himself, so to speak, one monstrous organ. Surely, for man himself, a *uniform* cultivation of his strengths is more useful and beneficial, for every talent is a vampire that sucks blood and strength out of the remaining strengths; and excessive productivity can bring the most gifted man almost to madness. Even within the arts, extreme natures attract notice much too much, but a much lesser culture is also necessary to let itself be captivated by them. Men submit from habit to anything that wants to have power.

## 261

*Tyrants of the spirit.* The life of the Greeks shines bright only when the ray of myth falls on it; otherwise it is gloomy. Now, the Greek philosophers rob themselves of precisely this mythology; is it not as if they wanted to move out of the sunlight into the shadow, the gloom? But no plant wants to avoid light: actually, those philosophers were only seeking a *brighter* sun; mythology was not pure or shining enough for them. They found the light they sought in their knowledge, in what each of them called his "truth." But knowledge shone ever brighter at that time; it was still young, and still knew too little of all the difficulties and dangers of its ways; it could still hope to reach the midpoint of all being with a single bound, and from there solve the riddle of the world. These philosophers had a firm belief in themselves and in their "truth," and with it they overcame all their neighbors and predecessors; each of them was a combative and violent *tyrant.* Perhaps the happiness of believing oneself in possession of the truth was never greater in the world, but neither was the harshness, arrogance, tyranny, and evil of such a belief. They were tyrants, which is what every Greek wanted to be, and which each one was, if he was *able.* Perhaps only Solon[15] is an exception: in his poetry he tells how he despised personal tyranny. But he did it out of love for his work, for his lawgiving; and to be a lawgiver is a sublimated form of tyranny. Parmenides, too, gave laws, probably Pythagoras and Empedocles as well; Anaximander founded a city. Plato was the incarnate wish to become the greatest philosophical lawgiver and founding father of a state; he seems to have suffered terribly that his nature was not fulfilled, and towards the

---

15. Solon, Greek lawgiver (640–560 B.C.).

end, his soul became full of the blackest bile. The more Greek philosophy lost power, the more it suffered inwardly because of this bile and need to slander. When various sects finally fought for their truths in the streets, the souls of all these suitors of truth were completely clogged with jealousy and venom;[16] the tyrannic element raged like a poison in their bodies. These many petty tyrants would have liked to devour one another raw; there was not a spark of love left in them, and all too little joy in their own knowledge.

The tenet that tyrants are usually murdered and that their descendants live briefly is also generally true of the tyrants of the spirit. Their history is short, violent; their influence breaks off suddenly. One can say of almost all great Hellenes that they seem to have come too late, thus Aeschylus, Pindar, Demosthenes, Thucydides; one generation follows them—and then it is always over forever. That is the turbulent and uncanny thing about Greek history. These days, of course, we admire the gospel of the tortoise. To think historically these days almost means to imply that history was always made according to the principle, "As little as possible in the longest time possible!" Alas, Greek history goes so quickly! Never has life been lived so prodigally, so immoderately. I cannot convince myself that the history of the Greeks took that *natural* course for which it is so famous. They were much too diversely gifted to be *gradual* in a step-by-step manner, like the tortoise racing with Achilles,[17] and that is what is called natural development. With the Greeks, things go forward swiftly, but also as swiftly downwards; the movement of the whole mechanism is so intensified that a single stone, thrown into its wheels, makes it burst. Such a stone was Socrates, for example; in one night, the development of philosophical science, until then so wonderfully regular but, of course, all too swift, was destroyed.[18] It is no idle question to wonder whether Plato, if he had stayed free of the Socratic spell, might not have found an even higher type of the philosophical man, now lost to us forever. We look into the ages before him as into a sculptor's workshop, full of such

16. *Eifer-und Geifersucht*

17. In *The Achilles,* Zeno (c. 490 B.C.) recounts the paradox of Achilles' race with a tortoise, cited in Aristotle's *Physics* 239b 15–18 and in Plato's *Parmenides* 128c.

18. Cf. *The Birth of Tragedy,* secs. 13–15, especially.

types. The sixth and fifth centuries, however, seem to promise even more and greater things than they produced; but it remained at promises and declarations. And yet there is hardly a heavier loss than the loss of a type, the loss of a new, previously undiscovered, supreme *possibility of philosophical life*. Even of the older types, most have been handed down to us inadequately; it seems to me extraordinarily difficult to see any philosopher from Thales to Democritus[19] clearly; but the man who is successful in recreating these figures strolls among creatures of the mightiest and purest type. Of course, this ability is rare; even the later Greeks who studied the older philosophers did not have it. Aristotle, particularly, seems not to have his eyes in his head when he is faced with them. And so it seems as if these marvelous philosophers had lived in vain, or even as if they had only been meant to prepare the way for the combative and garrulous hordes of the Socratic schools. As we said, there is a gap here, a break in development; some great misfortune must have occurred, and the sole statue in which we might have recognized the sense and purpose of that great creative preparatory exercise must have broken or been unsuccessful. What actually happened has remained forever a secret of the workshop.

What took place with the Greeks (that each great thinker, believing he possessed absolute truth, became a tyrant, so that Greek intellectual history has had the violent, rash, and dangerous character evident in its political history) was not exhausted with them. Many similar things have come to pass right up to the most recent times, although gradually less often, and hardly any longer with the Greek philosophers' pure, naive conscience. For the opposite doctrine and skepticism have, on the whole, too powerful and loud a voice. The period of the spiritual tyrants is over. In the domain of higher culture there will of course always have to be an authority, but from now on this authority lies in the hands of the *oligarchs of the spirit*. Despite all spatial and political separation, they form a coherent society, whose members *recognize* and *acknowledge* each other, whatever

19. For more about Nietzsche and the pre-Socratic philosophers, see Nietzsche's *Philosophy in the Tragic Age of the Greeks,* Marianne Cowan, trans. (Chicago: Gateway, 1962). For more about Nietzsche and Socrates, see Werner J. Dannhauser, *Nietzsche's View of Socrates* (Ithaca, N.Y.: Cornell University Press, 1974).

favorable or unfavorable estimations may circulate due to public opinion and the judgments of the newspaper and magazine writers. The spiritual superiority which formerly caused division and enmity now tends to *bind:* how could individuals assert themselves and swim through life along their own way, against all currents, if they did not see their like living here and there under the same circumstances and grasp their hands in the struggle as much against the ochlocratic nature of superficial minds and superficial culture as against the occasional attempts to set up a tyranny with the help of mass manipulation? Oligarchs need each other; they are their own best friends; they understand their insignias—but nevertheless each of them is free; he fights and conquers on *his* ground, and would rather perish than submit.

## 262

*Homer.* Even now, the greatest fact about Greek culture is that Homer became Panhellenic so soon. All the spiritual and human freedom the Greeks attained goes back to this fact. But at the same time it was also the actual doom of Greek culture, for, by centralizing, Homer made shallow and dissolved the more serious instincts of independence. From time to time an opposition to Homer arose from the depths of Hellenic feeling; but he always triumphed. All great spiritual powers exercise a suppressing effect in addition to their liberating one; but of course it makes a difference whether it is Homer or the Bible or science tyrannizing men.

## 263

*Talent.* In such a highly developed humanity as the present one, each man by nature has access to many talents. Each has *inborn talent,* but only a few have inherited and cultivated such a degree of toughness, endurance, and energy that they really become a talent, *become* what they *are*[20]—that is, release it in works and actions.

## 264

*The witty man*[21] *either overestimated or underestimated.* Unscientific, but gifted men esteem any sign of wit,[22] whether it is

20. One of Nietzsche's favorite citations from Pindar.
21. *der Geistreiche*
22. *Geist*

on the right or the wrong track. Above all, they want the man who goes about with them to entertain them well with his wit, spur them on, ignite them, move them to seriousness and levity, and, in any case, protect them from boredom like a most powerful amulet. A scientific nature, on the other hand, knows that the gift of having all kinds of ideas must be reined in most severely by the scientific spirit; not what glitters, shines, and excites, but rather the often plain truth is the fruit he wishes to shake off the Tree of Knowledge. Like Aristotle, he may make no distinction between "boring" and "witty" men; his daemon takes him through the desert as well as through tropical vegetation, so that wherever he goes he will take pleasure only in what is real, tenable, genuine.

In insignificant scholars, this results in a distrust and suspicion of all things witty; and conversely, witty people often have a distaste for science, as do, for example, almost all artists.

## 265

*Reason in school.* Schooling has no more important task than to teach rigorous thinking, careful judgment, logical conclusions; that is why it must refrain from every thing which is not suitable for these operations—religion, for example. It can count on the fact that later, human opacity, habit, and need will again slacken the bow of all-too-taut thinking. But as long as its influence lasts, schooling should force into being what is essential and distinguishing in man: "Reason and science, the *supreme* strength of man," in Goethe's judgment, at least.[23]

The great natural scientist von Baer[24] finds all Europeans' superiority, compared to Asians, in their learned ability to give reasons for what they believe, which Asians are wholly incapable of doing. Europe has gone to the school of logical and critical thinking; Asia still does not know how to distinguish between truth and poetry, and does not perceive whether its convictions stem from its own observation and proper thinking, or from fantasies.

Reason in the schools has made Europe into Europe. In the Middle Ages, it was on its way to becoming a part and appendage of Asia again, that is, to forfeiting the scientific sense that it owed to the Greeks.

23. Spoken by Mephistopheles in Goethe's *Faust I,* "Studierzimmer," 1851f.
24. See n. 11 to Section Two.

## 266

*Underestimated effect of Gymnasium instruction.* One seldom looks for the value of the Gymnasium in the things that are really learned there, never to be forgotten, but rather in those things that are taught but which the pupil assimilates only with reluctance, to shake off as soon as he can. As it is carried out everywhere, reading the Classics is an odious procedure (as every educated man will admit): for young people who are in no respect ready for it, by teachers who by their every word, and often by their appearance, throw a blight over a good author. But therein lies the value that is generally underestimated: that these teachers speak the *abstract language of higher culture,* ponderous and hard to understand though it is, but an elevated exercise[25] of the brain; that concepts, technical terms, methods, and allusions continually occur in their language which young people almost never hear in the conversations of their relatives or in the streets. If pupils only *listen,* their intellect will be automatically preformed to a scientific way of thinking. It is not possible to emerge from this training as a pure child of nature, fully untouched by abstraction.

## 267

*Learning many languages.* To learn many languages fills the memory with words instead of with facts and ideas, even though in every man, memory is a vessel that can take in only a certain limited amount of content. Also, learning many languages is harmful in that it makes a man believe he is accomplished, and actually does lend a certain seductive prestige in social intercourse; it also does harm indirectly by undermining his acquisition of well-founded knowledge and his intention to earn men's respect in an honest way. Finally, it is the axe laid to the root of any finer feeling for language within the native tongue; that is irreparably damaged and destroyed. The two peoples who produced the greatest stylists, the Greeks and the French, did not learn any foreign languages.

But because the commerce of men must become increasingly cosmopolitan and, for example, a proper merchant in London must be able to make himself understood orally and in writing in eight languages, the learning of many languages is, of course, a

25. *Gymnastik*

necessary *evil*. When it finally reaches an extreme, it will force mankind to find a remedy for it, and in some far-off future time everyone will know a new language, a language of commerce at first, then a language of intellectual intercourse generally, and this as surely as there will one day be aerial navigation. Why else would the science of linguistics have studied the laws of language for a century and assessed what is necessary, valuable, and successful about each separate language!

## 268

*On the martial history of the individual.* We find the battle that usually takes place between two generations, between father and son, compressed into any single human life that crosses several cultures. A close relationship *heightens* this battle because each party mercilessly draws in the inner self of the other party, which it knows so well; and thus this battle will be most embittered within the individual; here each new phase strides on past the earlier ones with a cruel injustice, and with no appreciation for their means and ends.

## 269

*A quarter of an hour earlier.* Occasionally one finds a person whose views are before his time, but only to the extent that he anticipates the common views of the next decade. He holds the public opinion before it is public; that is, he has fallen into the arms of a view that deserves to become trite, one-quarter of an hour sooner than the others. But his fame tends to be much noisier than the fame of the truly great and superior.

## 270

*The art of reading.* Every strong orientation is one-sided; it approaches the orientation of a straight line, and, like it, is exclusive; that is, it does not touch on many other orientations, as weak parties and natures do in their wavelike vacillation. Thus one must excuse the philologists for being one-sided. The guild's century-long practice of producing and preserving texts, as well as explaining them, has finally permitted the discovery of the right methods. The whole Middle Ages was profoundly incapable of a strictly philological explanation, incapable, that is, of the simple wish to understand what the author says. It was something to find these methods; let us not underestimate it! All science has gained continuity and stability only because the art of reading correctly, that is, philology, attained its full power.

## 271

*The art of drawing conclusions.* The greatest progress men have made lies in their learning to *draw correct conclusions.* That is by no means so natural a thing as Schopenhauer assumes when he says, "Everyone is capable of drawing conclusions, only a few of judging";[26] rather, it is learned late and still has not come to prevail. False conclusions are the rule in older times. And all peoples' mythologies, magic, superstition, religious worship, and law—all are the inexhaustible sites of evidence for this thesis.

## 272

*Annual circles of individual culture.* Strength or weakness in intellectual productivity depends much less on inherited gift than on the inborn amount of *resilience.* Most young educated people thirty years of age go backwards at this spring solstice of their lives, and from then on are averse to new intellectual changes. That is why, for the health of a continually growing culture, a new generation is then necessary which, however, also does not get very far: for in order to *catch up* to the father's culture, the son must consume almost the same amount of inherited energy that the father himself possessed at that stage of life when he begot his son; with his little surplus, the son goes farther (for since the path is being taken for the second time, he goes a little faster; to learn what the father knew, the son does not use up quite so much energy). Very resilient men, like Goethe, for example, traverse almost more than four generations in a row can do; but for that reason they get ahead too quickly, so that other men catch up to them only in the next century, and perhaps never entirely, because frequent interruptions have weakened cultural unity and developmental consistency.

With ever greater speed, men are repeating the usual phases of the spiritual culture that has been attained in the course of history. Presently, they begin to enter the culture as children moved by

26. Schopenhauer, *Ethics,* 114.

religion, and in their tenth year of life, perhaps, those feelings attain the greatest vitality; then they make the transition to weaker forms (pantheism) as they approach science; they get quite beyond God, immortality, and the like, but yield to the spells of a metaphysical philosophy. This, too, they finally cease to find credible; art, on the other hand, seems to offer more and more, so that for a time metaphysics barely survives as a metamorphosis into art or as an artistically transfiguring mood. But the scientific sense grows ever more domineering, and leads the man on to natural science and history, and in particular to the most rigorous methods of knowledge, while art takes on an ever more subdued and modest meaning. All this tends to happen within a man's first thirty years. It is the recapitulation of a task at which mankind has been toiling for perhaps thirty thousand years.

## 273

*Going backward, not staying backward.* Anyone who still begins his development with religious feelings and then continues living in metaphysics and art for a long time, has of course gone some distance backward, and begins his race against other modern men with a handicap. He is apparently losing ground and time. But by having dwelled in those realms where heat and energy are unleashed, and power keeps streaming like a volcanic river out of an everflowing spring, he then, once having left those domains in time, comes the more quickly forward; his feet have wings; his breast has learned to breathe more peacefully, longer, with more endurance.

He has drawn back, only in order to have enough room for his leap: so there can even be something terrible or threatening about his retrogression.

## 274

*A section of our self as an artistic object.* It is a sign of superior culture when men consciously remember and sketch a true picture of certain periods of their development, which lesser men live through almost without thought, wiping them off their soul's tablet; this is the higher kind of painting, which only few people understand. To do it, it is necessary to isolate those phases artificially. Historical studies develop the capacity for this form of painting, for they continually exhort us, when occasioned by a period of history, or a people—or a human life, to imagine a quite definite horizon of thoughts, a definite intensity of feelings, the predominance of some, and the withdrawal of others. Historical sense consists of being able, when there is the occasion, to reconstruct quickly such systems of thought and feeling, like impressions of a temple from some random remaining columns and pieces of wall. The immediate result is that we understand our fellow men to be such definite systems, and representatives of various cultures; that is, necessary, but changeable. And conversely, we can separate out sections of our own development and set them down as autonomous.

## 275

*Cynics and epicureans.* The cynic knows the connection between the more highly cultivated man's stronger and more numerous pains, and his profuse needs; therefore he understands that manifold opinions about beauty, propriety, seemliness, and delight must give rise to very rich sources of pleasure, but also to sources of discontent. In accordance with this insight, the cynic educates himself retrogressively by giving up many of these opinions and withdrawing from certain demands of culture. In that way, he achieves a feeling of freedom and of strengthening; and gradually, when habit makes his way of life bearable, he does indeed feel discontent more rarely and less strongly than cultured men, and approximates a domesticated animal; in addition, everything charms him by its contrast and—he can also scold to his heart's content, so that in that way he again gets far beyond an animal's world of feelings.

The epicurean has the same point of view as the cynic; between the two there is usually only a difference in temperament. Furthermore, the epicurean uses his higher culture to make himself independent of prevailing opinions; he lifts himself above them, while the cynic merely remains in negation. He strolls as in calm, well-protected, half-dark passageways, while above him the treetops whip about in the wind, revealing to him how violently in motion is the world outside. The cynic, on the other hand, seems to walk about outside in the blowing wind naked, hardening himself until he is without feeling.

## 276

*Microcosm and macrocosm of culture.* Man makes the best discoveries about culture within himself when he finds two heterogeneous powers governing there. Given that a man loved the plastic arts or music as much as he was moved by the spirit of science, and that he deemed it impossible to end this contradiction by destroying the one and completely unleashing the other power; then, the only thing remaining to him is to make such a large edifice of culture out of himself that both powers can live there, even if at different ends of it; between them are sheltered conciliatory central powers, with the dominating strength to settle, if need be, any quarrels that break out. Such a cultural edifice in the single individual will have the greatest similarity to the cultural architecture of whole eras and, by analogy, provide continuous instruction about them. For wherever the great architecture of culture developed, it was its task to force opposing forces into harmony through an overwhelming aggregation of the remaining, less incompatible[27] powers, yet without suppressing or shackling them.

## 277

*Happiness and culture.* We are devastated by the sight of the scenes of our childhood: the garden house, the church with its graves, the pond and the woods—we always see them again as sufferers. We are gripped by self-pity, for what have we not suffered since that time! And here, everything is still standing so quiet, so eternal: we alone are so different, so in turmoil; we even rediscover some people on whom Time has sharpened its tooth no *more* than on an oak tree: peasants, fishermen, woodsmen—they are the same.

Devastation and self-pity in the face of the lower culture is the sign of higher culture—this shows that happiness, at least, has not been increased by the latter. Whoever wishes to harvest happiness and comfort from life, let him always keep out of the way of higher culture.

---

27. *unverträglich,* not *unerträglich* (unbearable) as in the Zimmern text.

## 278

*Analogy of the dance.*[28] Today we should consider it the decisive sign of great culture if someone possesses the strength and flexibility to pursue knowledge purely and rigorously and, at other times, to give poetry, religion, and metaphysics a handicap, as it were, and appreciate their power and beauty. A position of this sort, between two such different claims, is very difficult, for science urges the absolute dominion of its method, and if this is not granted, there exists the other danger of a feeble vacillation between different impulses. Meanwhile (to open up a view to the solution of this difficulty by means of an analogy, at least) one might remember that *dancing* is not the same thing as staggering wearily back and forth between different impulses. High culture will resemble a daring dance, thus requiring, as we said, much strength and flexibility.

## 279

*On easing life.* One principal means to ease life is to idealize all its processes; but from painting one should be well aware what idealization means. The painter requires that the viewer not look too hard or too close; he forces him back to a certain distance to view from there; he is obliged to presuppose that a viewer is at a fixed distance from his picture; indeed, he must even assume an equally fixed amount of visual acuity in his viewer; he may on no account waver about such things. So anyone who wants to idealize his life must not desire to see it too closely, and must keep his sight back at a certain distance. Goethe, for example, knew this trick well.

## 280

*Aggravating as easing,*[29] *and vice versa.* Much that aggravates man's life at certain stages eases it at a higher stage because such men have come to know life's more severe aggravations. The reverse also occurs: thus religion, for example, has a double face,

28. The metaphor of the dance assumes ever greater importance for Nietzsche: cf. *The Gay Science,* bk. 5, par. 381.

29. *Erschwerung als Erleichterung*

depending on whether a man is looking up to it, in order to have his burden and misery taken from him, or whether he is looking down on it, as on a chain laid on him so that he may not rise too high into the air.

## 281

*Higher culture is inevitably misunderstood.* A man who has strung his instrument with only two strings (as do scholars who, in addition to the *scientific drive,* have only an acquired *religious* drive) does not understand the kind of man who can play on more strings. It is in the nature of the higher, *many-stringed and many-sided*[30] culture that it is always misinterpreted by the lower, as happens, for example, when art is taken for a disguised form of religion. Indeed, people who are religious only, understand even science as a search for religious feeling, just as deaf-mutes do not know what music is, if not visible movement.

## 282

*Lament.* It is perhaps the advantages of our times that bring with them a decline and occasional underestimation of the *vita contemplativa.* But one must admit to himself that our age is poor in great moralists, that Pascal, Epictetus, Seneca, and Plutarch are now read but little, that work and industry (formerly attending the great goddess Health) sometimes seem to rage like a disease. Because there is no time for thinking, and no rest in thinking, we no longer weigh divergent views: we are content to hate them. With the tremendous acceleration of life, we grow accustomed to using our mind and eye for seeing and judging incompletely or incorrectly, and all men are like travelers who get to know a land and its people from the train. An independent and cautious scientific attitude is almost thought to be a kind of madness: the free spirit is brought into disrepute, particularly by scholars who miss their own thoroughness and antlike industry in his talent for observation, and would gladly confine him to a single corner of science; while he has the quite different and higher task of commanding the entire *arrière-ban*[31] of scientific and

30. *vielsaitiger:* literally "more multi-stringed," also a pun on the word *vielseitiger,* which means "more multi-sided."

31. *arrière-ban:* the body of vassals summoned to military service.

learned men from his remote outpost, and showing them the ways and ends of culture.

A lament like this one just sung will probably have its day and, at some time when the genius of meditation makes a powerful return, cease of itself.

## 283

*Main deficiency of active people.* Active men are usually lacking in higher activity—I mean individual activity. They are active as officials, businessmen, scholars, that is, as generic beings, but not as quite particular, single and unique men. In this respect they are lazy.

It is the misfortune of active men that their activity is almost always a bit irrational. For example, one must not inquire of the money-gathering banker what the purpose for his restless activity is: it is irrational. Active people roll like a stone, conforming to the stupidity of mechanics.

Today as always, men fall into two groups: slaves and free men. Whoever does not have two-thirds of his day for himself, is a slave, whatever he may be: a statesman, a businessman, an official, or a scholar.

## 284

*In favor of the idle.* An indication that esteem for the meditative life has decreased is that scholars today compete with active men in a kind of hasty enjoyment, so that they seem to value this kind of enjoying more than the kind that actually befits them and, in fact, offers much more enjoyment. Scholars are ashamed of *otium*. But leisure and idleness[32] are a noble thing.

If idleness is really the *beginning* of all vices,[33] it is at least located in the closest vicinity to all the virtues: the idle man is still a better man than the active man.

You don't think that by leisure and idling I'm talking about you, do you, you lazybones?

## 285

*Modern restlessness.* The farther West one goes, the greater modern agitation becomes; so that to Americans the inhabitants

32. *Musse und Müssiggehen*

33. "Müssigang ist aller Laster Anfang" (idleness is the beginning of all vices), German saying.

of Europe appear on the whole to be peace-loving, contented beings, while in fact they too fly about pell-mell, like bees and wasps. This agitation is becoming so great that the higher culture can no longer allow its fruits to ripen; it is as if the seasons were following too quickly on one another. From lack of rest, our civilization is ending in a new barbarism. Never have the active, which is to say the restless, people been prized more. Therefore, one of the necessary correctives that must be applied to the character of humanity is a massive strengthening of the contemplative element. And every individual who is calm and steady in his heart and head, already has the right to believe that he possesses not only a good temperament, but also a generally useful virtue, and that in preserving this virtue, he is even fulfilling a higher duty.

## 286

*To what extent the active man is lazy.* I believe that each person must have his own opinion about every thing about which it is possible to have an opinion, because he himself is a special, unique thing that holds a new, previously nonexistent view about all other things. But laziness, which is at the bottom of the active man's soul, hinders man from drawing water out of his own well.

It is the same with freedom of opinions as with health: both are individual; no generally valid concept can be set up about either. What one individual needs for his health will make another ill, and for more highly developed natures, many means and ways to spiritual freedom may be ways and means to bondage.

## 287

*Censor vitae.*[34] For a long time, the inner state of a man who wants to become free in his judgments about life will be characterized by an alternation between love and hatred; he does not forget, and resents everything, good as well as evil. Finally, when the whole tablet of his soul is written full with experiences, he will neither despise and hate existence nor love it, but rather lie above it, now with a joyful eye, now with a sorrowful eye, and, like nature, be now of a summery, now of an autumnal disposition.

---

34. *Censor vitae:* critic of life.

## 288

*Secondary result.* Whoever seriously wants to become free, will in the process also lose, uncoerced, the inclination to faults and vices; he will also be prey ever more rarely to annoyance and irritation. For his will desires nothing more urgently than knowledge, and the means to it—that is, the enduring condition in which he is best able to engage in knowledge.

## 289

*The value of illness.* The man who lies ill in bed sometimes perceives that it is usually his office, business, or society that has made him ill and caused him to lose all clear-mindedness about himself; he gains this wisdom from the leisure forced upon him by his illness.

## 290

*Feeling in the country.* If one does not have stable, calm lines on the horizon of his life, like lines of mountaintops or trees, then man's innermost will itself becomes restless, distracted, and covetous, like the city dweller's character: he knows no happiness, and gives none.

## 291

*Caution of free spirits.* Free-spirited people, living for knowledge alone, will soon find they have achieved their external goal in life, their ultimate position vis à vis society and the state, and gladly be satisfied, for example, with a minor position or a fortune that just meets their needs; for they will set themselves up to live in such a way that a great change in economic conditions, even a revolution in political structures, will not overturn their life with it. They expend as little energy as possible on all these things, so that they can plunge with all their assembled energy, as if taking a deep breath, into the element of knowledge. They can then hope to dive deep, and also get a look at the bottom.

Such a spirit will be happy to take only the corner of an experience; he does not love things in the whole breadth and prolixity of their folds; for he does not want to get wrapped up in them.

He, too, knows the week-days of bondage, dependence, and

service. But from time to time he must get a Sunday of freedom, or else he will not endure life.

It is probable that even his love of men will be cautious and somewhat shortwinded, for he wants to engage himself with the world of inclination and blindness only as far as is necessary for the sake of knowledge. He must trust that the genius of justice will say something on behalf of its disciple and protégé, should accusatory voices call him poor in love.

In his way of living and thinking, there is a *refined heroism;* he scorns to offer himself to mass worship, as his cruder brother does, and is used to going quietly through the world and out of the world. Whatever labyrinths he may wander through, among whatever rocks his river may at times have forced its tortured course—once he gets to the light, he goes his way brightly, lightly, and almost soundlessly, and lets the sunshine play down to his depths.

## 292

*Onwards.* And so onwards along the path of wisdom, with a hearty tread, a hearty confidence! However you may be, be your own source of experience! Throw off your discontent about your nature; forgive yourself your own self, for you have in it a ladder with a hundred rungs, on which you can climb to knowledge. The age into which you feel yourself thrown with sorrow calls you blessed because of this stroke of fortune; it calls to you so that you may share in experiences that men of a later time will perhaps have to forego. Do not disdain having once been religious; investigate thoroughly how you once had a genuine access to art. Do not these very experiences help you to pursue with greater understanding enormous stretches of earlier humanity? Have not many of the most splendid fruits of older culture grown up on *that* very ground that sometimes displeases you, on the ground of impure thinking? One must have loved religion and art like one's mother or wet-nurse—otherwise one cannot become wise. But one must be able to look beyond them, outgrow them; if one stays under their spell, one does not understand them. Likewise, you must be familiar with history and the delicate game with the two scales: "on the one hand—on the other hand." Stroll backwards, treading in the footprints in which humanity made its great and sorrowful passage through the desert of the past; then you have been instructed most surely about the places where all later humanity cannot or may not go again. And by wanting with all your strength to detect in advance how the knot of the future will be tied, your own life takes on the value of a tool and means to knowledge. You have it in your power to merge everything you have lived through—attempts, false starts, errors, delusions, passions, your love and your hope—into your goal, with nothing left over: you are to become an inevitable chain of culture-rings, and on the basis of this inevitability, to deduce the inevitable course of culture in general. When your sight has become good enough to see the bottom in the dark well of your being and knowing, you may also see in its mirror the distant constellations of future cultures. Do you think this kind of life with this kind of goal is too arduous, too bereft of all comforts? Then you have not yet learned that no honey is sweeter than that of knowledge, and that the hanging clouds of sadness must serve you as an udder, from which you will squeeze the milk to refresh yourself. Only when you are older will you perceive properly how you listened to the voice of nature, that nature which rules the whole world through pleasure. The same life that comes to a peak in old age also comes to a peak in wisdom, in that gentle sunshine of continual spiritual joyfulness; you encounter both old age and wisdom on *one* ridge of life—that is how nature wanted it. Then it is time, and no cause for anger that the fog of death is approaching. Towards the light—your last movement; a joyful shout of knowledge—your last sound.

# SECTION SIX

## Man in Society

### 293

*Benevolent dissembling.* In interaction with people, a benevolent dissembling is often required, as if we did not see through the motives for their behavior.

### 294

*Copies.* Not infrequently, one encounters copies of important people; and, as with paintings, most people prefer the copy to the original.

### 295

*The speaker.* We can speak very appropriately and yet in such a way that all the world cries out the reverse: that is when we are not speaking to all the world.

### 296

*Lack of intimacy.* Lack of intimacy among friends is a mistake that cannot be censured without becoming irreparable.

### 297

*On the art of giving.* To have to reject a gift, simply because it was not offered in the proper way, embitters us towards the giver.

### 298

*The most dangerous partisan.* In every party there is one person who, by his all-too-devout enunciation of party principles, provokes the other members to defect.

## 299

*Advisor to the ill.* Whoever gives an ill man advice gains a feeling of superiority over him, whether the advice is accepted or rejected. For that reason, irritable and proud ill people hate advisors even more than their illness.

## 300

*Twofold kind of equality.* The craving for equality can be expressed either by the wish to draw all others down to one's level (by belittling, excluding, tripping them up) or by the wish to draw oneself up with everyone else (by appreciating, helping, taking pleasure in others' success).

## 301

*Countering embarrassment.* The best way to come to the aid of someone who is very embarrassed and to soothe him is to praise him resolutely.

## 302

*Preference for certain virtues.* We lay no special value on the possession of a virtue until we perceive its complete absence in our opponent.

## 303

*Why one contradicts.* We often contradict an opinion, while actually it is only the tone with which it was advanced that we find disagreeable.

## 304

*Trust and intimacy.*[1] If someone assiduously seeks to force intimacy with another person, he usually is not sure whether he possesses that person's trust. If someone is sure of being trusted, he places little value on intimacy.

## 305

*Balance of friendship.* Sometimes in our relationship to another person, the right balance of friendship is restored when we put a few grains of injustice[2] on our own side of the scale.

---

1. *Vertrauen und Vertraulichkeit*
2. *Unrecht*

## 306

*The most dangerous doctors.* The most dangerous doctors are those born actors who imitate born doctors with perfect deceptive art.

## 307

*When paradoxes are appropriate.* At times, one can win clever people over to a principle merely by presenting it in the form of an outrageous paradox.

## 308

*How brave people are won over.* Brave people are persuaded to an action when it is represented as more dangerous than it is.

## 309

*Courtesies.* We count the courtesies shown to us by unpopular people as offenses.

## 310

*Making them wait.* A sure way to provoke people and to put evil thoughts into their heads is to make them wait a long time. This gives rise to immorality.

## 311

*Against trusting people.* People who give us their complete trust believe that they therefore have a right to our own. This conclusion is false: rights are not won by gifts.

## 312

*Means of compensation.* If we have injured someone, giving him the opportunity to make a joke about us is often enough to provide him personal satisfaction, or even to win his good will.

## 313

*Vanity of the tongue.* Whether a man hides his bad qualities and vices or confesses them openly, his vanity wants to gain an advantage by it in both cases: just note how subtly he distinguishes between those he will hide his bad qualities from and those he will face honestly and candidly.

### 314

*Considerate.* The wish not to annoy anyone or injure anyone can be an equally good indication of a just, as of a fearful disposition.

### 315

*Required for debate.* Whoever does not know how to put his thoughts on ice should not engage in the heat of argument.

### 316

*Milieu and arrogance.* One unlearns arrogance when he knows he is always among men of merit; solitude breeds presumption. Young people are arrogant because they go about with their own kind, each of whom is nothing, but wishes to be important.

### 317

*Motive for attack.* We attack not only to hurt a person, to conquer him, but also, perhaps, simply to become aware of our own strength.

### 318

*Flattery.* People who want to flatter us to dull our caution in dealing with them are using a very dangerous tool, like a sleeping potion which, if it does not put us to sleep, keeps us only the more awake.

### 319

*Good letter-writer.* The man who writes no books, thinks a lot, and lives in inadequate society will usually be a good letter-writer.

### 320

*Most ugly.* It is to be doubted whether a well-traveled man has found anywhere in the world regions more ugly than in the human face.

### 321

*The sympathetic.* Sympathetic natures, always helpful in a misfortune, are rarely the same ones who share our joy: when others are happy, they have nothing to do, become superfluous, do not feel in possession of their superiority, and therefore easily show dissatisfaction.

## 322

*Relatives of a suicide.* The relatives of a suicide resent him for not having stayed alive out of consideration for their reputation.

## 323

*Anticipating ingratitude.* The man who gives a great gift encounters no gratitude; for the recipient, simply by accepting it, already has too much of a burden.

## 324

*In dull society.* No one thanks the witty man for the courtesy of adapting himself to a society in which it is not courteous to display wit.

## 325

*Presence of witnesses.* One is twice as happy to dive after a man who has fallen into the water if people are present who do not dare to.

## 326

*Silence.* For both parties, the most disagreeable way of responding to a polemic is to be angry and keep silent: for the aggressor usually takes the silence as a sign of disdain.

## 327

*The friend's secret.* There will be but few people who, when at a loss for topics of conversation, will not reveal the more secret affairs of their friends.

## 328

*Humanity.* The humanity of famous intellectuals consists in graciously losing the argument when dealing with the nonfamous.

## 329

*The inhibited one.* Men who do not feel secure in social situations take every opportunity to demonstrate superiority over an intimate to whom they are superior; this they do publicly, before the company—by teasing, for example.

## 330

*Thanks.* A refined soul is distressed to know that someone owes it thanks; a crude soul is distressed that it owes thanks.

## 331

*Indication of alienation.* The clearest sign that two people hold alienated views is that each says ironic things to the other, but neither of the two feels the other's irony.

## 332

*Arrogance after achievements.* Arrogance after achievements offends even more than arrogance in men of no achievement; for the achievement itself offends.

## 333

*Danger in the voice.* Sometimes in conversation the sound of our own voice confuses us and misleads us to assertions that do not at all reflect our opinion.

## 334

*In conversation.* In conversation, it is largely a matter of habit whether one decides mainly for or against the other person: both make sense.

## 335

*Fear of one's neighbor.*[3] We fear the hostile mood of our neighbor because we are afraid that this mood will help him discover our secrets.

## 336

*To distinguish by censure.* Very respected people confer even their censure in such a way as to distinguish us by it. It is supposed to make us aware how earnestly they are concerned with us. We quite misunderstand them if we take their censure as a matter of fact and defend ourselves against it; we annoy them by doing so and alienate them.

---

3. In the religious sense.

## 337

*Vexation at the goodwill of others.* We are wrong about the degree to which we believe ourselves hated or feared; for we ourselves know well the degree of our divergence from a person, a direction, or a party, but those others know us only very superficially, and therefore also hate us only superficially. Often we encounter goodwill which we cannot explain; but if we understand it, it offends us, for it shows that one doesn't take us seriously or importantly enough.

## 338

*Clashing vanities.* Two people with equally great vanity retain a bad impression of one another after they meet, because each one was so busy with the impression he wanted to elicit in the other that the other made no impression on him; finally both notice that their efforts have failed and blame the other for it.

## 339

*Bad manners as a good sign.* The superior spirit takes pleasure in ambitious youths' tactless, arrogant, even hostile behavior toward him; it is the bad behavior of fiery horses who still have carried no rider, and yet will in a short time be so proud to carry him.

## 340

*When it is advisable to be wrong.* It is good to accept accusations without refuting them, even when they do us wrong, if the accuser would see an even greater wrong on our part were we to contradict him, or indeed refute him. In this way, of course, one can always be in the wrong, and always gain one's point, and, finally, with the best conscience in the world, become the most intolerable tyrant and pest; and what is true of the individual can also occur in whole classes of society.

## 341

*Too little honored.* Very conceited people to whom one has given fewer signs of regard than they expected will try to mislead themselves and others about this for a long time; they become casuistic psychologists in order to prove that they were indeed honored sufficiently; if they do not achieve their goal, if the veil of deception is torn away, they indulge in a rage all the greater.

## 342

*Primeval states echoed in speech.* In the way men make assertions in present-day society, one often hears an echo of the times when they were better skilled in arms than in anything else; sometimes they handle assertions as poised archers their weapons; sometimes one thinks he hears the whir and clatter of blades; and with some men an assertion thunders down like a heavy cudgel.

Women, on the other hand, speak like creatures who sat for thousands of years at the loom, or did sewing, or were childish with children.

## 343

*The narrator.* It is easy to tell whether a narrator is narrating because the subject matter interests him or because he wants to evoke interest through his narrative. If the latter is the case, he will exaggerate, use superlatives, etc. Then he usually narrates the worse, because he is not thinking so much about the story as about himself.

## 344

*Reading aloud.* Whoever reads dramatic poetry aloud makes discoveries about his own character. He finds his voice more natural for certain moods and scenes than for others—for everything pathetic or for the farcical, for example; whereas in his usual life, he may not have had the opportunity to indicate pathos or farce.

## 345

*A comedy scene which occurs in life.* Someone thinks of a clever opinion about a matter in order to expound it in company. Now, in a comedy we would hear and see how he sets all sails to get to the point, and tries to steer the company to where he can make his remark; how he continually pushes the conversation toward one destination, sometimes losing his direction, finding it again, finally reaching the moment; his breath almost fails him—then someone from the company takes his words out of his mouth. What will he do? Oppose his own opinion?

## 346

*Unintentionally impolite.* If we unintentionally treat another impolitely, do not greet him, for example, because we do not recognize him, this riles us, even though we cannot reproach our own good intentions; the bad opinion that we engendered in the other fellow irks us, or we fear the consequences of ill feeling, or we are pained at having hurt the other fellow—thus vanity, fear, or pity can be aroused, and perhaps all three together.

## 347

*Traitor's tour-de-force.* To express to your fellow conspirator the hurtful suspicion that he might be betraying you, and this at the very moment when you are yourself engaged in betraying him, is a tour-de-force of malice, because it makes the other person aware of himself and forces him to behave very unsuspiciously and openly for a time, giving you, the true traitor, a free hand.

## 348

*To offend and be offended.* It is much more agreeable to offend and later ask forgiveness than to be offended and grant forgiveness. The one who does the former demonstrates his power and then his goodness. The other, if he does not want to be thought inhuman, *must* forgive; because of this coercion, pleasure in the other's humiliation is slight.

## 349

*In a dispute.* When someone contradicts an opinion and develops his own at the same time, his incessant consideration of the other opinion usually causes the natural presentation of his own to go awry: it appears more intentional, cutting, perhaps a bit exaggerated.

## 350

*Trick.* A man who wishes to demand something difficult from another man must not conceive of the matter as a problem, but rather simply lay out his plan, as if it were the only possibility; when an objection or contradiction glimmers in the eye of his opponent, he must know how to break off the conversation quickly, leaving him no time.

## 351

*Pangs of conscience after parties.* Why do we feel pangs of conscience after ordinary parties? Because we have taken important matters lightly; because we have discussed people with less than complete loyalty, or because we were silent when we should have spoken; because we did not on occasion jump up and run away; in short, because we behaved at the party as if we belonged to it.

## 352

*One is judged wrongly.* He who listens to how he is judged will always be annoyed. For we are sometimes judged wrongly even by those who are closest to us ("who know us best"). Even good friends release their annoyance in an envious word; and would they be our friends if they knew us completely?

The judgment of disinterested people hurts a great deal, because it sounds so uninhibited, almost objective. But if we notice that an enemy knows one of our secret characteristics as well as we know ourselves—how great our annoyance is then!

## 353

*Tyranny of the portrait.* Artists and statesmen, who quickly put together the whole picture of a person or event from individual characteristics, are usually unjust, in that they demand afterwards that the event or person really must be the way they painted it; they virtually demand that a person be as gifted, cunning, or unjust as he is in their imagination.

## 354

*The relative as best friend.* The Greeks, who knew so well what a friend is (they alone of all peoples have a deep, many-sided, philosophical discussion of friendship; so that they are the first, and thus far are the last, to consider the friend as a problem worthy of solution), these same Greeks called *relatives* by a term that is the superlative of the word "friend." I find this inexplicable.

## 355

*Unrecognized honesty.* If someone quotes himself in conversation ("I used to say . . ." "I always say . . ."), this gives the impression of arrogance, whereas it more often stems from precisely the opposite source, or at least from an honesty that does not wish to embellish or adorn the moment with ideas that belong to a previous moment.

## 356

*The parasite.* It shows a complete lack of noble character when someone prefers to live in dependence, at the expense of others, in order not to work at any cost, and usually with a secret bitterness towards those on whom he is dependent.

This kind of character is much more common in women than in men, and also much more forgivable (for historical reasons).

## 357

*On the altar of conciliation.* There are circumstances when one obtains an object from a person only by offending him and antagonizing him; this feeling of having an enemy torments the man so that he gladly seizes the first sign of a milder mood to bring about conciliation, and on the altar of this conciliation sacrifices the object which was earlier of such great importance to him that he did not want to give it up at any price.

## 358

*Demanding pity as a sign of arrogance.* There are people, who, when they become angry and offend others, demand first that nothing be held against them, and second, that they be pitied because they are prey to such violent attacks. Human arrogance can go that far.

## 359

*Bait.* "Every man has his price"[4]—that is not true. But every one has a bait into which he must bite. Thus, to win certain people to a matter, one need only paint it as human, noble, charitable, self-sacrificing—and what matter could not be painted thus? It is the sweet candy of *their* souls: others have another.

## 360

*Behavior when praised.* When good friends praise a talented man's nature, he often appears pleased about it out of politeness

---

4. Attributed to Oliver Cromwell (1599–1658).

and good will, but in truth it is a matter of indifference to him. His real nature is quite sluggish about it, and cannot be dragged one step out of the sun or shade in which it lies; but men want to give joy by praising, and we would sadden them if we did not take pleasure in their praise.

## 361

*What Socrates found out.* If someone has mastered one subject, it usually has made him a complete amateur in most other subjects; but people judge just the reverse, as Socrates found out. This is the drawback that makes associating with masters disagreeable.

## 362

*Means of bestialization.*[5] In the struggle with stupidity the fairest and gentlest people finally become brutal. Perhaps that is the right way for them to defend themselves; for by rights the argument against a stupid brow is a clenched fist. But because, as we said, they have a fair and gentle disposition, this means of self-defense makes their own suffering greater than the suffering they inflict.

## 363

*Curiosity.* If there were no curiosity, nothing much would be done for the good of one's neighbor. But, using the name of Duty or Pity, Curiosity sneaks into the house of the unfortunate and needy.

Perhaps even in the much-celebrated matter of motherly love, there is a good bit of curiosity.

## 364

*Miscalculating in society.* One person wants to be interesting by virtue of his judgments, another by his likes and dislikes, a third by his acquaintances, a fourth by his isolation—and all of them are miscalculating. For the person for whom they are putting on the spectacle thinks that he himself is the only spectacle that counts.

---

5. *Vertierung.* In Zimmern's text *Verteidigung* (defense).

## 365

*Duel.* It can be said in favor of all duels and affairs of honor, that if a man is so sensitive as not to want to live if so-and-so said or thought this-and-that about him, then he has a right to let the matter be settled by the death of one man or the other. We cannot argue about his being so sensitive; in that regard we are the heirs of the past, its greatness as well as its excesses, without which there can never be any greatness. Now, if a canon of honor exists that allows blood to take the place of death, so that the heart is relieved after a duel according to the rules, then this is a great blessing, because otherwise many human lives would be in danger.

Such an institution, by the way, educates men to be cautious in their remarks, and makes associating with them possible.

## 366

*Nobility and gratitude.* A noble soul will be happy to feel itself bound in gratitude and will not try anxiously to avoid the occasions when it may be so bound; it will likewise be at ease later in expressing gratitude; while cruder souls resist being bound in any way, or are later excessive and much too eager in expressing their gratitude. This last, by the way, also occurs in people of low origin or oppressed station: they think a favor shown to *them* is a miracle of mercy.

## 367

*The hours of eloquence.* In order to speak well, one person needs someone who is definitely and admittedly superior to him; another person can speak completely freely and turn a phrase with eloquence only in front of someone whom he surpasses; the reason is the same in both cases: each of them speaks well only when he speaks *sans gêne,*[6] the one because he does not feel the stimulus of rivalry or competition vis à vis the superior man, the other for the same reason vis à vis the lesser man.

Now, there is quite another category of men who speak well only when they speak in competition, intending to win. Which of the two categories is the more ambitious: the one that speaks well

6. without embarrassment

when ambition is aroused, or the one that, out of precisely the same motives, speaks badly or not at all?

## 368

*The talent for friendship.* Among men who have a particular gift for friendship, two types stand out. The one man is in a continual state of ascent, and finds an exactly appropriate friend for each phase of his development. The series of friends that he acquires in this way is only rarely interconnected, and sometimes discordant and contradictory, quite in accordance with the fact that the later phases in his development invalidate or compromise the earlier phases. Such a man may jokingly be called a *ladder.*

The other type is represented by the man who exercises his powers of attraction on very different characters and talents, thereby winning a whole circle of friends; and these come into friendly contact with one another through him, despite all their diversity. Such a man can be called a *circle;* for in him, that intimate connection of so many different temperaments and natures must somehow be prefigured.

In many people, incidentally, the gift of having good friends is much greater than the gift of being a good friend.

## 369

*Tactics in conversation.* After a conversation with someone, one is best disposed towards his partner in conversation if he had the opportunity to display to him his own wit and amiability in its full splendor. Clever men who want to gain someone's favor use this during a conversation, giving the other person the best opportunities for a good joke and the like. One could imagine an amusing conversation between two very clever people, both of whom want to gain the other's favor and therefore toss the good conversational opportunities back and forth, neither one accepting them—so that the conversation as a whole would proceed without wit or amiability because each one was offering the other the opportunity to demonstrate wit and amiability.

## 370

*Releasing ill humor.* The man who fails at something prefers to attribute the failure to the bad will of another rather than to chance. His injured sensibility is relieved by imagining a person, not a thing, as the reason for his failure. For one can avenge oneself on people, but one must choke down the injuries of coincidence. Therefore, when a prince fails at something, his court habitually points out to him a single person as the alleged cause, and sacrifices this person in the interest of all the courtiers; for the prince's ill humor would otherwise be released on them all, since he can, of course, take no vengeance on Dame Fortune herself.

## 371

*Assuming the colors of the environment.* Why are likes and dislikes so contagious that one can scarcely live in proximity to a person of strong sensibilities without being filled like a vessel with his pros and cons? First, it is very hard to withhold judgment entirely, and sometimes it is virtually intolerable for our vanity. It can look like poverty of thought and feeling, fearfulness, unmanliness; and so we are persuaded at least to take a side, perhaps against the direction of our environment if our pride likes this posture better. Usually, however (this is the second point), we are not even aware of the transition from indifference to liking or disliking, but gradually grow used to the sentiments of our environment; and because sympathetic agreement and mutual understanding are so pleasant, we soon wear all its insignias and party colors.

## 372

*Irony.* Irony is appropriate only as a pedagogical tool, used by a teacher interacting with pupils of whatever sort; its purpose is humiliation, shame, but the salubrious kind that awakens good intentions and bids us offer, as to a doctor, honor and gratitude to the one who treated us so. The ironic man pretends to be ignorant, and, in fact, does it so well that the pupils conversing with him are fooled and become bold in their conviction about their better knowledge, exposing themselves in all kinds of ways; they lose caution and reveal themselves as they are—until the rays of the torch that they held up to their teacher's face are suddenly reflected back on them, humiliating them.

Where there is no relation as between teacher and pupil, irony is impolite, a base emotion. All ironic writers are counting on that silly category of men who want to feel, along with the author, superior to all other men, and regard the author as the spokesman for their arrogance.

Incidentally, the habit of irony, like that of sarcasm, ruins the character; eventually it lends the quality of a gloating superiority; finally, one is like a snapping dog, who, besides biting, has also learned to laugh.

## 373

*Arrogance.* Man should beware of nothing so much as the growth of that weed called arrogance, which ruins every one of our good harvests;[7] for there is arrogance in warmheartedness, in marks of respect, in well-meaning intimacy, in caresses, in friendly advice, in confession of errors, in the pity for others—and all these fine things awaken revulsion when that weed grows among them. The arrogant man, that is, the one who wants to be more important than he is *or is thought to be,* always miscalculates. To be sure, he enjoys his momentary success, to the extent that the witnesses of his arrogance usually render to him, out of fear or convenience, that amount of honor which he demands. But they take a nasty vengeance for it, by subtracting just the amount of excess honor he demands from the value they used to attach to him. People make one pay for nothing so dearly as for humiliation. An arrogant man can make his real, great achievement so suspect and petty in the eyes of others that they tread upon it with dust-covered feet.

One should not even allow himself a proud bearing, unless he can be quite sure that he will not be misunderstood and considered arrogant—with friends or wives, for example. For in associating with men, there is no greater foolishness than to bring on oneself a reputation for arrogance; it is even worse than not having learned to lie politely.

## 374

*Dialogue.* A dialogue is the perfect conversation because everything that the one person says acquires its particular color, sound, its accompanying gesture *in strict consideration of the other person* to whom he is speaking; it is like letter-writing, where one and

---

7. *in uns jede gute Ernte verdirbt;* in some other editions *uns jede gute Ernte verdirbt.*

the same man shows ten ways of expressing his inner thoughts, depending on whether he is writing to this person or to that. In a dialogue, there is only one single refraction of thought: this is produced by the partner in conversation, the mirror in which we want to see our thoughts reflected as beautifully as possible. But how is it with two, or three, or more partners? There the conversation necessarily loses something of its individualizing refinement; the various considerations clash, cancel each other out; the phrase that pleases the one, does not accord with the character of the other. Therefore, a man interacting with several people is forced to fall back upon himself, to present the facts as they are, but rob the subject matter of that scintillating air of humanity that makes a conversation one of the most agreeable things in the world. Just listen to the tone in which men interacting with whole groups of men tend to speak; it is as if the ground bass[8] of all speech were: "That is who *I* am; that is what *I* say; now you think what you will about it!" For this reason, clever women whom a man has met in society are generally remembered as strange, awkward, unappealing: it is speaking to and in front of many people that robs them of all intelligent amiability and turns a harsh light only on their conscious dependence on themselves, their tactics, and their intention to triumph publicly; while the same women in a dialogue become females again and rediscover their mind's gracefulness.

## 375

*Posthumous fame.* It makes sense to hope for recognition in a distant future only if one assumes that mankind will remain essentially unchanged and that all greatness must be perceived as great, not for one time only, but for all times. However, this is a mistake; in all its perceptions and judgments of what is beautiful and good, mankind changes very greatly; it is fantasy to believe of ourselves that we have a mile's head start and that all mankind is following *our* path. Besides, a scholar who goes unrecognized may certainly count on the fact that other men will also make the same discovery he did, and that in the best case a historian will later acknowledge that he already knew this or the other thing

8. Recurrent short musical phrase, played against the melodies of the upper voices.

but was not capable of winning belief for his theory. Posterity always interprets lack of recognition as a lack of strength.

In short, one should not speak so quickly in favor of arrogant isolation. Incidentally, there are exceptions; but usually it is our errors, weaknesses, or follies that keep our great qualities from being recognized.

## 376

*About friends.* Just think to yourself some time how different are the feelings, how divided the opinions, even among the closest acquaintances; how even the same opinions have quite a different place or intensity in the heads of your friends than in your own; how many hundreds of times there is occasion for misunderstanding or hostile flight. After all that, you will say to yourself: "How unsure is the ground on which all our bonds and friendships rest; how near we are to cold downpours or ill weather; how lonely is every man!" If someone understands this, and also that all his fellow men's opinions, their kind and intensity, are as inevitable and irresponsible as their actions; if he learns to perceive that there is this inner inevitability of opinions, due to the indissoluble interweaving of character, occupation, talent, and environment— then he will perhaps be rid of the bitterness and sharpness of that feeling with which the wise man called out: "Friends, there are no friends!"[9] Rather, he will admit to himself that there are, indeed, friends, but they were brought to you by error and deception about yourself; and they must have learned to be silent in order to remain your friend; for almost always, such human relationships rest on the fact that a certain few things are never said, indeed that they are never touched upon; and once these pebbles are set rolling, the friendship follows after, and falls apart. Are there men who cannot be fatally wounded, were they to learn what their most intimate friends really know about them?

By knowing ourselves and regarding our nature itself as a changing sphere of opinions and moods, thus learning to despise it a bit, we bring ourselves into balance with others again. It is true, we have good reason to despise each of our acquaintances, even the greatest; but we have just as good reason to turn this feeling against ourselves.

9. Attributed to Aristotle.

And so let us bear with each other, since we do in fact bear with ourselves; and perhaps each man will some day know the more joyful hour in which he says:

"Friends, there are no friends!" the dying wise man shouted.
"Enemies, there is no enemy!" shout I, the living fool.

# SECTION SEVEN
## Woman and Child

### 377
*The perfect woman.* The perfect woman is a higher type of human than the perfect man, and also something much more rare.

The natural science of animals offers a means to demonstrate the probability of this tenet.

### 378
*Friendship and marriage.* The best friend will probably get the best wife, because a good marriage is based on a talent for friendship.

### 379
*Parents live on.* Unresolved dissonances in the relation of the character and disposition of the parents continue to reverberate in the nature of the child, and constitute his inner sufferings.

### 380
*From the mother.* Everyone carries within him an image of woman that he gets from his mother; that determines whether he will honor women in general, or despise them, or be generally indifferent to them.

### 381
*To correct nature.* If someone does not have a good father, he should acquire one.

### 382
*Fathers and sons.* Fathers have much to do to make amends for the fact that they have sons.

## 383

*Refined women's error.* Refined women think that a subject does not exist at all if it is not possible to speak about it in society.

## 384

*A male's disease.* The surest aid in combating the male's disease of self-contempt is to be loved by a clever woman.

## 385

*A kind of jealousy.* Mothers are easily jealous of their sons' friends if they are exceptionally successful. Usually a mother loves *herself* in her son more than she loves the son himself.

## 386

*Reasonable unreason.* When his life and reason are mature, man comes to feel that his father was wrong to beget him.

## 387

*Maternal goodness.* Some mothers need happy, respected children; some need unhappy children: otherwise they cannot demonstrate their goodness as mothers.

## 388

*Different sighs.* A few men have sighed because their women were abducted; most, because no one wanted to abduct them.

## 389

*Love matches.* Marriages that are made for love (so-called love matches) have Error as their father and Necessity (need)[1] as their mother.

## 390

*Women's friendship.* Women can very well enter into a friendship with a man, but to maintain it—a little physical antipathy must help out.

---

1. *die Not (das Bedürfnis): die Not* can mean both "necessity" and "misery" (cf. n. 24 to Section Two).

## 391

*Boredom.* Many people, especially women, do not experience boredom, because they have never learned to work properly.

## 392

*An element of love.* In every kind of female love, something of maternal love appears also.

## 393

*Unity of place, and drama.* If spouses did not live together, good marriages would be more frequent.

## 394

*Usual consequences of marriage.* Every association that does not uplift, draws downwards, and vice versa; therefore men generally sink somewhat when they take wives, while wives are somewhat elevated. Men who are too intellectual need marriage every bit as much as they resist it like a bitter medicine.

## 395

*Teaching to command.* Children from humble families must be educated to command, as much as other children to obey.

## 396

*To want to be in love.* Fiancés who have been brought together by convenience often try to *be* in love in order to overcome the reproach of cold, calculating advantage. Likewise, those who turn to Christianity for their advantage try to become truly pious, for in that way the religious pantomime is easier for them.

## 397

*No standstill in love.* A musician who *loves* the slow tempo will take the same pieces slower and slower. Thus there is no standstill in any love.

## 398

*Modesty.* Women's modesty generally increases with their beauty.

## 399

*Long-lasting marriage.* A marriage in which each wants to attain an individual goal through the other holds together well, for example, when the woman wants to be famous through the man, or the man popular through the woman.

## 400

*Proteus nature.* For the sake of love, women wholly become what they are in the imagination of the men who love them.

## 401

*Loving and possessing.* Women usually love an important man in such a way that they want to have him to themselves. They would gladly put him under lock and key, if their vanity, which wants him to appear important in front of others, too, did not advise against it.

## 402

*Test of a good marriage.* A marriage is proved good by its being able to tolerate an "exception."

## 403

*Means to bring everyone to everything.* One can so tire and weaken any man, by disturbances, fears, excessive work and ideas, that he no longer resists any apparently complex matter, but rather gives in to it—that is something diplomats and women know.

## 404

*Honor and honesty.*[2] Those girls who want to owe their whole life's maintenance to their youthful charms alone, and whose cunning is prompted by their shrewd mothers, want the same thing as courtesans—only the girls are more clever and less honest.

## 405

*Masks.* There are women who have no inner life wherever one looks for it, being nothing but masks. That man is to be pitied who lets himself in with such ghostly, necessarily unsatisfying creatures; but just these women are able to stimulate man's desire

2. *Ehrbarkeit und Ehrlichkeit*

most intensely: he searches for their souls—and searches on and on.

## 406

*Marriage as a long conversation.* When entering a marriage, one should ask the question: do you think you will be able to have good conversations with this woman right into old age? Everything else in marriage is transitory, but most of the time in interaction is spent in conversation.

## 407

*Girls' dreams.* Inexperienced girls flatter themselves with the notion that it is within their power to make a man happy; later they learn that it amounts to disdaining a man to assume that he needs no more than a girl to make him happy.

Women's vanity demands that a man be more than a happy husband.

## 408

*Faust and Gretchen dying out.* As one scholar very insightfully remarks, educated men in present-day Germany resemble a combination of Mephistopheles and Wagner,[3] but certainly not Faust, whom their grandfathers (in their youth at least) felt rumbling within them. So (to continue the idea), *Gretchens* do not suit them for two reasons. And because they are no longer desired, it seems that they are dying out.

## 409

*Girls as Gymnasium students.* For heaven's sake, do not pass our Gymnasium education on to girls too! For it often turns witty, inquisitive, fiery youths—into copies of their teachers!

## 410

*Without rivals.* Women easily notice whether a man's soul is already appropriated; they want to be loved without rivals, and resent the goals of his ambition, his political duties, his science and art, if he has a passion for such things. Unless he is dis-

---

3. The scholar referred to is Paul de Lagarde (1827–91). Wagner is Faust's pedantic assistant and comic relief in *Faust.*

tinguished because of them: then they hope an amorous tie to him will also make *them* more distinguished; when that is the case, they encourage their lover.

### 411

*The female intellect.* Women's intellect is manifested as perfect control, presence of mind, and utilization of all advantages. They bequeath it as their fundamental character to their children, and the father furnishes the darker background of will. His influence determines the rhythm and harmony, so to speak, to which the new life is to be played out; but its melody comes from the woman.

To say it for those who know how to explain a thing: women have the intelligence, men the heart and passion. This is not contradicted by the fact that men actually get so much farther with their intelligence: they have the deeper, more powerful drives; these take their intelligence, which is in itself something passive, forward. Women are often privately amazed at the great honor men pay to their hearts. When men look especially for a profound, warm-hearted being, in choosing their spouse, and women for a clever, alert, and brilliant being, one sees very clearly how a man is looking for an idealized man, and a woman for an idealized woman—that is, not for a complement, but for the perfection of their own merits.

### 412

*A judgment of Hesiod's[4] confirmed.* An indication of the cleverness of women is that, almost everywhere, they have known how to have others support them, like drones in a beehive. Just consider the original meaning of this, and why men do not have women support them. It is certainly because male vanity and ambition are greater than female cleverness; for, through submission, women have known how to secure for themselves the preponderant advantage, indeed domination. Originally, clever women could use even the care of children to excuse their avoiding work as much as possible. Even now, if they are really active, as house-

---

4. In summer 1878, Nietzsche lectured on his *Works and Days,* in which Hesiod asserts that no horror is like a gluttonous wife, who reclines to eat and ages a husband before his time (702–705).

keepers, for example, they know how to make a disconcerting fuss about it, so that men tend to overestimate the merit of their activity tenfold.

## 413

*Short-sighted people are amorous.* Sometimes just a stronger pair of glasses will cure an amorous man; and if someone had the power to imagine a face or form twenty years older, he might go through life quite undisturbed.

## 414

*When women hate.* When feeling hatred, women are more dangerous than men. First and foremost because once their hostile feeling has been aroused, they are inhibited by no considerations of fairness but let their hatred swell undisturbed to the final consequences; and second, because they are practiced in finding sore spots (which every man, every party has) and stabbing there: then their rapier-sharp mind performs splendid services for them (while men, when they see wounds, become restrained, often generous and conciliatory).

## 415

*Love.* The idolatry that women practice when it comes to love is fundamentally and originally a clever device, in that all those idealizations of love heighten their own power and portray them as ever more desirable in the eyes of men. But because they have grown accustomed over the centuries to this exaggerated estimation of love, it has happened that they have run into their own net and forgotten the reason behind it. They themselves are now more deceived than men, and suffer more, therefore, from the disappointment that almost inevitably enters the life of every woman—to the extent that she even has enough fantasy and sense to be able to be deceived and disappointed.[5]

## 416

*On the emancipation of women.* Can women be just at all, if they are so used to loving, to feeling immediately pro or con? For this reason they are also less often partial to causes, more often to

---

5. *getäuscht und enttäuscht*

people; but if to a cause, they immediately become partisan, thereby ruining its pure, innocent effect. Thus, there is a not insignificant danger when they are entrusted with politics or certain areas of science (history, for example). For what would be more rare than a woman who really knew what science is? The best even nourish in their hearts a secret disdain for it, as if they were somehow superior. Perhaps all this can change; for the time being it is so.

### 417

*Inspiration in the judgments of women.* Those sudden decisions about pro and con which women tend to make, the lightning-fast illuminations of personal relationships by their eruptions of liking and disliking, in short, the proofs of female injustice have been enwreathed by loving men with a glow, as if all women had inspirations of wisdom, even without the Delphic cauldron and the laurel: long afterwards, their statements are interpreted and explained like a sibyl's oracle. However, if one considers that something positive can be said for any person or cause, and likewise something against it, that all matters are not only two-sided, but three or four-sided, then it is almost difficult to go completely astray by such sudden decisions; indeed, one could say that the nature of things is arranged in such a way that women always win the argument.

### 418

*Letting oneself be loved.* Because one of the two loving people is usually the lover, the other the beloved, the belief has arisen that in every love affair the amount of love is constant: the more of it one of the two grabs to himself, the less remains for the other person. Sometimes, exceptionally, it happens that vanity convinces each of the two people that *he* is the one who has to be loved, so that both want to let themselves be loved: in marriage, especially, this results in some half-droll, half-absurd scenes.

### 419

*Contradictions in female heads.* Because women are so much more personal than objective, their range of ideas can tolerate tendencies that are logically in contradiction with one another; they tend to be enthusiastic about the representatives of these tendencies, one after the other, and accept their systems wholesale; but in such a way that a dead place arises whenever a new personality later gains the upper hand. It could happen that all of the philosophy in the head of an old woman consists of nothing but such dead places.

### 420

*Who suffers more?* After a personal disagreement and quarrel between a woman and a man, the one party suffers most at the thought of having hurt the other; while that other party suffers most at the thought of not having hurt the first enough; for which reason it tries by tears, sobs, and contorted features, to weigh down the other person's heart, even afterwards.

### 421

*Opportunity for female generosity.* Once a man's thoughts have gone beyond the demands of custom, he might consider whether nature and reason do not dictate that he marry several times in succession, so that first, aged twenty-two years, he marry an older girl who is spiritually and morally superior to him and can guide him through the dangers of his twenties (ambition, hatred, self-contempt, passions of all kinds). This woman's love would later be completely transformed into maternal feeling, and she would not only tolerate it, but promote it in the most salutary way, if the man in his thirties made an alliance with a quite young girl, whose education he himself would take in hand.

For one's twenties, marriage is a necessary institution; for one's thirties, it is useful, but not necessary; for later life, it often becomes harmful and promotes a husband's spiritual regression.

### 422

*Tragedy of childhood.* Not infrequently, noble-minded and ambitious men have to endure their harshest struggle in childhood, perhaps by having to assert their characters against a low-minded father, who is devoted to pretense and mendacity, or by living, like Lord Byron, in continual struggle with a childish and wrathful mother. If one has experienced such struggles, for the rest of his life he will never get over knowing who has been in reality his greatest and most dangerous enemy.

## 423

*Parents' foolishness.* The grossest errors in judging a person are made by his parents; this is a fact, but how is one to explain it? Do the parents have too much experience of the child, and can they no longer compose it into a unity? We notice that travelers in a strange land grasp correctly the common, distinctive traits of a people only in the first period of their stay; the more they get to know a people, the more they forget how to see what is typical and distinctive about it. As soon as they see up close, they stop being farsighted. Might parents judge their child wrongly because they have never stood far enough off from him?

A quite different explanation would be the following: men tend to stop thinking about things that are closest to them, and simply accept them. When parents are required to judge their children, it is perhaps their customary thoughtlessness that makes them judge so mistakenly.

## 424

*From the future of marriage.* Those noble, free-minded women who set themselves the task of educating and elevating the female sex should not overlook one factor: marriage, conceived of in its higher interpretation, the spiritual friendship of two people of opposite sexes, that is, marriage as hoped for by the future, entered into for the purpose of begetting and raising a new generation. Such a marriage, which uses sensuality as if it were only a rare, occasional means for a higher end, probably requires and must be provided with a natural aid: *concubinage.* For if, for reasons of the man's health, his wife is also to serve for the sole satisfaction of his sexual need, a false point of view, counter to the goals we have indicated, will be decisive in choosing a wife. Posterity becomes a coincidental objective; its successful education, highly improbable. A good wife, who should be friend, helpmate, child-bearer, mother, head of the family, manager, indeed, who perhaps has to run her own business or office separate from her husband, cannot be a concubine at the same time: it would usually be asking too much of her. Thus, the opposite of what happened in Pericles' times in Athens could occur in the future: men, whose wives were not much more than concubines then, turned to Aspasias[6] as

6. Aspasia (470?–410 B.C.): Pericles' clever, influential mistress. Used as a generic term for *hetaerae.*

well, because they desired the delights of a mentally and emotionally liberating sociability, which only the grace and spiritual flexibility of women can provide. All human institutions, like marriage, permit only a moderate degree of practical idealization, failing which, crude measures immediately become necessary.

## 425

*Women's period of storm and stress.* In the three or four civilized European countries, one can in a few centuries educate women to be anything one wants, even men—not in the sexual sense, of course, but certainly in every other sense. At some point, under such an influence, they will have taken on all male virtues and strengths, and of course they will also have to take male weaknesses and vices into the bargain. This much, as I said, one can bring about by force. But how will we endure the intermediate stage it brings with it, which itself can last a few centuries, during which female follies and injustices, their ancient birthright, still claim predominance over everything they will have learned or achieved? This will be the time when anger will constitute the real male emotion, anger over the fact that all the arts and sciences will be overrun and clogged up by shocking dilettantism; bewildering chatter will talk philosophy to death; politics will be more fantastic and partisan than ever; society will be in complete dissolution because women, the preservers of the old custom, will have become ludicrous in their own eyes, and will be intent on standing outside custom in every way. For if women had their greatest power *in* custom, where will they not have to reach to achieve a similar abundance of power again, after they have given up custom?

## 426

*Free spirit and marriage.* Will free spirits live with women? In general, I believe that, as the true-thinking, truth-speaking men of the present, they must, like the prophetic birds of ancient times, prefer *to fly alone.*

## 427

*Happiness of marriage.* Everything habitual draws an ever tighter net of spiderwebs around us; then we notice that the fibres have become traps, and that we ourselves are sitting in the middle, like a spider that got caught there and must feed on its own blood. That is why the free spirit hates all habits and rules, everything enduring and definitive; that is why, again and again, he painfully tears apart the net around him, even though he will suffer as a consequence from countless large and small wounds—for he must tear those fibres *away from himself*, from his body, his soul. He must learn to love where he used to hate, and vice versa. Indeed, nothing may be impossible for him, not even to sow dragons' teeth on the same field where he previously emptied the cornucopias of his kindness.

From this one can judge whether he is cut out for the happiness of marriage.

## 428

*Too close.* If we live in too close proximity to a person, it is as if we kept touching a good etching with our bare fingers; one day we have poor, dirty paper in our hands and nothing more. A human being's soul is likewise worn down by continual touching; at least it finally *appears* that way to us—we never see its original design and beauty again.

One always loses by all-too-intimate association with women and friends; and sometimes one loses the pearl of his life in the process.

## 429

*The golden cradle.* The free spirit will always breathe a sigh of relief when he has finally decided to shake off the maternal care and protection administered by the women around him. What is the harm in the colder draft of air that they had warded off so anxiously? What does one real disadvantage, loss, accident, illness, debt, or folly more or less in his life matter, compared with the bondage of the golden cradle, the peacock-tail fan, and the oppressive feeling of having to be actually grateful because he is waited upon and spoiled like an infant? That is why the milk offered him by the maternal disposition of the women around him can so easily turn to bile.

## 430

*Voluntary sacrificial animal.* Significant women bring relief to the lives of their husbands, if the latter are famous and great, by nothing so much as by becoming a vessel, so to speak, for other people's general ill-will and occasional bad humor. Contemporaries tend to overlook their great men's many mistakes and follies, even gross injustices, if only they can find someone whom they may abuse and slaughter as a veritable sacrificial animal to relieve their feelings. Not infrequently a woman finds in herself the ambition to offer herself for this sacrifice, and then the man can of course be very contented—in the case that he is egoist enough to tolerate in his vicinity such a voluntary conductor of lightning, storm, and rain.

## 431

*Pleasant adversaries.* Women's natural inclination to a quiet, regular, happily harmonious existence and society, the oil-like and calming aspect of their influence on the sea of life, automatically works against the heroic inner urgency of the free spirit. Without noticing it, women act as if they were removing the stones from the traveling mineralogist's path so that he will not bump his foot against them—while he has set out precisely *in order* to bump into them.

## 432

*Dissonance of two consonants.* Women want to serve, and therein lies their happiness; and the free spirit wants not to be served, and therein lies his happiness.

## 433

*Xanthippe.* Socrates found the kind of woman he needed—but not even he would have sought her out had he known her well enough; not even the heroism of this free spirit would have gone that far. In fact, Xanthippe drove him more and more into his strange profession, by making his house and home inhospitable and unhomely; she taught him to live in the back streets, and anywhere where one could chatter and be idle, and in that way formed him into Athens' greatest backstreet dialectician, who finally had to compare himself to a pesky horsefly, set by a god on the neck of the beautiful horse Athens to keep it from coming to rest.[7]

7. Cf. *Apology* 30e; 20c–23c.

## 434

*Blind at a distance.* Just as mothers cannot really perceive or see more than the perceptible and visible pains of their children, so wives of very ambitious men cannot bring themselves to see their husbands suffering, in want, and even disdained; while perhaps all this is not only the sign that they have chosen their way of life correctly, but also the guarantee that their goals will *have* to be attained sooner or later. Women always intrigue secretly against their husband's higher soul; they want to cheat it out of its future for the sake of a painless, comfortable present.

## 435

*Power and freedom.* As greatly as women honor their husbands, they honor the powers and ideas recognized by society even more; for thousands of years they have been used to walking bowed over in front of all forms of rule, with their hands folded on their breast, disapproving of any revolt against public power. That is why, without even intending to, but rather as if out of instinct, they drop themselves like a drag onto the wheels of any freethinking, independent striving, and in some circumstances make their husbands most impatient, especially when the husbands convince themselves that it is love that is really spurring the wives on. To disapprove of women's methods and generously to honor the motives for these methods: that is man's way, and often enough man's despair.

## 436

*Ceterum censeo.*[8] It is ludicrous when a have-not society declares the abolition of inheritance rights, and no less ludicrous when childless people work on the practical laws of a country: they do not have enough ballast in their ship to be able to sail surely into the ocean of the future. But it seems just as nonsensical if a man who has chosen as his task the acquisition of the most general knowledge and the evaluation of the whole of existence weighs himself down with personal considerations of a family, a

8. "Incidentally, I am of the opinion." Cato the Elder closed all his speeches with the line "Ceterum censeo Carthaginem esse delendam." (Incidentally, I am of the opinion that Carthage must be destroyed.) Cf. Plutarch on Cato the Elder (*Lives,* par. 27).

livelihood, security, respect of his wife and child; he is spreading out over his telescope a thick veil, which scarcely any rays from the distant heavens are able to penetrate. So I, too, come to the tenet that in questions of the highest philosophical kind, all married people are suspect.

## 437

*Finally.* There are many kinds of hemlock, and fate usually finds an opportunity to set a cup of this poison to the lips of the free spirit—to "punish" him, as everyone then says. What do the women around him do then? They will cry and lament and per-haps disturb the thinker's twilight peace, as they did in the prison of Athens. "O Crito, have someone take these women away!" said Socrates at last.[9]

9. Cf. *The Phaedo,* 116.

# SECTION EIGHT
## A Look at the State

### 438

*Leave to speak.* All political parties today have in common a demagogic character and the intention of influencing the masses; because of this intention, all of them are obliged to transform their principles into great frescos of stupidity, and paint them that way on the wall. Nothing more can be changed about this—indeed, it is superfluous even to lift a finger against it; for what Voltaire says applies here: "Quand la populace se mêle de raissoner, tout est perdu."[1] Now that this has happened, one must adapt to the new conditions, as one adapts when an earthquake has moved the old limits and outlines of the land, and changed the value of property. Moreover, if the business of all politics is to make life tolerable for the greatest number, this greatest number may also determine what they understand by a tolerable life; if they think their intellect capable of finding the right means to this goal, what good would it do to doubt it? They simply *want* to be the architects of their own fortune and misfortune;[2] and if this feeling of self-determination, this pride in the five or six concepts their heads contain and can bring to light, does indeed make their life so agreeable that they gladly bear the fatal consequences of their narrowness, then there is little to object to, provided that their narrowness does not go so far as to demand that *everything* should become politics in their sense, and that *everyone* should live and act according to their standard. For, first of all, some people must be

---

1. "Once the populace begins to reason, all is lost." Letter to Danilaville, April 1, 1766.

2. "Jeder ist seines Glückes Schmied"(each man is the architect of his own fortune), German saying.

allowed (now, more than ever) to keep out of politics and stand aside a little; the pleasure of self-determination is driving these people, too, and there may even be a little pride involved in being silent when too many—or only many—are speaking. Second, one must overlook it if these few do not take the happiness of the many (whether defined as peoples, or classes of population) so seriously, and are now and then guilty of an ironic attitude; for them, seriousness lies elsewhere; they have a different concept of happiness; their goal cannot be embraced by any clumsy hand with just five fingers. Finally (and certainly this is hardest to grant them, but must also be granted), they too have an occasional moment when they emerge from their silent isolation and try the power of their lungs again; then they call to each other, like men lost in a forest, to make themselves known and encourage each other; of course, when they do, various things are heard that sound bad to ears not meant to hear them.

Soon afterwards, it is quiet in the forest again, so quiet that one can again hear clearly the buzzing, humming, and fluttering of the innumerable insects that live in, above, and below it.

### 439

*Culture and caste.* A higher culture can come into being only where there are two castes of society: the working caste and the idle caste, capable of true leisure; or, to express it more emphatically, the caste of forced labor and the caste of free labor. The distribution of happiness is not a crucial factor when it is a matter of engendering a higher culture, but the caste of the idle is in fact the more capable of suffering and does suffer more; its contentment in existence is slighter; its task greater. Now, if there should be an exchange between the two castes, so that duller, less spiritual individuals and families from the higher caste are demoted into the lower, and, conversely, the freer people from that caste gain admission to the higher: then a condition has been achieved beyond which only the open sea of indefinite desires is still visible.

Thus the fading voice of the old era speaks to us; but where are the ears left to hear it?

### 440

*Of blood.* Men and women of blood have an advantage over others, giving them an indubitable claim to higher esteem, because they possess two arts, increasingly heightened through inheritance: the art of being able to command, and the art of proud obedience.

Now, wherever commanding is part of the daily routine (as in the great world of big business and industry), something similar to those generations "of blood" comes into being, but they lack the noble bearing in obedience, which the former inherited from feudal conditions, and which will no longer grow in our cultural climate.

## 441

*Subordination.* The subordination that is valued so highly in military and bureaucratic states will soon become as unbelievable to us as the secret tactics of the Jesuits have already become; and when this subordination is no longer possible, it will no longer be possible to achieve a number of its most astonishing consequences, and the world will be the poorer. Subordination must vanish, for its basis is vanishing: belief in absolute authority, in ultimate truth. Even in military states, physical coercion is not sufficient to produce subordination; rather it requires an inherited adoration of princeliness, as of something superhuman.

In *freer* situations, one subordinates himself only on conditions, as a consequence of a mutual contract, that is, without any prejudice to self-interest.

## 442

*Conscript army.* The greatest disadvantage of the conscript army, now so widely acclaimed, consists in the squandering of men of the highest civilization; they exist at all only when every circumstance is favorable—how sparingly and anxiously one should deal with them, since it requires great periods of time to create the chance conditions for the production of such delicately organized brains! But just as the Greeks wallowed in Greek blood, so Europeans are now wallowing in European blood; and, in fact, it is the men of highest culture who are always sacrificed in the relatively greatest number, the men who guarantee an abundant and good posterity; for these men stand as commanders in the front lines of a battle, and moreover, because of their greater ambition, expose themselves most to dangers.

Nowadays, when quite different and higher tasks are set than *patria* and *honor,* crude Roman patriotism is either something dishonest, or a sign of backwardness.

## 443

*Hope as arrogance.* Our social order will slowly melt away, as all earlier orders have done when the suns of new ideas shone forth with new warmth over the people. One can *desire* this melting only in that one has hope; and one may reasonably have hope only if one credits his own heart and head, and that of his equals, with more strength than one credits to the representatives of the existing order. Usually, then, this hope will be *arrogance,* an *overestimation.*

## 444

*War.* One can say against war that it makes the victor stupid and the vanquished malicious. In favor of war, one can say that it barbarizes through both these effects and thus makes man more natural; war is the sleep or wintertime of culture: man emerges from it with more strength, both for the good and for the bad.

## 445

*In the service of princes.* In order to act with complete inconsideration, a statesman will do best to carry out his work not for himself, but for his prince. The spectator's eye will be so blinded by the shine of this overall selflessness that he will not see the wiles and severities which the statesman's work brings with it.

## 446

*A question of power, not justice.* For men who always consider the higher usefulness of a matter, socialism, if it *really* is the uprising against their oppressors of people oppressed and kept down for thousands of years, poses no problem of *justice* (with the ludicrous, weak question: "How far *should* one yield to its demands?"), but only a problem of *power* ("To what extent *can* one use its demands?"). So it is like a natural power—steam, for example—which is either forced by man, as a god of machines, into his service, or, when there are mistakes in the machine (that is, errors of human calculation in its construction), wrecks itself and the human with it. To solve that question of power, one must know how strong socialism is, and in which of its modifications it can still be used as a mighty lever within the current political power game; in some circumstances one would even have to do everything possible to strengthen it. With every great force (even the most dangerous), humanity must think how to make it into a tool of its own intentions.

Socialism gains a right only when the two powers, the representatives of the old and new, seem to have come to war, but then both parties prudently calculate how they may preserve themselves to best advantage, and this results in their desire for a treaty. No justice without a treaty. Until now, however, there has been neither war in the indicated territory, nor treaties, and thus no rights, and no "ought" either.

## 447

*Use of the smallest dishonesty.* The power of the press consists in the fact that every individual who serves it feels only slightly pledged or bound to it. He usually gives *his* opinion, but sometimes does *not* give it, in order to help his party or the politics of his country, or even himself. Such little misdemeanors of dishonesty, or perhaps only of dishonest reticence, are not hard for the individual to bear; and yet the consequences are extraordinary, because these little misdemeanors are committed by many people at the same time. Each of these people says to himself, "For such petty services I live better and can make my livelihood; if I fail in such little considerations, I make myself impossible." Because it almost seems that writing one line more or less, and perhaps even without a signature, makes no difference morally, a man who has money and influence can turn any opinion into the public one. Whoever realizes that most people are weak in small things, and wants to attain his own purposes through them, is always a dangerous human being.

## 448

*Complaining too loudly.* When the description of an emergency (the crimes of an administration, or bribery and favoritism in political or scholarly corporations, for example) is greatly exaggerated, it does of course have less of an effect on insightful people, but it has all the greater effect on the uninsightful (who would have remained indifferent to a careful, measured presentation). But since the uninsightful are considerably in the majority, and

harbor within themselves greater strength of will and a more vehement desire for action, the exaggeration will lead to investigations, punishments, promises, and reorganizations.

To that extent, it is useful to exaggerate when describing
emergencies.

### 449

*The apparent weather-makers of politics.* Just as people secretly
assume that a man who knows something about the weather and
can predict it a day in advance actually makes the weather, so
even educated and learned men, calling on superstitious belief,
attribute all the important changes and conjunctures that occurred during the government of great statesmen to them, as their
own work, when it is only too clear that they knew something
about it sooner than the others and made their calculations accordingly; thus they, too, are taken as weather-makers—and this
belief is not the least tool of their power.

### 450

*New and old concept of government.* To differentiate between
government and people, as if two separate spheres of power, one
stronger and higher, the other weaker and lower, were negotiating and coming to agreement, is a bit of inherited political sensibility that still accords exactly with the historical establishment
of the power relationship in *most* states. When, for example,
Bismarck describes the constitutional form as a compromise between government and people, he is speaking according to a principle that has its reason in history (which is, of course, also the
source for that portion of unreason, without which nothing
human can exist). By contrast, we are now supposed to learn (according to a principle that has sprung from the *head* alone, and is
supposed to *make* history) that government is nothing but an
organ of the people, and not a provident, honorable "Above" in
relationship to a habitually humble "Below." Before one accepts
this formulation of the concept of government, which is as yet
unhistorical and arbitrary, if more logical, we might consider the
consequences: for the relationship between people and government is the strongest model relationship, according to which the
interactions between teacher and pupil, head of the house and
servants, father and family, commander-in-chief and soldier, mas-

ter and apprentice, are automatically patterned. All these relationships are now being slightly transformed, under the influence of the prevailing constitutional form of government: they *are becoming* compromises. But how will they have to reverse and displace themselves, changing name and nature, when that very newest concept of government has captured everyone's mind! But it will probably take another century for that. In this regard, there is nothing to wish for *more* than caution and slow development.

## 451

*Justice as a party's lure.* Noble (if not exactly very insightful) representatives of the ruling class may well vow to treat people as equals, and grant them equal rights. To that extent, a socialistic way of thought, based on *justice,* is possible; but, as we said, only within the ruling class, which in this case *practices* justice by its sacrifices and renunciations. On the other hand, to *demand* equality of rights, as do the socialists of the subjugated caste, never results from justice but rather covetousness.

If one shows the beast bloody pieces of meat close by, and then draws them away again until it finally roars, do you think this roar means justice?

## 452

*Possession and justice.* When socialists prove that the distribution of wealth in present-day society is the consequence of countless injustices and atrocities, rejecting *in summa* the obligation towards anything so unjustly established, they are seeing one particular thing only. The whole past of the old culture is built on violence, slavery, deception, error; but we, the heirs of all these conditions, indeed the convergence of that whole past, cannot decree ourselves away, and cannot want to remove one particular part. The unjust frame of mind lies in the souls of the "have-nots," too; they are no better than the "haves," and have no special moral privilege, for at some point their forefathers were "haves," too. We do not need forcible new distributions of property, but rather gradual transformations of attitude; justice must become greater in everyone, and the violent instinct weaker.

## 453

*The helmsman of passions.* The statesman creates public passions in order to profit from the counterpassion they awaken. To take an example: a German statesman knows well that the Catholic Church will never have the same plans as Russia, indeed that it would much rather ally itself with the Turks than with Russia; he likewise knows that Germany is greatly threatened by the danger of an alliance of France with Russia. Now, if he can succeed in making France the hearth and home of the Catholic Church, he will have eliminated this danger for a long time to come. Thus he has an interest in showing hatred towards the Catholics and, by hostilities of all kinds, transforming believers in the Pope's authority into a passionate political power that is inimical to German politics and must naturally merge with France, as Germany's adversary. He aims as necessarily at the Catholicization of France, as Mirabeau[3] saw the salvation of his fatherland in its de-Catholicization.

Thus, one state desires to cloud millions of minds in another state, in order to derive its benefit from this clouding. This is the same attitude that supports the neighboring states' republican form of government—"le désorde organisé,"[4] as Merimée says—for the sole reason that it assumes it will make the people weaker, more divided, and less able to wage war.

### 454

*Dangerous subversive spirits.* One can divide those who are intent on overthrowing society into the ones who want to gain something for themselves, and the ones who want to gain it for their children and grandchildren. The latter are the more dangerous; for they have faith, and the good conscience of selflessness. The others can be diverted: the ruling society is still rich and clever enough for that. Danger begins when goals become impersonal; revolutionaries whose interest is impersonal may regard all defenders of the existing order as having a personal interest, and may therefore feel superior to them.

### 455

*Political value of paternity.* If a man has no sons, he has no full right to speak about the needs of a single matter of state. He has to

---

3. Honorè Gabriel de Riqueti, Count de Mirabeau (1749–91), French statesman.

4. "organized disorder" (*Lettres à une inconnue*, 2, 372).

have risked with the others what is most precious to him; only then is he bound firmly to the state. One must consider the happiness of one's descendants, and so, above all, have descendants, in order to take a proper, natural part in all institutions and their transformation. The development of higher morality depends on a man's having sons: this makes him unselfish, or, more exactly, it expands his selfishness over time, and allows him seriously to pursue goals beyond his individual lifetime.

## 456

*Pride in ancestors.* One can justly be proud of an unbroken line *of good ancestors,* up to one's father—but not proud of the line, for everyone has that. The descent from good ancestors makes up true nobility of birth; one single interruption in that chain, one evil ancestor, and the nobility of birth is cancelled out. Everyone who speaks of his nobility should be asked whether he has no violent, greedy, dissolute, malicious, or cruel man among his ancestors. If he can thereupon answer "no" in good conscience, one should court his friendship.

## 457

*Slaves and workers.* That we lay more value on satisfying our vanity than on all other comforts (security, shelter, pleasure of all kinds) is revealed to a ludicrous degree by the fact that (except for political reasons) everyone desires the abolition of slavery, and utterly abhors bringing men into this state: while each of us must admit that slaves live more securely and happily than the modern worker in all regards, and that slave labor is very little labor, compared to that of the "worker." One protests in the name of human dignity, but expressed more plainly, that is that good old vanity, which experiences Not-being-equal-to or Publicly-being-esteemed-lower as the harshest fate.

The cynic thinks differently about the matter, because he scorns honor—and so for a time Diogenes[5] was a slave and a tutor.

## 458

*Guiding minds and their tools.* We see that great statesmen, and in general all those who must use many men to execute their

5. Greek Cynic philosopher (412?–323 B.C.).

plans, proceed now in one way, now in another: either they choose very subtly and carefully the men who suit their plans, and then give them relatively great freedom, knowing that the nature of these select men is driving them exactly to where they themselves wish to have them; or else they choose badly, indeed, take whatever falls into their hands, but then form each piece of clay into something fit for their purposes. This last sort is the more violent; they also desire more submissive tools; their knowledge of human psychology is usually much less, their disdain for humans greater than among the first-named minds; but the machine that they construct usually works better than the machine from the workshops of the former.

## 459

*Arbitrary law necessary.* Lawyers argue whether that law which is most thoroughly thought out, or that which is easiest to understand should prevail in a people. The first type, whose greatest model is Roman law, seems incomprehensible to the layman and therefore no expression of his sense of justice. Popular laws, like the Germanic, for example, were crude, superstitious, illogical, in part silly, but they reflected quite specific inherited native customs and feelings.

But when law is no longer a tradition, as in our case, it can only be *commanded,* or forced; none of us has a traditional sense of justice any longer; therefore we must content ourselves with *arbitrary laws,* which express the necessity of *having to have* a law. Then, the most logical law is the most acceptable, because it is the *most impartial,* even admitting that, in the relationship of crime and punishment, the smallest unit of measure is always set arbitrarily.

## 460

*The great man of the masses.* It is easy to give the recipe for what the masses call a great man. By all means, supply them with something that they find very pleasant, or, first, put the idea into their heads that this or that would be very pleasant, and then give it to them. But on no account immediately: let it rather be won with great exertion, or let it seem so. The masses must have the impression that a mighty, indeed invincible, strength of will is present; at least it must seem to be there. Everyone admires a strong will, because no one has it, and everyone tells himself that, if he had it, there would be no more limits for him and his egoism. Now, if it appears that this strong will is producing something very pleasant for the masses, instead of listening to its own covetous desires, then everyone admires it all the more, and congratulates himself. For the rest, let him have all the characteristics of the masses: the less they are ashamed before him, the more popular he is. So, let him be violent, envious, exploitative, scheming, fawning, grovelling, puffed up, or, according to the circumstances, all of the above.

## 461

*Prince and God.* Men often deal with their princes in a similar way as with their God, since after all the Prince was often God's representative, or at least his high priest. This almost uncanny feeling of reverence and fear and shame had, and has, become much weaker, but sometimes it flares up and attaches to powerful people generally. Worship of the genius is an echo of this reverence for gods and princes. Wherever one endeavors to elevate individual men to the superhuman, the tendency also exists to imagine whole classes of people as rougher and more base than they really are.

## 462

*My utopia.* In a better social order, the hard work and misery of life will be allotted to the man who suffers least from it, that is, to the dullest man, and so on step by step upwards to the man who is most sensitive to the highest, most sublimated kind of suffering, and therefore suffers even when life is most greatly eased.

## 463

*A delusion in the theory of subversion.* There are political and social visionaries who hotly and eloquently demand the overthrow of all orders, in the belief that the proudest temple of fair humanity would then immediately rise up on its own. In these dangerous dreams, there is still the echo of Rousseau's superstition, which believes in a wondrous, innate, but, as it were, *repressed* goodness of human nature, and attributes all the blame for that repression to the institutions of culture, in society, state, and education.[6] Unfortunately, we know from historical experience that every such overthrow once more resurrects the wildest energies, the long since buried horrors and extravagances of most distant times. An overthrow can well be a source of energy in an exhausted human race, but it can never be an organizer, architect, artist, perfecter of the human character.

It is not *Voltaire's* temperate nature, inclined to organizing, cleansing, and restructuring, but rather *Rousseau's* passionate idiocies and half-truths that have called awake the optimistic spirit of revolution, counter to which I shout: "Ecrasez l'infame!"[7] Because of him,[8] the *spirit of enlightenment and of progressive development* has been scared off for a long time to come: let us see (each one for himself) whether it is not possible to call it back again!

## 464

*Moderation.* Complete decisiveness in thought and inquiry— that is, free-thinking, when it has become a quality of character— makes men moderate in behavior: for it reduces covetousness, draws much of the available energy to itself in order to advance spiritual ends, and shows what is half-useful or useless and dangerous about all sudden changes.

## 465

*Resurrection of the spirit.* On its political sickbed, a people usually regenerates itself and finds its spirit again, which had been lost gradually in the seeking and claiming of power. Culture owes its highest achievements to politically weakened times.

## 466

*New beliefs in the old house.* The overthrow of beliefs is not immediately followed by the overthrow of institutions; rather, the new beliefs live for a long time in the now desolate and eerie house of their predecessors, which they themselves preserve, because of the housing shortage.

6. Cf. Jean-Jacques Rousseau's *Discourses,* on arts and sciences (1749), and on the origin of inequality (1755).

7. "Crush the infamous thing!" In his letter to d'Alembert on November 28, 1762, Voltaire was referring to superstition.

8. *Durch ihn* could mean either "because of him," i.e., Rousseau, or "because of it," i.e., the spirit of revolution.

## 467

*The educational system.* The educational system in large states will always be mediocre at best, for the same reason that the cooking in large kitchens is at best mediocre.

## 468

*Innocent corruption.* In all institutions that do not feel the sharp wind of public criticism (as, for example, in scholarly organizations and senates), an innocent corruption grows up, like a mushroom.

## 469

*Scholars as politicans.* Scholars who become politicians are usually given the comic role of having to be the good conscience of a policy.

## 470

*The wolf hidden behind the sheep.* In certain situations, almost every politician needs an honest man so badly that, like a ravenous wolf, he breaks into a sheeppen: not, however, in order to eat the ram he has stolen, but rather to hide behind its woolly back.

## 471

*Happy times.* A happy era is completely impossible, because men want only to desire it, but not to have it, and every individual, if he has good days, learns virtually to pray for unrest and misery. The destiny of men is designed for *happy moments* (every life has those), but not for happy eras. Nevertheless, this idea, as a heritage of past ages,[9] will endure in the human imagination as "the place beyond the mountains," for since ancient times, the concept of the age of happiness has been inferred from that state when, after powerfully exerting himself in hunting or war, man surrenders to rest, stretches his limbs, and hears the wings of slumber rustle around him. It is a false conclusion when man imagines, according to that old habit of mind, that *after whole periods* of misery and toil, he could experience such a state of happiness *in corresponding intensity and duration.*

9. *Vorzeiten.* In some editions *Urväter* (ancestors).

## 472

*Religion and government.* As long as the state, or more precisely, the government knows that it is appointed as trustee on behalf of a group of people in their minority, and for their sake considers the question whether religion is to be preserved or eliminated, it will most probably always decide to preserve religion. For religion appeases the individual soul in times of loss, privation, fear, or mistrust, that is, when government feels itself unable to do anything directly to alleviate the private man's inner suffering; even during universal, inevitable, and initially unpreventable misfortunes (famines, financial crises, wars), religion gives the masses a calm, patient and trusting bearing. Wherever the necessary or coincidental failings of a state government, or the dangerous consequences of dynastic interests catch the eye of a man of insight and make him recalcitrant, the uninsightful will think they are seeing the finger of God, and will submit patiently to the directives from *Above* (in which concept, divine and human ways of government are usually merged). Thus the citizens' inner peace and a continuity of development will be preserved. Religion protects and seals the power that lies in the unity of popular sentiment, in identical opinions and goals for all, discounting those rare cases when a priesthood and the state power cannot agree about the price and enter into battle. Usually, the state will know how to win the priests over, because it needs their most private, secret education of souls and knows how to appreciate servants who seem outwardly to represent a quite different interest. Without the help of priests, no power can become "legitimate" even now—as Napoleon understood.

Thus, absolute tutelary government and the careful preservation of religion necessarily go together. It is to be presumed that ruling persons and classes will be enlightened about the benefit provided them by religion, and thus feel somewhat superior to it, in that they are using it as a tool: and this is the origin of freethinking.

But what if a quite different view of the concept of government, as it is taught in *democratic* states, begins to prevail? If one sees in government nothing but the instrument of popular will, no Above in contrast to a Below, but solely a function of the single sovereign, the people? Then the government can only take the same position

toward religion that the people hold; any spread of enlightenment
will have to reverberate right into its representatives; it will not be
so easy to use or exploit religious energies and comforts for state
purposes (unless powerful party leaders occasionally exert an influence similar to that of enlightened despotism). But if the state may
no longer draw any use from religion itself, or if the people think so
variously about religious matters that the government cannot take
uniform, unified measures regarding religion, then the necessary
alternative will appear to be to treat religion as a private matter and
consign it to the conscience and habits of each individual. At the
very first, the result is that religious feeling appears to be strengthened, to the extent that hidden or repressed stirrings of it, which
the state had unwittingly or deliberately stifled, now break out and
exceed all limits; later, it turns out that religion is overrun with
sects, and that an abundance of dragon's teeth had been sown at the
moment when religion was made a private affair. Finally, the sight
of the strife, and the hostile exposure of all the weaknesses of
religious confessions allow no other alternative but that every superior and more gifted man makes irreligiosity his private concern.
Then this attitude also prevails in the minds of those who govern,
and gives, almost against their will, an antireligious character to
the measures they take. As soon as this happens, the people who
are still moved by religion, and who used to adore the state as
something half-divine or wholly divine, develop an attitude decid-
edly *hostile to the state;* they attack government measures, try to
impede, cross, disturb as much as they can, and because their
opposition is so heated, they drive the other party, the irreligious
one, into an almost fanatical enthusiasm *for* the state; also contrib-
uting secretly to this is the fact that, since they parted from religion,
the nonreligious have had a feeling of emptiness and are provision-
ally trying to create a substitute, a kind of fulfillment, through
devotion to the state. After these transitional struggles, which may
last a long time, it is finally decided whether the religious parties
are still strong enough to resurrect an old state of affairs and turn
the wheel back—in which case, the state inevitably falls into the
hands of enlightened despotism (perhaps less enlightened and
more fearful than before)—or whether the nonreligious parties
prevail, undermining and finally thwarting the propagation of
their opponents for a few generations, perhaps by means of schools
and education. Yet their enthusiasm for the state will also diminish

then. It becomes more and more clear that when religious adoration, which makes the state into a *mysterium,* a transcendent institution, is shaken, so is the reverent and pious relationship to the state. Henceforth, individuals see only the side of it that can be helpful or harmful to them; they press forward with all the means in their power to get an influence over it. But soon this competition becomes too great; men and parties switch too quickly; too impetuously, they throw each other down from the mountain, after they have scarcely arrived at the top. There is no guarantee that any measure a government puts through will endure; people shy away from undertakings that would have to grow quietly over decades or centuries in order to produce ripe fruit. No longer does anyone feel an obligation toward a law, other than to bow instantaneously to the power that introduced it; at once, however, people begin to undermine it with a new power, a new majority yet to be formed. Finally (one can state it with certainty) the distrust of anything that governs, the insight into the uselessness and irritation of these short-lived struggles, must urge men to a quite new decision: the abolition of the concept of the state, the end of the antithesis "private and public." Step by step, private companies incorporate state businesses; even the most stubborn vestige of the old work of governing (for example, that activity which is supposed to secure private parties against other private parties) will ultimately be taken care of by private contractors. Neglect, decline, and *death of the state,* the unleashing of the private person (I am careful not to say "of the individual")—this is the result of the democratic concept of the state; this is its mission. If it has fulfilled its task (which, like everything human, includes much reason and unreason), if all the relapses of the old illness have been overcome, then a new leaf in the storybook of humanity will be turned; on it one will read all sorts of strange histories, and perhaps some good things as well.

To recapitulate briefly, the interests of tutelary government and the interests of religion go together hand in hand, so that if the latter begins to die out, the foundation of the state will also be shaken. The belief in a divine order of political affairs, in a *mysterium* in the existence of the state, has a religious origin; if religion disappears, the state will inevitably lose its old veil of Isis[10] and

10. Egyptian fertility goddess, whose cult spread throughout the Roman Empire.

no longer awaken awe. The sovereignty of the people, seen closely, serves to scare off even the last trace of magic and superstition
contained in these feelings; modern democracy is the historical
form of the *decline of the state.*

But the prospect resulting from this certain decline is not an
unhappy one in every respect: of all their qualities, men's cleverness and selfishness are the best developed; when the state no
longer satisfies the demands of these energies, chaos will be the
last thing to occur. Rather, an invention even more expedient than
the state will triumph over the state. Mankind has already seen
many an organizational power die out, for example, associations
by sex, which for thousands of years were much more powerful
than the family, indeed held sway and organized society long before the family existed. We ourselves are witnessing how the significant legal and political idea of the family, which once ruled as
far as Roman culture reached, is growing ever fainter and feebler.
Thus a later generation will also see the state become meaningless
in certain stretches of the earth—an idea that many men today can
hardly contemplate without fear and abhorrence. To be sure, to
*work* on the spread and realization of this idea is something else
again: one must have a very arrogant opinion of his own reason
and only a superficial understanding of history to set his hand to
the plough right now—while there is still no one who can show
us the seeds that are to be strewn afterwards on the ravaged earth.
So let us trust to "men's cleverness and selfishness" that the state
will *still* endure for a good while, and that the destructive efforts
of overzealous and rash pretenders to knowledge will be repulsed!

## 473

*Socialism in respect to its means.* Socialism is the visionary
younger brother of an almost decrepit despotism, whose heir it
wants to be. Thus its efforts are reactionary in the deepest sense.
For it desires a wealth of executive power, as only despotism had
it; indeed, it outdoes everything in the past by striving for the
downright destruction of the individual, which it sees as an un-
justified luxury of nature, and which it intends to improve into an
expedient *organ of the community.* Socialism crops up in the
vicinity of all excessive displays of power because of its relation to
it, like the typical old socialist Plato, at the court of the Sicilian

tyrant;[11] it desires (and in certain circumstances, furthers) the Caesarean power state of this century, because, as we said, it would like to be its heir. But even this inheritance would not suffice for its purposes; it needs the most submissive subjugation of all citizens to the absolute state, the like of which has never existed. And since it cannot even count any longer on the old religious piety towards the state, having rather always to work automatically to eliminate piety (because it works on the elimination of all existing *states*), it can only hope to exist here and there for short periods of time by means of the most extreme terrorism. Therefore, it secretly prepares for reigns of terror, and drives the word "justice" like a nail into the heads of the semieducated masses, to rob them completely of their reason (after this reason has already suffered a great deal from its semieducation), and to give them a good conscience for the evil game that they are supposed to play.

Socialism can serve as a rather brutal and forceful way to teach the danger of all accumulations of state power, and to that extent instill one with distrust of the state itself. When its rough voice chimes in with the battle cry *"As much state as possible,"* it will at first make the cry noisier than ever; but soon the opposite cry will be heard with strength the greater: *"As little state as possible."*

## 474

*The development of the spirit, feared by the state.* Like every organizational political power, the Greek *polis* spurned and distrusted the increase of culture among its citizens; its powerful natural impulse was to do almost nothing but cripple and obstruct it. The *polis* did not want to permit to culture any history or evolution; the education determined by the law of the land was intended to bind all generations and keep them at one level. Later, Plato, too, wanted it no different for his ideal state. So culture developed *in spite of* the *polis; the polis* helped indirectly, of course, and involuntarily, because in it an individual's ambition was stimulated greatly, so that once he had come to the path of intellectual devel-

---

11. In 388 B.C. Plato visited the court of the Sicilian tyrant Dionysius the Elder in Syracuse, where he returned in 367 and 361 B.C., hoping to realize his political ideals there.

opment, he pursued that, too, as far as it would go. One should not evoke Pericles' panegyric[12] as refutation, for it is only a great, optimistic delusion about the allegedly necessary connection between the *polis* and Athenian civilization; just before the night falls on Athens (the plague and the break with tradition), Thucydides lets it[13] shine resplendent once again, like a transfiguring sunset, at whose sight we are to forget the bad day that went before it.

## 475

*The European man and the destruction of nations.* Commerce and industry, traffic in books and letters, the commonality of all higher culture, quick changes of locality and landscape, the present-day nomadic life of all nonlandowners—these conditions necessarily bring about a weakening and ultimately a destruction of nations, or at least of European nations; so that a mixed race, that of the European man, has to originate out of all of them, as the result of continual crossbreeding. The isolation of nations due to engendered *national* hostilities now works against this goal, consciously or unconsciously, but the mixing process goes on slowly, nevertheless, despite those intermittent countercurrents; this artificial nationalism, by the way, is as dangerous as artificial Catholicism was, for it is in essence a forcible state of emergency and martial law, imposed by the few on the many, and requiring cunning, lies, and force to remain respectable. It is not the self-interest of the many (the people), as one would have it, that urges this nationalism, but primarily the self-interest of certain royal dynasties, as well as that of certain commercial and social classes; once a man has understood this, he should be undaunted in presenting himself as a *good European,* and should work actively on the merging of nations. The Germans, because of their age-old, proven trait of being the *nations' interpreter and mediator,* will be able to help in this process.

Incidentally, the whole problem of the *Jews* exists only within national states, inasmuch as their energy and higher intelligence, their capital of spirit and will, which accumulated from genera-

12. In Thucydides, 2.35–46 (cf. n. 12 to Section Five).
13. "It" can refer either to "civilization" or "panegyric."

tion to generation in the long school of their suffering, must pre-
dominate to a degree that awakens envy and hatred; and so, in the
literature of nearly all present-day nations (and, in fact, in proportion to their renewed nationalistic behavior), there is an increase
in the literary misconduct that leads the Jews to the slaughter-
house, as scapegoats for every possible public and private misfortune. As soon as it is no longer a matter of preserving nations, but
rather of producing the strongest possible mixed European race,
the Jew becomes as useful and desirable an ingredient as any
other national quantity. Every nation, every man has disagreeable, even dangerous characteristics; it is cruel to demand that the
Jew should be an exception. Those characteristics may even be
especially dangerous and frightful in him, and perhaps the
youthful Jew of the stock exchange is the most repugnant invention of the whole human race. Nevertheless, I would like to
know how much one must excuse in the overall accounting of a
people which, not without guilt on all our parts, has had the most
sorrowful history of all peoples, and to whom we owe the noblest
human being (Christ), the purest philosopher (Spinoza), the
mightiest book, and the most effective moral code in the world.
Furthermore, in the darkest medieval times, when the Asiatic
cloud had settled heavily over Europe, it was the Jewish free-
thinkers, scholars, and doctors, who, under the harshest personal
pressure, held fast to the banner of enlightenment and intellectual
independence, and defended Europe against Asia; we owe to
their efforts not least, that a more natural, rational, and in any
event unmythical explanation of the world could finally triumph
again, and that the ring of culture which now links us to the
enlightenment of Greco-Roman antiquity, remained unbroken. If
Christianity did everything possible to orientalize the Occident,
then Judaism helped substantially to occidentalize it again and
again, which, in a certain sense, is to say that it made Europe's
history and task into a *continuation of the Greek.*

## 476

*Apparent superiority of the Middle Ages.* The Middle Ages offers
in the church an institution with a quite universal goal, com-
prehending all men, and aimed at their (supposed) highest interest; in contrast to it, the goals of states and nations, which modern history offers, make a disheartening impression; they appear

petty, low, materialistic, geographically narrow. But we should not form our judgments because of these different impressions on our imagination; for the universal institution of the church was reflecting artificial needs, based on fictions, which, if they were not yet present, it first had to produce (need for redemption). The new institutions help in real states of need; and the time is coming when institutions will be formed in order to serve the common, true needs of all men, and to place that fantastic prototype, the Catholic Church, into the shadows of oblivion.

## 477

*War essential.* It is vain rhapsodizing and sentimentality[14] to continue to expect much (even more, to expect a very great deal) from mankind, once it has learned not to wage war. For the time being, we know of no other means to imbue exhausted peoples, as strongly and surely as every great war does, with that raw energy of the battleground, that deep impersonal hatred, that murderous coldbloodedness with a good conscience, that communal, organized ardor in destroying the enemy, that proud indifference to great losses, to one's own existence and to that of one's friends, that muted, earthquakelike convulsion of the soul. Afterwards, if conditions are favorable, the brooks and streams that have broken forth, rolling stones and all kinds of debris along with them, and destroying the meadows of delicate cultures, will start to turn the wheels in the workshops of the spirit with new strength. Culture absolutely cannot do without passions, vices, and acts of malice.

When the Imperial Romans had tired somewhat of wars, they tried to gain new strength by animal-baiting, gladiator contests, and the persecution of Christians. The present-day English, who seem in general also to have renounced war, are using another means to produce anew those fading strengths: they have undertaken dangerous voyages of discovery, crossed oceans, climbed mountains—for scientific purposes, as is said, in truth to bring surplus energy home with them from every sort of adventure and danger. People will discover many other such surrogates for war, but perhaps that will make them understand ever more clearly that such a highly cultivated, and therefore necessarily weary humanity as that of present-day Europe, needs not only wars but the

14. *eitel Schwärmerei und Schönseelenthum*

greatest and most terrible wars (that is, occasional relapses into barbarism) in order not to forfeit to the means of culture its culture and its very existence.

## 478

*Industriousness in South and North.* Industriousness comes about in two very different ways. Craftsmen in the South do not become industrious from an acquisitive drive, but rather from the constant needs of others. Because someone is always coming to have his horse shod, or his wagon repaired, the smith is industrious. If no one came, he would lie about the marketplace. It is not so difficult to subsist in a fertile land; to do so, he would need only a very small amount of work, and certainly no industriousness; in the end, he would go begging and be content.

The industriousness of an English worker, on the other hand, has acquisitiveness behind it: he is aware of himself and his goals; he wants to attain power with his property, and, with his power, the greatest possible freedom and individual distinction.

## 479

*Wealth as the source of a nobility of the blood.* Wealth necessarily produces an aristocracy of race, for it permits one to select the most beautiful women and to pay the best teachers; it allows a person to be clean, to have time for physical exercise, and, above all, to avoid dulling physical labor. It provides all the conditions to enable men, in a few generations, to move and even behave elegantly and beautifully: greater freedom of feeling, the absence of miserable pettiness, of degradation before one's employers, of penny thrift.

For a young man, precisely these negative advantages are the richest birthright of good fortune; a very poor man with a noble nature usually destroys himself: he does not advance and acquires nothing; his race is not viable.

But one must also remember that the effects of wealth are almost the same if a man is permitted to consume three hundred talers a year, or thirty thousand: then we no longer find any substantial heightening of favorable conditions. But to have less, to beg as a boy, and to debase oneself, is terrible, though it may be the right point of departure for those who want to try their luck in the splendor of the courts, in submission to the mighty and influential, or for those who want to be heads of churches. (It teaches how to slink bent over into the underground passageways of favor.)

## 480

*Envy and sloth in different directions.* The two opposing parties, the socialistic and the nationalistic (or however they are called in Europe's various countries) deserve one another: in both of them, envy and laziness are the moving powers. In the one camp, people want to work as little as possible with their hands; in the other, as little as possible with their heads; in nationalism, men hate and envy the outstanding individuals who develop on their own and are not willing to let themselves be placed into the rank and file for the purpose of a mass action; in socialism, men hate and envy the better caste of society, outwardly in a more favorable position, whose actual duty—the production of the highest goods of culture—makes life inwardly all the more difficult and painful. Of course, if one can succeed in turning that spirit of mass action into the spirit of the higher social classes, then the socialistic throngs are quite right to try to bring themselves, externally too, to the level of the former, since inwardly, in heart and head, they are already on the same level.

Live as higher men, and persist in doing the deeds of higher culture—then everything alive will grant you your rights, and the social order, whose peak you represent, will be preserved from any evil eye or hand.

## 481

*Great politics and its losses.* War and readiness for war do not cause a people to suffer its greatest losses because of the costs, the obstructions in trade and commerce, or the need to provide for the standing armies (however great these losses may be now, when eight European states spend the sum of two to three billion on them annually). Rather, its greatest loss is that, year in and year out, the ablest, strongest, most industrious men are taken in extraordinary numbers from their own occupations and professions in order to be soldiers. Similarly, a people that prepares to engage in great politics and secure a decisive voice among the mightiest states does not suffer its greatest losses in the most obvious place. It is true that thenceforth it continually sacrifices a large number of its most outstanding talents on the "Altar of the Fatherland," or to national ambition, while earlier, instead of being devoured by politics, they had other spheres of action open to them. But off to the side from these public hecatombs, and fundamentally much more frightful, a show goes on continually in one hundred thousand simultaneous acts: each able, industrious, intelligent, ambitious man of a people greedy for political glory is ruled by this greed and no longer belongs entirely to his own cause, as he did before; every day, new questions and cares of the public good consume a daily tribute, taken from every citizen's mental and emotional capital: the sum of all these sacrifices and losses of individual energy and labor is so enormous, that, almost necessarily, the political flowering of a people is followed by an intellectual impoverishment and exhaustion, a decreased ability to produce works that demand great concentration and singlemindedness. Finally, one may ask whether all this blossoming and splendor of the whole (which, after all, is only expressed as other states' fear of the new colossus, and the patronage, wrung from abroad, of national commerce and trade)—whether it is *worth* it, if all the nobler, more tender and spiritual plants once produced in such abundance on its soil have to be sacrificed to this gross and gaudy national flower.

## 482

*To say it again.* Public opinions—private laziness.[15]

15. Nietzsche is quoting this line from the third of his *Untimely Meditations,* "Schopenhauer as Educator." It is also the subtitle of *The Fable of the Bees* by Bernard de Mandeville (1670–1733).

# SECTION NINE
## Man Alone with Himself

### 483

*Enemies of truth.* Convictions are more dangerous enemies of truth than lies.

### 484

*Topsy-turvy world.* We criticize a thinker more sharply when he proposes a tenet that is disagreeable to us; and yet it would be more reasonable to do this when we find his tenet agreeable.

### 485

*A person of character.* It is much more common for a person to appear to have character because he always acts in accord with his temperament, rather than because he always acts in accord with his principles.

### 486

*The one necessary thing.* A person must have one or the other: either a disposition which is easygoing by nature, or else a disposition eased by art and knowledge.

### 487

*Passion for things.* He who directs his passion to things (the sciences, the national good, cultural interests, the arts) takes much of the fire out of his passion for people (even when they represent those things, as statesmen, philosophers, and artists represent their creations).

### 488

*Calm in action.* As a waterfall becomes slower and more floating as it plunges, so the great man of action will act with *greater* calm than could be expected from his violent desire before the deed.

## 489

*Not too deep.* People who comprehend a matter in all its depth seldom remain true to it forever. For they have brought its depths to the light; and then there is always much to see about it that is bad.

## 490

*Idealists' delusion.* All idealists imagine that the causes they serve are significantly better than the other causes in the world; they do not want to believe that if their cause is to flourish at all, it needs exactly the same foul-smelling manure that all other human undertakings require.

## 491

*Self-observation.* Man is very well defended against himself, against his own spying and sieges; usually he is able to make out no more of himself than his outer fortifications. The actual stronghold is inaccessible to him, even invisible, unless friends and enemies turn traitor and lead him there by a secret path.

## 492

*The right profession.* Men seldom endure a profession if they do not believe or persuade themselves that it is basically more important than all others. Women do the same with their lovers.

## 493

*Nobility of mind.* To a great degree, nobility of mind consists of good nature and lack of distrust, and thus contains precisely that which acquisitive and successful people so like to treat with superiority and scorn.

## 494

*Destination and paths.* Many people are obstinate about the path once it is taken, few people about the destination.

## 495

*The infuriating thing about an individual way of living.* People are always angry at anyone who chooses very individual standards for his life; because of the extraordinary treatment which that man grants to himself, they feel degraded, like ordinary beings.

## 496

*Privilege of greatness.* It is the privilege of greatness to grant supreme pleasure through trifling gifts.

## 497

*Unwittingly noble.* A man's behavior is unwittingly noble if he has grown accustomed never to want anything from men, and always to give to them.

## 498

*Condition for being a hero.* If a man wants to become a hero, the snake must first become a dragon: otherwise he is lacking his proper enemy.[1]

## 499

*Friend.* Shared joy, not compassion,[2] makes a friend.

## 500

*Using high and low tides.* For the purpose of knowledge, one must know how to use that inner current that draws us to a thing, and then the one that, after a time, draws us away from it.

## 501

*Delight in oneself.*[3] "Delight in an enterprise," they say; but in truth it is delight in oneself, by means of an enterprise.

## 502

*The modest one.* He who is modest with people shows his arrogance all the more with things (the city, state, society, epoch, or mankind). That is his revenge.

## 503

*Envy and jealousy.* Envy and jealousy are the pudenda of the human soul. The comparison can perhaps be pursued further.

1. Cf. Schopenhauer, *The World as Will and Idea,* 1:173.
2. *Mitfreude, nicht Mitleiden*
3. *Freude an sich* is ambiguous: it could also mean "joy in and of itself."

## 504

*The most refined hypocrite.* To speak about oneself not at all is a very refined form of hypocrisy.

## 505

*Annoyance.* Annoyance is a physical illness that is by no means ended simply by eliminating the cause of the annoyance.

## 506

*Representatives of truth.* The champions of truth are hardest to find, not when it is dangerous to tell it, but rather when it is boring.

## 507

*More troublesome than enemies.* When some reason (e.g., gratitude) obliges us to maintain the appearance of unqualified congeniality with people about whose own congenial behavior we are not entirely convinced, these people torment our imagination much more than do our enemies.

## 508

*Out in nature.* We like to be out in nature so much because it has no opinion about us.

## 509

*Everyone superior in one thing.* In civilized circumstances, everyone feels superior to everyone else in at least one way; this is the basis of the general goodwill, inasmuch as everyone is someone who, under certain conditions, can be of help, and need therefore feel no shame in allowing himself to be helped.

## 510

*Reasons for consolation.* When someone dies, we usually need reasons to be consoled, not so much to soften the force of our pain, as to excuse the fact that we feel consoled so easily.

## 511

*Loyal to their convictions.* The man who has a lot to do usually keeps his general views and opinions almost unchanged; as does each person who works in the service of an idea. He will never test the idea itself any more; he no longer has time for that. Indeed, it is contrary to his interest even to think it possible to discuss it.

## 512

*Morality and quantity.* One man's greater morality, in contrast to another's, often lies only in the fact that his goals are quantitatively larger. The other man is pulled down by occupying himself with small things, in a narrow sphere.

## 513

*Life as the product of life.* However far man may extend himself with his knowledge, however objective he may appear to himself—ultimately he reaps nothing but his own biography.

## 514

*Iron necessity.* Over the course of history, men learn that iron necessity is neither iron nor necessary.

## 515

*From experience.* That something is irrational is no argument against its existence, but rather a condition for it.

## 516

*Truth.* No one dies of fatal truths nowadays: there are too many antidotes.

## 517

*Basic insight.* There is no preestablished harmony[4] between the furthering of truth and the good of mankind.

## 518

*Human lot.* Whoever thinks more deeply knows that he is always wrong, whatever his acts and judgments.

## 519

*Truth as Circe.* Error has turned animals into men; might truth be capable of turning man into an animal again?

4. Preestablished harmony: Liebniz's concept describing the harmony of parts of a composed whole, especially the monads making up the world substance.

### 520

*Danger of our culture.* We belong to a time in which culture is in danger of being destroyed by the means of culture.

### 521

*Greatness means: to give a direction.* No river is great and bounteous through itself alone, but rather because it takes up so many tributaries and carries them onwards: that makes it great. It is the same with all great minds. All that matters is that one man give the direction, which the many tributaries must then follow; it does not matter whether he is poorly or richly endowed in the beginning.

### 522

*Weak conscience.* Men who talk about their importance for mankind have a weak conscience about their common bourgeois honesty in keeping contracts or promises.

### 523

*Wanting to be loved.* The demand to be loved is the greatest kind of arrogance.

### 524

*Contempt for people.* The least ambiguous sign of a disdain for people is this: that one tolerates everyone else only as a means to *his* end, or not at all.

### 525

*Disciples out of disagreement.* Whoever has brought men to a state of rage against himself has always acquired a party in his favor, too.

### 526

*Forgetting one's experiences.* It is easy for a man who thinks a lot—and objectively—to forget his own experiences, but not the thoughts that were evoked by them.

### 527

*Adhering to an opinion.* One man adheres to an opinion because he prides himself on having come upon it by himself; another because he has learned it with effort, and is proud of having grasped it: thus both out of vanity.

## 528

*Shunning the light.* The good deed shuns the light as anxiously as the evil deed: the latter fears that, if it is known, pain (as punishment) will follow; the former fears that, if it is known, joy (that pure joy in oneself, which ceases as soon as it includes the satisfaction of one's vanity) will disappear.

## 529

*The day's length.* If a man has a great deal to put in them, a day will have a hundred pockets.

## 530

*Tyrant-genius.* If the soul stirs with an ungovernable desire to assert itself tyranically, and the fire is continually maintained, then even a slight talent (in politicians or artists) gradually becomes an almost irresistible force of nature.

## 531

*The life of the enemy.* Whoever lives for the sake of combating an enemy has an interest in the enemy's staying alive.

## 532

*More important.* The unexplained, obscure matter is taken as more important than the explained, clear one.

## 533

*Evaluating services rendered.* We evaluate services someone renders us according to the value that person places on them, not according to the value they have for us.

## 534

*Unhappiness.* The distinction that lies in being unhappy (as if to feel happy were a sign of shallowness, lack of ambition, ordinariness) is so great that when someone says, "But how happy you must be!" we usually protest.

## 535

*Fantasy of fear.* The fantasy of fear is that malevolent, apelike goblin which jumps onto man's back just when he already has the most to bear.

## 536

*Value of insipid opponents.* Sometimes we remain true to a cause only because its opponents will not stop being insipid.

## 537

*Value of a profession.* A profession makes us thoughtless: therein lies its greatest blessing. For it is a bulwark, behind which we are allowed to withdraw when qualms and worries of a general kind attack us.

## 538

*Talent.* The talent of some men appears slighter than it is because they have always set themselves tasks that are too great.

## 539

*Youth.* The time of youth is disagreeable, for then it is not possible, or not reasonable, to be productive in any sense.

## 540

*Goals too great.* Who publicly sets himself great goals, and later realizes privately that he is too weak to accomplish them, does not usually have enough strength to revoke those goals publicly, either, and then inevitably becomes a hypocrite.

## 541

*In the stream.* Strong currents draw many stones and bushes along with them; strong minds many stupid and muddled heads.

## 542

*Danger of intellectual liberation.* When a man tries earnestly to liberate his intellect, his passions and desires secretly hope to benefit from it also.

## 543

*Embodiment of the spirit.* When a man thinks much and cleverly, not only his face, but also his body takes on a clever look.

## 544

*Seeing poorly and hearing poorly.* He who sees little, always sees less; he who hears poorly, always hears something more.

## 545

*Self-enjoyment in vanity.* The vain man wants not only to stand out, but also to feel outstanding, and therefore rejects no means to deceive and outwit himself. Not the opinion of others, but his opinion of their opinion is what he cares about.

## 546

*Vain by way of an exception.* When he is physically ill, the man who is usually self-sufficient is vain by way of an exception and responsive to fame and praise. In the proportion that he is losing himself, he must try to regain himself from the outside, using strangers' opinions.

## 547

*The "witty" ones.* The man who seeks wit has no wit.

## 548

*Hint for party chiefs.* If we can force people to declare themselves publicly for something, we have usually also brought them to the point of declaring themselves for it privately; they want to continue to be perceived as consistent.

## 549

*Contempt.* Man is more sensitive to contempt from others than to contempt from himself.

## 550

*Rope of gratitude.* There are slavish souls who carry their thanks for favors so far that they actually strangle themselves with the rope of gratitude.

## 551

*Trick of the prophet.* In order to predict the behavior of ordinary men, we must assume that they always expend the least possible amount of intellect to free themselves from a disagreeable situation.

## 552

*The only human right.* He who strays from tradition becomes a sacrifice to the extraordinary; he who remains in tradition is its slave. Destruction follows in any case.

## 553

*Lower than the animal.* When man howls with laughter, he surpasses all animals by his coarseness.

## 554

*Superficial knowledge.* He who speaks a bit of a foreign language has more delight in it than he who speaks it well; pleasure goes along with superficial knowledge.

## 555

*Dangerous helpfulness.* There are people who want to make men's lives more difficult for no other reason than afterwards to offer them their prescriptions for making life easier—their Christianity, for example.

## 556

*Industriousness and conscientiousness.* Industriousness and conscientiousness are often antagonists, in that industriousness wants to take the fruits off the tree while still sour, but conscientiousness lets them hang too long, until they drop off the tree and come to nothing.

## 557

*Suspicion.* People whom we cannot tolerate, we try to make suspect.

## 558

*Lacking the circumstances.* Many men wait all their lives for the opportunity to be good in *their* way.

## 559

*Want of friends.* A want of friends points to envy or arrogance. Many a man owes his friends simply to the fortunate circumstance that he has no cause for envy.

## 560

*Danger in multiplicity.* With one talent the more, one often stands less secure than with one talent the less: as the table stands better on three legs than on four.

## 561

*Model for others.* He who wants to set a good example must add a grain of foolishness to his virtue; then others can imitate and, at the same time, rise above the one being imitated—something which people love.

## 562

*Being a target.* Often, other people's vicious talk about us is not actually aimed at us, but expresses their annoyance or ill humor arising from quite different reasons.

## 563

*Easily resigned.* A man suffers little from unfulfilled wishes if he has trained his imagination to think of the past as hateful.

## 564

*In danger.* When we have just gotten out of the way of a vehicle, we are most in danger of being run over.

## 565

*The role according to the voice.* He who is forced to speak more loudly than is his habit (as in front of someone hard of hearing, or before a large audience) generally exaggerates what he has to communicate.

Some people become conspirators, malicious slanderers, or schemers, merely because their voice is best suited to a whisper.

## 566

*Love and hatred.* Love and hatred are not blind, but are blinded by the fire they themselves carry with them.

## 567

*Made an enemy to one's advantage.* Men who are unable to make their merit completely clear to the world seek to awaken an intense enmity towards themselves. Then they have the comfort of thinking that this stands between their merit and its recognition—and that other people assume the same thing, which is of great advantage to their own importance.

## 568

*Confession.* We forget our guilt when we have confessed it to another, but usually the other person does not forget it.

## 569

*Self-sufficiency.* The golden fleece of self-sufficiency protects against thrashings, but not against pin-pricks.

## 570

*Shadow in the flame.* The flame is not so bright to itself as to those on whom it shines: so too the wise man.

## 571

*Our own opinions.* The first opinion that occurs to us when we are suddenly asked about a matter is usually not our own, but only the customary one, appropriate to our caste, position, or parentage; our own opinions seldom swim near the surface.

## 572

*Origin of courage.* The ordinary man is courageous and invulnerable like a hero when he does not see the danger, when he has no eyes for it. Conversely, the hero's one vulnerable spot is on his back; that is, where he has no eyes.

## 573

*Danger in the doctor.* A man is either born for his doctor, or else he perishes by his doctor.

## 574

*Magical vanity.* He who has boldly prophesied the weather three times and has been successful, believes a bit, at the bottom of his heart, in his own prophetic gift. We do not dispute what is magical or irrational when it flatters our self-esteem.

## 575

*Profession.* A profession is the backbone of life.

## 576

*Danger of personal influence.* He who feels that he exercises a great inner influence on another must leave him quite free rein, indeed must look with favor on his occasional resistance and even bring it about: otherwise he will inevitably make himself an enemy.

## 577

*Giving the heir his due.* Whoever has established something great with a selfless frame of mind takes care to bring up heirs. It is the sign of a tyrannical and ignoble nature to see one's opponents in all the possible heirs of one's work and to live in a state of self-defense against them.

## 578

*A little knowledge.* A little knowledge is more successful than complete knowledge: it conceives things as simpler than they are, thus resulting in opinions that are more comprehensible and persuasive.

## 579

*Not suited to be a party member.* He who thinks much is not suited to be a party member: too soon, he thinks himself through and beyond the party.

## 580

*Bad memory.* The advantage of a bad memory is that, several times over, one enjoys the same good things for the first time.

## 581

*Causing oneself pain.* Inconsiderate thinking is often the sign of a discordant inner state which craves numbness.

## 582

*Martyr.* The disciple of a martyr suffers more than the martyr.

## 583

*Residual vanity.* The vanity of some people, who should not need to be vain, is the left-over and full-grown habit stemming from that time when they still had no right to believe in themselves, and only acquired their belief from others, by begging it in small change.

## 584

*Punctum saliens[5] of passion.* He who is about to fall into a state of anger or violent love reaches a point where his soul is full like a vessel; but it needs one more drop of water: the good will to passion (which is generally also called the bad will). Only this little point is necessary; then the vessel runs over.

## 585

*Bad-tempered thought.* People are like piles of charcoal in the woods. Only when young people have stopped glowing, and carbonized, as charcoal does, do they become *useful.* As long as they smolder and smoke they are perhaps more interesting, but useless, and all too often troublesome.

Mankind unsparingly uses every individual as material to heat its great machines; but what good are the machines when all individuals (that is, mankind) serve only to keep them going? Machines that are their own end—is that the *umana commedia?*[6]

## 586

*The hour-hand of life.* Life consists of rare, isolated moments of the greatest significance, and of innumerably many intervals, during which at best the silhouettes of those moments hover about us. Love, springtime, every beautiful melody, mountains, the moon, the sea—all these speak completely to the heart but once, if in fact they ever do get a chance to speak completely. For many men do not have those moments at all, and are themselves intervals and intermissions in the symphony of real life.

5. the salient point
6. human comedy

## 587

*To set against or set to work.*[7] We often make the mistake of actively opposing a direction, or party, or epoch, because we coincidentally get to see only its superficial side, its stunted aspect, or the inescapable "faults of its virtues,"[8]—perhaps because we ourselves have participated to a large degree in them. Then we turn our back on them and seek an opposite direction; but it would be better to look for the strong, good sides, or to develop them in ourselves. To be sure, it takes a stronger gaze and a better will to further that which is evolving and imperfect, rather than to penetrate its imperfection and reject it.

## 588

*Modesty.* True modesty (that is, the knowledge that we are not our own creations) does exist, and it well suits the great mind, because he particularly can comprehend the thought of his complete lack of responsibility (even for whatever good he creates). One does not hate the great man's immodesty because he is feeling his strength, but rather because he wants to feel it primarily by wounding others, treating them imperiously and watching to see how much they can stand. Most often, this actually proves that he lacks a secure sense of his strength, and makes men doubt his greatness. To this extent, cleverness would strongly advise against immodesty.

## 589

*The first thought of the day.* The best way to begin each day well is to think upon awakening whether we could not give at least one person pleasure on this day. If this practice could be accepted as a substitute for the religious habit of prayer, our fellow men would benefit by this change.

## 590

*Arrogance as the last means of comfort.* If a man accounts for a misfortune, or his intellectual inadequacies, or his illness by seeing them as his predetermined fate, his ordeal, or mysterious punishment for something he had done earlier, he is thereby mak-

7. *Angreifen oder eingreifen*
8. After George Sand: "Chacun a les défauts de ses vertus."

ing his own nature interesting, and imagining himself superior to his fellow men. The proud sinner is a familiar figure in all religious sects.

## 591

*Growth of happiness.* Near to the sorrow of the world, and often upon its volcanic earth, man has laid out his little gardens of happiness; whether he approaches life as one who wants only knowledge from existence, or as one who yields and resigns himself, or as one who rejoices in a difficulty overcome—everywhere he will find some happiness sprouting up next to the trouble. The more volcanic the earth, the greater the happiness will be—but it would be ludicrous to say that this happiness justified suffering per se.

## 592

*The street of one's ancestors.* It is reasonable to develop further the *talent* that one's father or grandfather worked hard at, and not switch to something entirely new; otherwise one is depriving himself of the chance to attain perfection in some one craft. Thus the saying: "Which street should you take?—that of your ancestors."

## 593

*Vanity and ambition as educators.* So long as a man has not yet become the instrument of the universal human good, ambition may torment him; but if he has achieved that goal, if of necessity he is working like a machine for the good of all, then vanity may enter; it will humanize him in small matters, make him more sociable, tolerable, considerate, once ambition has completed the rough work (of making him useful).

## 594

*Philosophical novices.* If we have just partaken of a philosopher's wisdom, we go through the streets feeling as if we had been transformed and had become great men; for we encounter only people who do not know this wisdom, and thus we have to deliver a new, unheard-of judgment about everything; because we have acknowledged a book of laws, we also think we now have to act like judges.

## 595

*Pleasing by displeasing.* People who prefer to be noticed, and thereby displease, desire the same thing as those who do not want to be noticed, and want to please, only to a much greater degree and indirectly, by means of a step that seems to be distancing them from their goal. Because they want to have influence and power, they display their superiority, even if it is felt as disagreeable: for they know that the man who has finally gained power pleases in almost everything he does and says, that even when he displeases, he seems nevertheless to be pleasing.

Both the free spirit and the true believer want power, too, in order to use it to please; if they are threatened because of their doctrines with a dire fate, persecution, prison, or execution, they rejoice at the thought that this will enable their doctrines to be engraved and branded upon mankind; although it is delayed acting, they accept it as a painful but potent means to attain power after all.

## 596

*Casus belli[9] and the like.* The prince who discovers a *casus belli* for an earlier decision to wage war against his neighbor is like a father who imposes a mother upon his child, to be henceforth accepted as such. And are not almost all publicly announced motives for our actions such imposed mothers?

## 597

*Passions and rights.* No one speaks more passionately about his rights than the man who, at the bottom of his heart, doubts them. In drawing passion to his side, he wants to deaden reason and its doubts: he thus gains a good conscience, and, along with it, success with his fellow men.

## 598

*The renouncing man's trick.* He who protests against marriage, in the manner of Catholic priests, will seek to understand it in its lowest, most vulgar sense. Likewise, he who refuses the respect of his contemporaries will conceive it in a base way; he thus makes his renunciation of it and the fight against it easier for himself.

9. cause of war

Incidentally, he who denies himself much in large matters will easily indulge himself in small matters. It is conceivable that the man who is above the applause of his contemporaries is nevertheless unable to refuse himself the satisfaction of little vanities.

## 599

*The age of arrogance.* The true period of arrogance for talented men comes between their twenty-sixth and thirtieth year; it is the time of first ripeness, with a good bit of sourness still remaining. On the basis of what one feels inside himself, one demands from other people, who see little or nothing of it, respect and humility; and because these are not at first forthcoming, one takes vengeance with a glance, an arrogant gesture, or a tone of voice. This a fine ear and eye will recognize in all the products of those years, be they poems, philosophies, or paintings and music. Older, experienced men smile about it, and remember with emotion this beautiful time of life, in which one is angry at his lot of having to *be* so much and *seem* so little. Later, one really *seems* to be more— but the faith in *being* much has been lost, unless one remain throughout his life vanity's hopeless fool.

## 600

*Deceptive and yet firm.* When walking around the top of an abyss, or crossing a deep stream on a plank, we need a railing, not to hold onto (for it would collapse with us at once), but rather to achieve the visual image of security. Likewise, when we are young, we need people who unconsciously offer us the service of that railing; it is true that they would not help us if we really were in great danger and wanted to lean on them; but they give us the comforting sensation of protection nearby (for example, fathers, teachers, friends, as we generally know all three).

## 601

*Learning to love.* We must learn to love, learn to be kind, and this from earliest youth; if education or chance give us no opportunity to practice these feelings, our soul becomes dry and unsuited even to understanding the tender inventions of loving people. Likewise, hatred must be learned and nurtured, if one wishes to become a proficient hater: otherwise the germ for that, too, will gradually wither.

## 602

*Ruins as decoration.* People who go through many spiritual changes retain some views and habits from earlier stages, which then jut out into their new thinking and acting like a bit of inexplicable antiquity and gray stonework, often ornamenting the whole region.

## 603

*Love and respect.*[10] Love desires; fear avoids. That is why it is impossible, at least in the same time span, to be loved and respected by the same person. For the man who respects another, acknowledges his power; that is, he fears it: his condition is one of awe.[11] But love acknowledges no power, nothing that separates, differentiates, ranks higher or subordinates. Because the state of being loved carries with it no respect, ambitious[12] men secretly or openly balk against it.

## 604

*Prejudice in favor of cold people.* People who catch fire rapidly quickly become cold, and are therefore by and large unreliable. Therefore, all those who are always cold, or act that way, benefit from the prejudice that they are especially trustworthy, reliable people: they are being confused with those others who catch fire slowly and burn for a long time.

## 605

*What is dangerous about free opinions.* The casual entertainment of free opinions is like an itch; giving in to it, one begins to rub the area; finally there is an open, aching wound; that is, the free opinion finally begins to disturb and torment us in our attitude to life, in our human relationships.

## 606

*Desire for deep pain.* When it has gone, passion leaves behind a dark longing for itself, and in disappearing throws us one last seductive glance. There must have been a kind of pleasure in having been beaten with her whip. In contrast, the more moderate

10. *Ehre*
11. *Ehr-Furcht:* respectful fear.
12. *ehrsüchtige*

feelings appear flat; apparently we still prefer a more violent displeasure to a weak pleasure.

## 607

*Annoyance with others and the world.* When, as happens so often, we let our annoyance out on others, while we are actually feeling it about ourselves, we are basically trying to cloud and delude our judgment; we want to motivate our annoyance *a posteriori* by the oversights and inadequacies of others, so we can lose sight of ourselves.

Religiously strict people, who judge themselves without mercy, are also those who have most often spoken ill of mankind in general. There has never been a saint who reserves sins to himself and virtues to others: he is as rare as the man who, following Buddha's precept, hides his goodness from people and lets them see of himself only what is bad.

## 608

*Cause and effect confused.* Unconsciously we seek out the principles and dogmas that are in keeping with our temperament, so that in the end it looks as if the principles and dogmas had created our character, given it stability and certainty, while precisely the opposite has occurred. It seems that our thinking and judging are to be made the cause of our nature after the fact, but actually our nature causes us to think and judge one way or the other.

And what decides us on this almost unconscious comedy? Laziness and convenience, and not least the vain desire to be considered consistent through and through, uniform both in character and thought: for this earns us respect, brings us trust and power.

## 609

*Age and truth.* Young people love what is interesting and odd, no matter how true or false it is. More mature minds love what is interesting and odd about truth. Fully mature intellects, finally, love truth, even when it appears plain and simple, boring to the ordinary person; for they have noticed that truth tends to reveal its highest wisdom in the guise of simplicity.

## 610

*People as bad poets.* Just as bad poets, in the second half of a line, look for a thought to fit their rhyme, so people in the second half of their lives, having become more anxious, look for the actions, attitudes, relationships that suit those of their earlier life, so that everything will harmonize outwardly. But then they no longer have any powerful thought to rule their life and determine it anew; rather, in its stead, comes the intention of finding a rhyme.

## 611

*Boredom and play.* Need forces us to do the work whose product will quiet the need; we are habituated to work by the ever-new awakening of needs. But in those intervals when our needs are quieted and seem to sleep, boredom overtakes us. What is that? It is the habit of working as such, which now asserts itself as a new, additional need; the need becomes the greater, the greater our habit of working, perhaps even the greater our suffering from our needs. To escape boredom, man works either beyond what his usual needs require, or else he invents play, that is, work that is designed to quiet no need other than that for working in general. He who is tired of play, and has no reason to work because of new needs, is sometimes overcome by the longing for a third state that relates to play as floating does to dancing, as dancing does to walking, a blissful, peaceful state of motion: it is the artist's and philosopher's vision of happiness.

## 612

*Instruction from pictures.* If we consider a series of pictures of ourselves from the time of childhood to that of manhood, we are agreeably surprised to find that the man resembles the child more than the adolescent: probably corresponding to this occurrence, then, there has been a temporary alienation from our basic character, now overcome again by the man's collected, concentrated strength. This perception agrees with the one that all those strong influences of our passions, our teachers, or political events, which pull us about in our adolescence, later seem to be reduced to a fixed measure. Certainly, they continue to live and act in us, but our basic feeling and basic thinking have the upper hand; these influences are used as sources of power, but no longer as regulators, as happens in our twenties. Thus man's thinking and feeling appear again more in accord with that of his childhood years—and this inner fact is expressed in the external one mentioned above.

## 613

*Voice of the years.* The tone adolescents use to speak, praise, blame, or invent displeases older people because it is too loud and yet at the same time muffled and unclear, like a tone in a vault, which gains resonance because of the emptiness. For most of what adolescents think has not flowed out of the fullness of their own nature, but rather harmonizes and echoes what is thought, spoken, praised, or blamed around them. But because the feelings (of inclination and disinclination) reverberate in them much more strongly than the reasons for these feelings, there arises, when they give voice to their feeling again, that muffled, ringing tone that indicates the absence or paucity of reasons. The tone of the more mature years is rigorous, sharply punctuated, moderately loud, but like everything clearly articulated, it carries very far. Finally, old age often brings a certain gentleness and indulgence to the sound and seems to sugar it: of course, in some cases it makes it sour, too.

## 614

*Backward and anticipating people.* The unpleasant personality who is full of mistrust, who reacts with envy to his competitors' and neighbors' successes, who flares up violently at divergent opinions, is showing that he belongs to an earlier stage of culture, and is thus a relic. For the way in which he interacts with people was proper and appropriate for the conditions of an age when rule by force prevailed: he is a *backward* person. A second personality, who shares profusely in others' joy, who wins friends everywhere, who is touched by everything that grows and evolves, who enjoys other people's honors and successes, and makes no claim to the privilege of alone knowing the truth, but instead is full of modest skepticism—he is an anticipator who is reaching ahead towards a higher human culture. The unpleasant personality grows out of times when the unhewn foundation of human intercourse had still to be laid; the other lives on its highest floors, as far away as possible from the wild animal that rages and howls locked up in the cellars, beneath the foundations of culture.

## 615

*Comfort for hypochondriacs.* When a great thinker is temporarily subjected to hypochondriacal self-torments, he may say to comfort himself: "This parasite is feeding and growing from your great strength; if that strength were less, you would have less to suffer." The statesman may speak likewise when his jealousy and vengeful feelings, in short, the mood of a *bellum omnium contra omnes,*[13] for which he as a nation's representative must necessarily have a great gift, occasionally intrude into his personal relations and make his life difficult.

## 616

*Alienated from the present.* There are great advantages in for once removing ourselves distinctly from our time and letting ourselves be driven from its shore back into the ocean of former world views. Looking at the coast from that perspective, we survey for the first time its entire shape, and when we near it again, we have the advantage of understanding it better on the whole than do those who have never left it.

## 617

*Sowing and reaping on personal inadequacies.* People like Rousseau know how to use their weaknesses, deficiencies, or vices as if they were the fertilizer of their talent. When Rousseau laments the depravity and degeneration of society as the unpleasant consequence of culture,[14] this is based on his personal experience, whose bitterness makes his general condemnation so sharp, and poisons the arrows he shoots. He is relieving himself first as an individual, and thinks that he is seeking a cure that will directly benefit society, but that will also indirectly, and by means of society, benefit him too.

## 618

*A philosophical frame of mind.* Generally we strive to acquire *one* emotional stance, *one* viewpoint for all life situations and events: we usually call that being of a philosophical frame of mind. But rather than making oneself uniform, we may find greater value for the enrichment of knowledge by listening to the soft voice of different life situations; each brings its own views with it. Thus we acknowledge and share the life and nature of

13. The war of each against all: coined by Thomas Hobbes (1588–1679).
14. See n. 6 to Section Eight.

many by not treating ourselves like rigid, invariable, single individuals.

## 619

*In the fire of contempt.* It is a new step towards independence, once a man dares to express opinions that bring disgrace on him if he entertains them; then even his friends and acquaintances begin to grow anxious. The man of talent must pass through this fire, too; afterwards he is much more his own person.

## 620

*Sacrifice.* If there is a choice, a great sacrifice will be preferred to a small one, because we compensate ourselves for a great sacrifice with self-admiration, and this is not possible with a small one.

## 621

*Love as a device.* Whoever wants really to get to *know* something new (be it a person, an event, or a book) does well to take up this new thing with all possible love, to avert his eye quickly from, even to forget, everything about it that he finds inimical, objectionable, or false. So, for example, we give the author of a book the greatest possible head start, and, as if at a race, virtually yearn with a pounding heart for him to reach his goal. By doing this, we penetrate into the heart of the new thing, into its motive center: and this is what it means to get to know it. Once we have got that far, reason then sets its limits; that overestimation, that occasional unhinging of the critical pendulum, was just a device to entice the soul of a matter out into the open.

## 622

*To think too well or too ill of the world.* Whether we think too well or too ill of things, we will always gain the advantage of reaping a greater pleasure: if our preconceived opinion is too good we are generally investing things (experiences) with more sweetness than they actually possess. If a preconceived opinion is overly negative, it leads to a pleasant disappointment: what was pleasurable in those things in and of themselves is increased through the pleasure of our surprise.

Incidentally, a morose temperament will experience the opposite in both cases.

### 623

*Profound people.* Those people whose strength lies in the profundity of their impressions (they are generally called "profound people") are relatively controlled and decisive when anything sudden happens: for in the first moment the impression was still shallow; only later does it *become* profound. But long-foreseen, anticipated things or people excite such natures most, and make them almost incapable of maintaining presence of mind when their wait is over.

### 624

*Traffic with one's higher self.* Everyone has his good day, when he finds his higher self; and true humanity demands that we judge someone only when he is in this condition, and not in his workdays of bondage and servitude. We should, for example, assess and honor a painter according to the highest vision he was able to see and portray. But people themselves deal very differently with this, their higher self, and often act out the role of their own self, to the extent that they later keep imitating what they were in those moments. Some regard their ideal with shy humility and would like to deny it: they fear their higher self because, when it speaks, it speaks demandingly. In addition, it has a ghostly freedom of coming or staying away as it wishes; for that reason it is often called a gift of the gods, while actually everything else is a gift of the gods (of chance): this, however, is the man himself.

### 625

*Solitary people.* Some people are so used to solitude with themselves that they never compare themselves to others, but spin forth their monologue of a life in a calm, joyous mood, holding good conversations with themselves, even laughing. But if they are made to compare themselves with others, they tend to a brooding underestimation of their selves: so that they have to be forced *to learn* again from others to have a good, fair opinion of themselves. And even from this learned opinion they will always want to detract or reduce something.

Thus one must grant certain men their solitude, and not be silly enough, as often happens, to pity them for it.

## 626

*Without melody.* There are people for whom a constant inner repose and a harmonious ordering of all their capabilities is so characteristic that any goal-directed activity goes against their grain. They are like a piece of music consisting entirely of sustained harmonious chords, with no evidence of even the beginning of a structured, moving melody. At any movement from the outside, their boat at once gains a new equilibrium on the sea of harmonic euphony. Modern people are usually extremely impatient on meeting such natures, who do not *become* anything—though it may not be said that they *are* not anything. In certain moods, however, their presence evokes that rare question: why have melody at all? Why are we not satisfied when life mirrors itself peacefully in a deep lake?

The Middle Ages was richer in such natures than we are. How seldom do we now meet a person who can keep living so peacefully and cheerfully with himself even amidst the turmoil, saying to himself like Goethe: "The best is the deep quiet in which I live and grow against the world, and harvest what they cannot take from me by fire or sword."[15]

## 627

*Life and experience.*[16] If one notices how some individuals know how to treat their experiences (their insignificant everyday experiences) so that these become a plot of ground that bears fruit three times a year; while others (and how many of them!) are driven through the waves of the most exciting turns of fate, of the most varied currents of their time or nation, and yet always stay lightly on the surface, like cork: then one is finally tempted to divide mankind into a minority (minimality) of those people who know how to make much out of little and a majority of those who know how to make a little out of much; indeed, one meets those perverse wizards who, instead of creating the world out of nothing, create nothing out of the world.

15. Goethe's diary, May 13, 1780.
16. *Leben und Erleben*

## 628

*Seriousness in play.* At sunset in Genoa, I heard from a tower a long chiming of bells: it kept on and on, and over the noise of the backstreets, as if insatiable for itself, it rang out into the evening sky and the sea air, so terrible and so childish at the same time, so melancholy. Then I thought of Plato's words and felt them suddenly in my heart: *all in all, nothing human is worth taking very seriously; nevertheless. . . .*[17]

## 629

*On convictions and justice.*[18] To carry out later, in coolness and sobriety, what a man promises or decides in passion: this demand is among the heaviest burdens oppressing mankind. To have to acknowledge for all duration the consequences of anger, of raging vengeance, of enthusiastic devotion—this can incite a bitterness against these feelings all the greater because everywhere, and especially by artists, precisely these feelings are the object of idol worship. Artists cultivate the *esteem for the passions,* and have always done so; to be sure, they also glorify the frightful satisfactions of passion, in which one indulges, the outbursts of revenge that have death, mutilation, or voluntary banishment as a consequence, and the resignation of the broken heart. In any event, they keep alive curiosity about the passions; it is as if they wished to say: without passions you have experienced nothing at all.

Because we have vowed to be faithful, even, perhaps, to a purely imaginary being, a God, for instance; because we have given our heart to a prince, a party, a woman, a priestly order, an artist, or a thinker, in the state of blind madness that enveloped us in rapture and let those beings appear worthy of every honor, every sacrifice: are we then inextricably bound? Were we not deceiving ourselves then? Was it not a conditional promise, under the assumption (unstated, to be sure) that those beings to whom we

17. Plato, *Republic* 10.604b. Also quoted in Schopenhauer's *Parerga and Paralipomena,* Nietzsche mentions such an evening in Genoa in a letter to his mother and sister on October 22, 1876.

18. In writing of faithfulness and betrayal, as Nietzsche does in the passage to come, he doubtless had his relationship with Wagner in mind. But he is also laying the groundwork for his theory of the transformation of the spirit (cf. *Thus spoke Zarathustra,* Part One, "Of the Three Metamorphoses").

dedicated ourselves really are the beings they appeared to be in our imaginations? Are we obliged to be faithful to our errors, even if we perceive that by this faithfulness we do damage to our higher self?

No—there is no law, no obligation of that kind; we *must* become traitors, act unfaithfully, forsake our ideals again and again. We do not pass from one period of life to another without causing these pains of betrayal, and without suffering from them in turn. Should we have to guard ourselves against the upsurging of our feeling in order to avoid these pains? Would not the world then become too bleak, too ghostly for us? We want rather to ask ourselves whether these pains at a change of conviction are *necessary,* or whether they do not depend on an *erroneous* opinion and estimation. Why do we admire the man who remains faithful to his conviction and despise the one who changes it? I fear the answer must be that everyone assumes such a change is caused only by motives of baser advantage or personal fear. That is, we believe fundamentally that no one changes his opinions as long as they are advantageous to him, or at least as long as they do him no harm. But if that is the case, it bears bad testimony to the *intellectual* meaning of all convictions. Let us test how convictions come into being and observe whether they are not vastly overrated: in that way it will be revealed that the *change* of convictions too is in any case measured by false standards and that until now we have tended to suffer too much from such changes.

## 630

Conviction is the belief that in some point of knowledge one possesses absolute truth. Such a belief presumes, then, that absolute truths exist; likewise, that the perfect methods for arriving at them have been found; finally, that every man who has convictions makes use of these perfect methods. All three assertions prove at once that the man of convictions is not the man of scientific thinking; he stands before us still in the age of theoretical innocence, a child, however grownup he might be otherwise. But throughout thousands of years, people have lived in such childlike assumptions, and from out of them mankind's mightiest sources of power have flowed. The countless people who sacrificed themselves for their convictions thought they were doing it for absolute truth. All of them were wrong: probably no man has ever sacrificed himself for truth; at least, the dogmatic expression of his belief will have been unscientific or half-scientific. But actually one wanted to be right because one thought he *had* to be right. To let his belief be torn from him meant perhaps to put his eternal happiness in question. With a matter of this extreme importance, the "will" was all too audibly the intellect's prompter. Every believer of every persuasion assumed he *could* not be refuted; if the counterarguments proved very strong, he could still always malign reason in general and perhaps even raise as a banner of extreme fanaticism the "credo quia absurdum est."[19] It is not the struggle of opinions that has made history so violent, but rather the struggle of belief in opinions, that is, the struggle of convictions. If only all those people who thought so highly of their conviction, who sacrificed all sorts of things to it and spared neither their honor, body nor life in its service, had devoted only half of their strength to investigating by what right they clung to this or that conviction, how they had arrived at it, then how peaceable the history of mankind would appear! How much more would be known! All the cruel scenes during the persecution of every kind of heretic would have been spared us for two reasons: first, because the inquisitors would above all have inquired within themselves, and got beyond the arrogant idea that they were defending the absolute truth; and second, because the heretics themselves would not have granted such poorly established tenets as those of all the sectarians and "orthodox" any further attention, once they had investigated them.

## 631

Stemming from the time when people were accustomed to believe that they possessed absolute truth is a deep *discomfort* with all skeptical and relativistic positions on any questions of knowledge; usually we prefer to surrender unconditionally to a conviction held by people of authority (fathers, friends, teachers, princes), and we have a kind of troubled conscience if we do not do so. This inclination is understandable and its consequences do not entitle us to violent reproaches against the development of human reason. But eventually the scientific spirit in man must bring forth that virtue of *cautious restraint,* that wise moderation that is

19. "I believe because it is absurd" (falsely attributed to Augustine).

better known in the realm of practical life than in the realm of theoretical life, and that Goethe, for example, portrayed in his Antonio, as an object of animosity for all Tassos,[20] that is, for those unscientific and also passive natures. The man of conviction has in himself a right not to understand the man of cautious thinking, the theoretical Antonio; the scientific man, on the other hand, has no right to scold him for this; he makes allowances for him and knows besides that, in certain cases, the man will cling to him as Tasso finally does to Antonio.

## 632

If one has not passed through various convictions, but remains caught in the net of his first belief, he is in all events, because of just this unchangeability, a representative of *backward* cultures; in accordance with this lack of education (which always presupposes educability), he is harsh, injudicious, unteachable, without gentleness, eternally suspect, a person lacking scruples, who reaches for any means to enforce his opinion because he simply cannot understand that there have to be other opinions. In this regard, he is perhaps a source of power, and even salutary in cultures grown too free and lax, but only because he powerfully incites opposition: for in that way the new culture's more delicate structure, which is forced to struggle with him, becomes strong itself.

## 633

Essentially, we are still the same people as those in the period of the Reformation—and how should it be otherwise? But we no longer allow ourselves certain means to gain victory for our opinion: this distinguishes us from that age and proves that we belong to a higher culture. These days, if a man still attacks and crushes opinions with suspicions and outbursts of rage, in the manner of men during the Reformation, he clearly betrays that he would have burnt his opponents, had he lived in other times, and that he would have taken recourse to all the means of the Inquisition, had he lived as an opponent of the Reformation. In its time, the Inquisition was reasonable, for it meant nothing other than the general martial law which had to be proclaimed over the whole do-

20. In Goethe's play *Tasso* (1790).

main of the church, and which, like every state of martial law, justified the use of the extremest means, namely under the assumption (which we no longer share with those people) that one *possessed* truth in the church and *had to* preserve it at any cost, with any sacrifice, for the salvation of mankind. But now we will no longer concede so easily that anyone has the truth; the rigorous methods of inquiry have spread sufficient distrust and caution, so that we experience every man who represents opinions violently in word and deed as any enemy of our present culture, or at least as a backward person. And in fact, the fervor about having the truth counts very little today in relation to that other fervor, more gentle and silent, to be sure, for seeking the truth, a search that does not tire of learning afresh and testing anew.

## 634

Incidentally, the methodical search for truth itself results from those times when convictions were feuding among themselves. If the individual had not cared about *his* "truth," that is, about his being right in the end, no method of inquiry would exist at all; but, given the eternal struggle of various individuals' claims to absolute truth, man proceeded step by step, in order to find irrefutable principles by which the justice of the claims could be tested and the argument settled. At first decisions were made according to authorities, later the ways and means with which the ostensible truth had been found were mutually criticized; in between, there was a period when the consequences of the opposing tenet were drawn and perhaps experienced as harmful and saddening; this was to result in everyone's judging that the opponent's conviction contained an error. Finally, the *thinkers' personal struggle* sharpened their methods so much that truths could really be discovered, and the aberrations of earlier methods were exposed to everyone's eye.

## 635

All in all, scientific methods are at least as important as any other result of inquiry; for the scientific spirit is based on the insight into methods, and were those methods to be lost, all the results of science could not prevent a renewed triumph of superstition and nonsense. Clever people may *learn* the results of science as much as they like, one still sees from their conversation, especially from their hypotheses in conversation, that they lack the scientific spirit. They do not have that instinctive mistrust of the wrong ways of thinking, a mistrust which, as a consequence of long practice, has put its roots deep into the soul of every scientific man. For them it is enough to find any one hypothesis about a matter; then they get fired up about it and think that puts an end to it. For them, to have an opinion means to get fanatical about it and cherish it in their hearts henceforth as a conviction. If a matter is unexplained, they become excited at the first notion resembling an explanation that enters their brain; this always has the worst consequences, especially in the realm of politics.

Therefore everyone should have come to know at least *one* science in its essentials; then he knows what method is, and how necessary is the most extreme circumspection. This advice should be given to women particularly, who are now the hopeless victims of all hypotheses, especially those which give the impression of being witty, thrilling, invigorating, or energizing. In fact, if one looks closer, one notices that the majority of all educated people still desire convictions and nothing but convictions from a thinker, and that only a slight minority want *certainty*. The former want to be forcibly carried away, in order to thus increase their own strength; the latter few have that matter-of-fact interest that ignores personal advantage, even the above-mentioned increase of strength. Wherever the thinker behaves like a *genius,* calling himself one, and looking down like a higher being who deserves authority, he is counting on the class in the overwhelming majority. To the extent that that kind of genius keeps up the heat of convictions and awakens distrust of the cautious and modest spirit of science, he is an enemy of truth, however much he may believe he is its suitor.

## 636

To be sure, there is also quite another category of genius, that of justice; and I can in no way see fit to esteem that kind lower than any philosophical, political, or artistic genius. It is its way to avoid with hearty indignation everything which blinds and confuses our judgment about things; thus it is an *enemy of convictions,* for it wants to give each thing its due, be it living or dead, real or fictive—and to do so it must apprehend it clearly. Therefore it places each thing in the best light and walks all around it with an attentive eye. Finally it will even give its due to its opponent, to blind or shortsighted "conviction" (as men call it; women call it "faith")—for the sake of truth.

## 637

Out of *passions* grow opinions; *mental sloth* lets these rigidify into *convictions*.

However, if one feels he is of a *free,* restlessly lively mind, he can prevent this rigidity through constant change; and if he is on the whole a veritable thinking snowball, then he will have no opinions at all in his head, but rather only certainties and precisely measured probabilities.

But we who are of a mixed nature, sometimes aglow with fire and sometimes chilled by intellect, we want to kneel down before justice, as the only goddess whom we recognize above us. Usually *the fire* in us makes us unjust, and in the sense of that goddess, impure; never may we touch her hand in this condition; never will the grave smile of her pleasure lie upon us. We honor her as our life's veiled Isis;[21] ashamed, we offer her our pain as a penance and a sacrifice, when the fire burns us and tries to consume us. It is the *intellect* that saves us from turning utterly to burnt-out coals; here and there it pulls us away from justice's sacrificial altar, or wraps us in an asbestos cocoon. Redeemed from the fire, we then stride on, driven by the intellect, from opinion to opinion, through the change of sides, as noble *traitors* to all things that can ever be betrayed—and yet with no feeling of guilt.

## 638

*The wanderer.* He who has come only in part to a freedom of reason cannot feel on earth otherwise than as a wanderer—though not as a traveler *towards* a final goal, for this does not exist. But he does want to observe, and keep his eyes open for everything that actually occurs in the world; therefore he must not attach his heart too firmly to any individual thing; there must be something wandering within him, which takes its joy in change and transitoriness. To be sure, such a man will have bad nights, when he is tired and finds closed the gates to the city that should offer him rest; perhaps in addition, as in the Orient, the desert reaches up to

21. Cf. n. 10 to Section Eight.

the gate; predatory animals howl now near, now far; a strong wind stirs; robbers lead off his pack-animals. Then for him the frightful night sinks over the desert like a second desert, and his heart becomes tired of wandering. If the morning sun then rises, glowing like a divinity of wrath, and the city opens up, he sees in the faces of its inhabitants perhaps more of desert, dirt, deception, uncertainty, than outside the gates—and the day is almost worse than the night. So it may happen sometimes to the wanderer; but then, as recompense, come the ecstatic mornings of other regions and days. Then nearby in the dawning light he already sees the bands of muses dancing past him in the mist of the mountains. Afterwards, he strolls quietly in the equilibrium of his forenoon soul, under trees from whose tops and leafy corners only good and bright things are thrown down to him, the gifts of all those free spirits who are at home in mountain, wood, and solitude, and who are, like him, in their sometimes merry, sometimes contemplative way, wanderers and philosophers. Born out of the mysteries of the dawn, they ponder how the day can have such a pure, transparent, transfigured and cheerful face between the hours of ten and twelve—they seek the *philosophy of the forenoon.*

# Among Friends
## An Epilogue

### 1

Fine, with one another silent,
Finer, with one another laughing—
Under heaven's silky cloth
Leaning over books and moss
With friends lightly, loudly laughing
Each one showing white teeth shining.

If I did well, let us be silent,
If I did badly, let us laugh
And do it bad again by half,
More badly done, more badly laugh,
Until the grave, when down we climb.

Friends! Well! What do you say?
Amen! Until we meet again!

### 2

Don't excuse it! Don't forgive!
You happy, heart-free people, give
This unreasonable book[1] of mine
Ear and heart and sheltering!
Truly, friends, my own unreason
Did not grow to earn a curse!

What *I* find, what *I* am seeking—
Was that ever in a book?
Honor one from the fools' legion!
Learn from out of this fool's book
How reason can be brought—"to reason"!

So then, friends, what do you say?
Amen! Until we meet again.

1. The book referred to was not *Human, All Too Human,* but rather a planned collection of songs and sayings to be called *The Book of Folly* (*Das Narrenbuch*).

# Index

Numbers refer to aphorism number.
P = Nietzsche's Preface.